D1626551

SCOTTISH ECCENTRICS

By the Same Author

Poetry

Sangschaw
Penny Wheep
To Circumjack Cencrastus
First Hymn to Lenin, and other Poems
A Drunk Man looks at the Thistle
Stony Limits, and other Poems

Fiction

Annals of the Five Senses

Translations

The Handmaid of the Lord (novel, from the Spanish of Ramon Maria de Tenreiro)
Birlinn Chlann-Rhagnaill (poem, from the Scots Gaelic of Alasdair Mac-Mhaighstir Alasdair)

Criticism

Contemporary Scottish Studies
Albyn: or Scotland and the Future
Scottish Scene (in collaboration with Lewis Grassic Gibbon)
At the Sign of the Thistle

etc. etc.

HUGH MacDIARMID

SCOTTISH ECCENTRICS

"They do not love liberty
who fear license"

LONDON
GEORGE ROUTLEDGE & SONS, LTD.
BROADWAY HOUSE: 68–74 CARTER LANE, E.C.
1936

PRINTED IN GREAT BRITAIN
BY R. & R. CLARK, LIMITED, EDINBURGH

TO

MY FRIEND AND FELLOW-COUNTRYMAN

A. J. B. PATERSON

WITH GRATITUDE AND AFFECTION

The hornless hart carries off the harem,
Magnificent antlers are nothing in love.
Great tines are only a drawback and danger
To the noble stag that must bear them.

Crowned as with an oaktree he goes,
A sacrifice for the ruck of his race,
Knowing full well that his towering points
Single him out, a mark for his foes.

Yet no polled head's triumphs since the world began
In love and war have made a high heart thrill
Like the sight of a Royal with its Rights and Crockets,
Its Pearls, and Beam, and Span.

AUTHOR'S NOTE

LIVING remote from library facilities, I have necessarily been greatly indebted in writing this book to friends who have hunted up essential references for me or forwarded to me on loan copies of volumes I required to consult. In this connection I must specially thank Dr. Mary Ramsay, Mr Francis George Scott, Mr John Tonge, Mr Robin M. Black, and Miss Helen B. Cruickshank.

HUGH MacDIARMID

Isle of Whalsay,
Shetland Islands

CONTENTS

SCOTTISH ECCENTRICS

LORD GEORGE GORDON

THE story of Lord George Gordon is a very sensational and very sad one. No British politician ever soared up into public notice like a rocket so spectacularly and none ever came down like the stick so quickly and so abjectly.

The third son of the third Duke of Gordon by his Duchess, Catherine, daughter of the Earl of Aberdeen, Lord George was born in Upper Brook Street, London, in December 1750 and George II stood as his sponsor or godfather at his baptism in the succeeding January. "Of his boyhood or education we know little or nothing; nor does there appear to have supervened any peculiar trait of conduct, or bias of disposition, during his juvenile years, to distinguish him from his compeers, or forebode the singular eccentricity and erratic waywardness of his future career."

Entering the navy, he rose to the rank of Lieutenant, but left the service to go into politics. In 1772 he went to reside in Inverness-shire with a view to standing in opposition to General Fraser of Lovat, as member for the county, at the next general election, which would of necessity take place in not more than two years thereafter. He made a model candidate and nursed the constituency to some tune. His project was, indeed, "bearding the lion in his den, and appeared almost as Quixotic an undertaking as that of displacing one of the chieftain's native mountains". Yet the unexpected happened; Inverness-shire witnessed a political equivalent of the fall of Goliath at the hands of David. Lord George was, nevertheless, not destined to enter Parliament for a Scottish seat.

The campaign and the result have been described as

follows: "Such were his ingratiating qualities, the frankness of his manners, the affability of his address, and his happy knack of accommodating himself to the humours of all classes that, when the day of election drew nigh, and the candidates began to number their strength, Lovat found to his unutterable confusion and vexation that his beardless competitor had actually succeeded in securing a majority of votes. Nor could the most distant imputations of bribery or undue influence be charged upon the young political aspirant. All was the result of his winning address and popular manners, superadded to his handsome countenance, which is said to have been of almost feminine beauty and delicacy. He played on the bagpipes and violin to those who loved music. He spoke Gaelic and wore the philabeg where these were in fashion. He made love to the young ladies, and listened with patience and deference to the garrulous sermonising of old age, and, finally, gave a splendid ball to the gentry at Inverness—one remarkable incident concerning which was his hiring a ship and bringing from the Isle of Skye the family of the McLeods, consisting of *fifteen* young ladies—the pride and admiration of the North. It was not to be tolerated, however, that the great feudal chieftain should thus be thrust from his hereditary political possession by a mere stripling. Upon an application to the Duke (Lord George's eldest brother had now succeeded their father) a compromise was agreed on by which it was settled that upon Lord George's relinquishing Inverness-shire General Fraser should purchase a seat for him in an English borough and he was accordingly returned for Ludgershall, the property of Lord Melbourne, at the election of 1744."

Little could the Inverness electors imagine—hardly can Lord George himself have had the first shadowy premonition—that the handsome, dashing, debonair young M.P. was six years later to head one of the greatest mob risings in British history and be the leader of a movement which resulted in what might easily have become a second

Great Fire of London; that he was to stand his trial and be acquitted on the charge of high treason; that he was seven years later to be convicted on other counts, flee the country to evade the sentences, and be brought back, a convert to Judaism, his beard hanging down on his breast, and his studiously sanctimonious deportment at appalling odds with the debonair and engaging figure he had cut on his first incursion into public affairs; that he was to linger in prison, sending out frenzied appeals and trying to negotiate for help with the French revolutionaries, until he died, at the early age of forty-three, of a fever in Newgate gaol, after three days' delirium. Yet such was his destined course.

In the few years before the shadows began to fall there was no sign of morbid tendency, unless an increasing independence of opinion which gave him an isolated place in Parliament is to be accounted as its earliest manifestation. It could not have been interpreted in that way at the time, and it is easy to be wise after the event.

It was immediately evident, at all events, that Lord George was not to be a silent or inactive member of the national assembly. He aligned himself at the outset with the Ministry of the day, but soon—it is alleged owing to the influence of his sister-in-law, the celebrated Duchess of Gordon—espoused the principles of the Opposition. "It was not long", we read, "ere, at the instigation of Governor Johnstone and Mr Burke, he fairly broke with the Ministry, upon their refusal to comply with a most unreasonable demand for promotion over the heads of older and abler officers, which the gentlemen just named had incited him to make." But this explanation of his change-over may be a partisan one, and even if he made any such unreasonable demand he may have put it forward as a mere pretext for changing his political colour. It is too early yet to charge him with displaying any of that unreasonableness which in the light of what followed can be all too readily adduced as an early symptom of his subsequent lamentable and disastrous trend.

However that may be, he came out as an energetic and outspoken opponent of the Government, particularly with regard to their policy towards America, where discontent against their measures was becoming increasingly rife and loud. His first speech was not made, however, until 1776, when he made a furious attack on the Ministers, alleging that they had made an infamous attempt to bribe him over to their side by the offer of a sinecure carrying with it a salary of £1000 a year. "Whether this charge was true or false, certain it is that Ministers felt the effects of the imputation so severely, reiterated and commented on as it was in the withering eloquence of Fox, Burke, and others, that an attempt was made to induce him to cede his seat in Parliament in favour of the famous Irish orator, Henry Flood, by the offer of the place of Vice-Admiral of Scotland, then vacant by the resignation of the Duke of Queensberry. Notwithstanding that Lord George's fortune was then scarcely £700 per annum he had the fortitude to resist the proffered bait, and seemed determined, like Andrew Marvel, to prefer dining for three days running on a single joint rather than sacrifice his independence by the acceptance of Court favour. His Lordship, indeed, soon began to estrange himself from both parties in the House, and to assume a position then entirely new in parliamentary tactics. Disclaiming all connection with either Whigs or Tories, he avowed himself as being devoted solely to the cause of the people. Continuing to represent the borough of Ludgershall, he persevered in animadverting with great freedom, and often with great wit, on the proceedings on both sides of the House, and became so marked that it was usual at that time to say that 'there were three parties in Parliament—the Ministry, the Opposition, and Lord George Gordon' ".

He had "gone his own gait" now but not yet entirely "kicked over the traces" in conventional opinion, and there was no indication so far of any interest in the particular cause which was shortly to lead to such amazing developments and carry him to a pinnacle of notoriety.

To read the beginnings of the mental alienation which eventually overcame him into even his earliest dissociations from both of the established parties, and to affect to trace the worsening of the disease into each successive step he took in his independent political reorientation, is carrying orthodox political prejudice to the point of insanity. And yet this has been done with dolorous head-shakings over the terrible dangers of the slightest departure from the safest ruts of conventionality. Lord George has been held up as a ghastly example of the perils of subversive activities, whereas the lamentable fact is rather that the ravages of his condition rendered him unable to stand by the position he assumed and hasten the collapse of the old system under the impact of the new forces he so signally heralded. The shake-up given to accepted conditions under his leadership would have been salutary enough if he had kept "health and harness" to see the matter through. His horrible misfortune was not an Act of God in favour of the stick-in-the-muds.

I am not suggesting that his cause—or the ostensible cause—which led to the riots was a good one. I do not think it was, but, on the contrary, that it was sufficiently bad to make it very easy for his opponents to attribute his advocacy of it to incipient lunacy. But it would be useful to those who are disposed to push back the inception of Lord George's malady to the earliest date at which he acted or spoke in a fashion counter to their rooted prejudices to recall that two of his great contemporaries, who had been, like him, most attractive and promising in their first manhood, were at this same time sharing his cruel misfortune.

Writing to Stephen Croft on Christmas Day, 1760, Laurence Sterne said that the young King, George III, "seems resolved to bring all things back to their original principles and to stop the torrent of corruption and laziness. He rises every morning at six to do business, rides out at eight to a minute, returns at nine to give himself up to his people. The King gives everything himself, knows everything, and weighs everything maturely, and then is inflexible—this puts old stagers off their game—how it will end we are all in the dark." But by 1788, when the hapless Lord George was lodged in Newgate prison, the King too "was in a state of mental alienation", and Bonnie Prince Charlie (Charles III), whose brain had long been decaying, had begun that same year with a paralytic stroke which disabled half his body, and died shortly afterwards.

This is to anticipate, however. Destiny was suddenly to declare itself for Lord George in a direction of which his antecedents had as yet vouchsafed no hint. Sir George Savile introduced a bill into Parliament in the session of 1778 for the relief of the Roman Catholics of England from some of the penalties to which they were subject under the test laws. In the following session it was proposed to extend the operation of similar measures to Scotland. This produced a crop of riots in Scotland, particularly in Edinburgh, where the mob destroyed some Popish chapels. The Scottish opposition spread to England. Protestant societies were speedily organised in both countries to demand the repeal of Savile's Act. The indifference with which the majority of the Scottish ministers treated the matter in the General Assembly of 1778, when the idea of a motion against the measure was coldly negatived, added fuel to the flame. The membership of the Protestant societies grew rapidly; inflammatory literature was distributed; large sums of money were contributed to carry on the campaign, and the English and Scottish societies arranged to work together for the common cause. Finally, in November 1779, Lord George accepted the Presidency of the whole movement.

The agitation came to a head on 2nd July 1780 when, on going to the House of Commons to present a "petition against the concessions to the Roman Catholics signed by 44,000 Protestants," Lord George was attended by an enormous crowd, stated in one quarter, no doubt by a considerable over-estimate, to number 100,000 persons.

This was the culmination of an intensive campaign which had led to the passing of resolutions of protest against Savile's Act by almost all the provincial synods of Scotland, most of the city incorporations, and the town council, of Edinburgh and Glasgow, and all manner of other public bodies. The newspaper publicity given to these developments propagated the ferment and fanned the public excitement into a blaze. Attacks were made on Catholic chapels and priests' houses, and liberal Protestants, known to favour toleration for the Catholics, were also assaulted in house and person. Edinburgh Town Council issued a proclamation assuring the people that no repeal of the statutes against Papists would take place and attributing the riots solely to the 'fears and distressed minds of well-meaning people'. Glasgow Town Council followed suit. The Home Secretary corroborated these assurances. Nevertheless the excitement throughout the country increased instead of abating. "At no period in our history has either branch of the legislature been addressed or spoken of in language half so daring, menacing, or contemptuous. The resolutions passed by the heritors and heads of families in the parish of Carluke, Lanarkshire, may vie with the most maledictory philippics poured forth on the heads of the 'Boroughmongers' in later days."

The Papists in turn memorialised Parliament, praying for protection for their lives and property, as well as redress for what they had already suffered. Burke laid this petition before the House, and it was in this debate that Lord George first emerged as the champion of the Protestant interests. The membership of the societies continued to swell; meetings and other forms of active propaganda were devoted to the cause. The failure of a Plymouth petition, presented by Lord George, praying for the repeal of Savile's Act was the last straw. The members of the Protestant Association determined to take other steps to secure their object. It was at a meeting held in Coachmakers' Hall that Lord George dilated on the growing menace of Popery and declared that their only recourse was to march in a body to the House of Commons and express their determination to protect their religious privileges with their lives. He swore that he would run all hazards with "the people" and that if they were too lukewarm to do the like with him they might choose another leader. He had struck the note his audience wanted. His speech was received with the utmost enthusiasm, and the arrangements were immediately put in hand to ensure the monster demonstration referred to which accompanied him to Parliament. The authorities were perfectly well aware of all that was going on, yet although the proposed gathering was illegal under the Act of 1661 they took no steps to prevent it or to warn its promoters to desist from their project.

Lord George's huge army of supporters assembled in St. George's Field, where he harangued them and gave them directions how to march—one section by London Bridge, another by Blackfriars, and a third, headed by himself, by Westminster Bridge. It is not surprising if, indeed, as has been said, Lord George's leadership of this great concourse "operated like quicksilver in his veins". The circumstances were sufficient to have intoxicated a much solider and abler politician. Nor would it have been natural for him at such a time to weigh the possible consequences; the support behind him must have seemed irresistible. He felt that he had a tremendous popular mandate.

The processions moved off. The die was cast, and wild scenes speedily ensued. On arriving at the Houses of Parliament the protesting army raised a mighty shout at which the historic walls might well have shuddered. Members of both Houses were abused and maltreated as they arrived. "Lord Boston, in particular, was so long in the hands of the mob that it was at one time proposed that the House should go out in a body to his rescue. He entered at last, unwigged, and with his clothes almost torn from his person."

Meanwhile unprecedented circumstances were developing within the precincts of the House of Commons, and we catch flying glimpses of Lord George's excited and intrepid figure here and there in the chaotic proceedings. "The rioters had got possession of the lobby, the doors of which they repeatedly tried to force open; and a scene of confusion, indignation, and uproar ensued in the House, almost rivalling that which was passing out of doors. Lord George, on first entering, had a blue cockade in his hat, but, upon this being commented on as a sign of riot, he drew it out. The greatest part of the day was consumed in debates (almost inaudible from the increasing roar of the multitude without) relative to the fearful state of affairs; but something like order being at last obtained, Lord George introduced the subject of the Protestant petition which, he stated, was signed by 120,000 Protestants, and moved that it be immediately brought up. Leave being given, he next moved that it be forthwith taken into consideration. This informal and unprecedented proposition was, of course, resisted; but Lord George nevertheless declared his determination of dividing the House on the subject, and a desultory but violent debate ensued, which was terminated by the motion being negatived by 192 to 9.

"During the course of the discussion, the riot outside became every moment more alarming, and Lord George was repeatedly called upon to disperse his followers But his manner of addressing the latter, which he did from the top of the gallery stairs, leaves it doubtful whether his intention was to quiet or irritate them still further. He informed them from time to time of the progress of the debate and mentioned by name (certainly, to put the best construction upon it, an extremely thoughtless proceeding) those members who opposed the immediate consideration of the petition, saying—'Mr So-and-So is now speaking against you.' He told them that it was proposed to adjourn the question to the following Tuesday, but that he did not like delays, that 'Parliament might be prorogued before that and there would be an end of the affair.' During his harangues, several members of the House warmly expostulated with him on the imprudence of his conduct; but to no purpose. General Grant attempted to draw him back, begging him 'for God's sake not to lead these poor deluded people into danger'. Colonel Gordon, a near relative of his (or, as other authorities say, Colonel Murray, uncle to the Duke of Atholl), demanded of him, 'Do you intend, my Lord George, to bring your rascally adherents into the House of Commons? If you do, the first man that enters I will plunge my sword not into his body but yours.' In this state matters continued until about nine o'clock at night, when a troop of horse and infantry arrived. Lord George then advised the mob to disperse quietly, observing 'that now their gracious king was made aware of the wishes and determination of his subjects he would no doubt compel his ministers to comply with their demands'."

It has been repeatedly asserted that only a tiny fraction of the demonstrators were genuinely actuated by Protestant passion and that the vast majority were only rascals out for mischief. This plan of construing popular demonstrations as hooliganism, or at least asserting that they give the hooligan element an excuse and result in excesses of all kinds, is still a favourite device of the authorities, and in these days of course the bulk of the people were regarded by their so-called superiors as just so many knaves and scoundrels. It is probably true that neither when it is on the side of law and order or organised against the authorities is "religious feeling" a real factor in public affairs. That was Bonnie Prince Charlie's conclusion, too. The authorities had reason to fear the populace. As late as 1787 Dr. Johnson observed: "If England were fairly polled, the present King would be sent away to-night, and his adherents hanged to-morrow". Lord George not only was a detested Scotsman, but he embodied that spirit which the authorities feared—that "all or nothing" spirit which could not sacrifice honour to respectability, antithetical to that Whiggery "used to designate a character made up of negatives, merely studying comfort and conveniency and more anxious for the absence of positive evil than the presence of relative good". In the cautious comments and disgraceful insinuations of some of the passages concerning him I am quoting, the cold, selfish, formal, cabbage-hearted spirit of the other side is all too clearly manifested. In any case it is absurd to say, as this writer does, that following Lord George's advice to the crowds to disperse quietly, "those who attended from purely religious motives, numbering not more than 600 or 700, immediately departed peaceably, first giving the magistrates and soldiers three cheers". Who counted them? Who knows what motives really actuated those who went away or the vastly greater number who remained. Nor, despite what happened, is there any good ground for declaring that the latter "soon began to display the villainous designs which had congregated them".

Whatever doubts there may be as to their character and motives, however, there are none as to what actually happened. In the same way there may be different opinions as to the motives of the authorities; what is not in question is simply that they were responsible "for the absence of everything like preparation for preserving the peace—aware, as they perfectly were, of the intended multitudinous procession". They had had all the afternoon and evening during which the crowds were besieging the Houses of Parliament to gauge their temper and take the necessary measures. It was only after the crowd, round about midnight, completely gutted the chapels of the Sardinian ambassador in Duke Street and of the Bavarian ambassador in Warwick Street, making bonfires of the furniture and other fittings, that a party of Guards arrived and succeeded in capturing thirteen of the rioters.

The following day (Saturday) passed without disturbance, but on the Sunday the Moorfields chapel was demolished and the altar, images, and pictures burned in open street—the Guards again arriving too late and manifesting a strangely lenient deportment by refraining from the use of either salvos or side-arms. On Monday matters got into full swing—a school-house, three dwelling-houses, and a valuable library, belonging to Catholics, were destroyed in Ropemaker's Alley. Sections of the rioters were now operating simultaneously in different parts of the city, and the houses of Sir George Savile and several other public and private gentlemen, together with various Romish chapels, were pillaged and put to fire. "The violence of the mob also received an accession of fury this day from two circumstances—a proclamation offering a reward of £500 for the discovery of those concerned in destroying the Bavarian and Sardinian chapels; and the public committal to Newgate of three of the supposed ringleaders on those occasions."

Early on the same morning the Protestant Association distributed a circular disclaiming all connection with the rioters and earnestly counselling all good Protestants to maintain peace and good order.

The Houses of Parliament were again besieged by great crowds on the Tuesday—the day appointed for consideration of the Protestant petition. "A disposition to outrage soon manifested itself, and Lord Sandwich with difficulty escaped with his life, by the aid of the military, his carriage being smashed to pieces. The House of Lords, after several of their Lordships had commented on the unprecedented circumstances in which they were placed, unanimously decided on the absurdity of transacting business while in a state of durance and restraint, and soon broke up, after adjourning proceedings till the Thursday following. In the House of Commons, after several remarks similar to those in the Upper House, and the passing of various resolutions to the same effect, a violent attack was made upon Ministers by Mr Burke, Mr Fox, and others of the Opposition, on account of the relaxed state of the police, which had left the legislature at the mercy of a reckless mob. Lord George Gordon said if the House would appoint a day for the discussion of the petition, and do it to the satisfaction of the people, he had no doubt they would quietly disperse. Colonel Herbert remarked that although Lord George disclaimed all connection with the rioters it was strange that he came into the House with their ensign of insurrection in his hat (a blue cockade), upon which his lordship pulled it out. A Committee was then appointed 'to inquire into the causes of the riot, etc.', and the House adjourned to Thursday. Upon the breaking up of the House, Lord George addressed the multitude, told them what had been done, and advised them to disperse quietly. In return they unharnessed his horses and drew him in triumph through the town."

Meantime Lord North's residence in Downing Street was attacked and only saved from destruction by the intervention of the military. In the evening Justice Hyde's residence was sacked and all the furniture, pictures, and books burned before the door. Newgate Jail, where some of the arrested rioters were imprisoned, was the next objective. The mob demanded admittance. When Mr Ackerman, the Governor, refused, they smashed his windows and began battering in the doors of the prison with pickaxes and sledge-hammers. Then they got flambeaux and threw them into his house, which, along with the chapel and other parts of the prison, was speedily in flames. The prison doors were soon consumed and the mob rushed in and released all the prisoners (including several under sentence of death) to the number of 300. "One most remarkable circumstance was that from a prison thus enveloped in flames, and in the midst of a scene of such uproar and confusion, such a number of prisoners (many of them shut in cells to which access was at all times most intricate and difficult) could escape without the loss of a single life or the fracture of a limb."

Equally remarkable, perhaps, was the fact that within a few days almost all the prisoners thus unexpectedly liberated had been recaptured and lodged either in their old or more secure quarters.

Many amusing and curious details come to light in

narratives of the proceedings of that and the following day. The following account may be quoted at some length, readers being left to discount for themselves some of the exaggerated language in which it is couched and to make what allowances they feel necessary for partisan feeling.

"Still more emboldened by this reinforcement of desperate confederates, the rioters proceeded in different detachments to the houses of Justice Cox and Sir John Fielding, as also to the public office in Bow Street and the new prison, Clerkenwell; all of which they broke in upon and gutted, liberating the prisoners in the latter places, and thereby gaining fresh numbers and strength. But the most daring act of all was their attacking the splendid mansion of Lord Chief Justice Mansfield,[1] in Bloomsbury Square. Having broken open the doors and windows, they proceeded, as was their custom, to fling all the rich and costly furniture into the street where it was piled into heaps and burned, amid the most exulting yells. The library, consisting of many thousands of volumes, rare MSS, title-deeds, etc., together with a splendid assortment of pictures—all were remorselessly destroyed. And all this passed, too, in the presence of between 200 and 300 soldiers, and under the eye of the Lord Chief Justice himself, who calmly permitted this destruction of his property rather than expose the wretched criminals to the vengeance of the military. At last, seeing preparations made to fire the premises, and not knowing where the conflagration might terminate, a magistrate read the Riot Act; but without effect. The military were then reluctantly ordered to fire; but although several men and women were shot, the desperadoes did not cease the work of destruction until nothing but the bare and smoking walls were left standing. At this time the British metropolis may be said to have been entirely in the hands of a lawless, reckless, and frenzied mob. The vilest of the

[1] Another Scotsman—born at Perth in 1704. He declined the offer of the Treasury to compensate him for the losses he had sustained by the actions of the mob in the riots with which we are dealing.

rabble possessed more power and authority than the King upon the throne; the functions of government were, for a time, suspended; and the seat of legislation had become the theatre of anarchy and misrule. So confident now were the rioters in their own irresistible strength that on the afternoon of the above day they sent notices round to the various prisons yet left standing to inform the prisoners at what hour they intended to visit and liberate them. If any one incident connected with a scene of such devastation, plunder, and triumphant villainy could raise a smile on the face of the reader or narrator, it would be the fact that the prisoners confined in the Fleet sent to request that they might not be turned out of their lodgings so late in the evening; to which a generous answer was returned that they would not be disturbed till next day. In order not to be idle, however, the considerate mob amused themselves during the rest of the evening in burning the houses of Lord Petre and about twenty other individuals of note—Protestant as well as Catholic—and concluded the labours of the day by ordering a general illumination in celebration of their triumph—an order which the inhabitants were actually compelled to obey. On Wednesday this horrible scene of tumult and devastation reached its acme. A party of the rioters paid a visit to Lord Mansfield's beautiful villa at Caen Wood in the forenoon and coolly began to regale themselves with the contents of his larder and wine-cellar, preparatory to their commencing the usual work of destruction. Their orgies were interrupted, however, by a party of military and they fled in all directions. It was not until the evening that the main body seriously renewed their diabolical work; and the scene which ensued is described by contemporary writers, who witnessed the proceedings, as being too frightful for the power of language to convey the slightest idea of. Detachments of military, foot and horse, had gradually been drawing in from different parts of the interior; the civic authorities, who up to that time had been solely occupied consulting and debating upon the course they should pursue in the awful and unparalleled circumstances in which they were placed, began to gather resolution, to concentrate their force, and to perceive the absolute necessity of acting with vigour and decision—a necessity which every moment increased. The strong arm of the law, which had so long hung paralysed over the heads of the wretched criminals, once more became nerved, and prepared to avenge the cause of justice, humanity, and social order. The struggle, however, as may well be conceived, was dreadful; and we gladly borrow the language of one who witnessed the awful spectacle in detailing the events of that ever-memorable night. The King's Bench, Fleet Prison, Borough Clink, and Surrey Bridewell, were all in flames at the same moment, and their inhabitants let loose to assist in the general havoc. No less than thirty-six fearful conflagrations in different parts of the metropolis were seen raging simultaneously '*licking up everything in their way, and hasting to meet each other*'.

" 'Let those', says this writer, 'call to their imagination flames ascending and rolling in vast voluminous clouds from the King's Bench and Fleet Prisons, the Surrey Bridewell, and the toll houses on Blackfriars Bridge; from houses in flames in every quarter of the city, and particularly from the middle and lower end of Holborn, where the premises of Messrs Langdale and Sons, eminent distillers, were blazing, as if the whole elements were one continued flame; the cries of men, women, and children, running up and down the street, with whatever, in their fright, they thought most necessary or most precious; the tremendous roar of the infernal miscreants inflamed with liquor, who aided the sly incendiaries, whose sole aim was plunder; and the repeated reports of the loaded musquetry dealing death and worse than death among the thronging multitude.'

"But it was not what was doing only, but what *might yet be done*, that roused the fears of all classes. When they beheld the very outcasts of society everywhere triumphant, and heard of their attempting the Bank, threatening

Doctors' Commons, the Exchange, the Pay-Office, in short every repository of treasure and office of record, men of every party and persuasion bitterly lamented the rise and progress of the bloody and fatal insurrection, and execrated the authors of it. Had the Bank and public offices been the first objects of attack, instead of the jails and houses of private individuals, there is not the smallest reason to doubt of their success. . . . The regulars and militia poured into the city in such numbers during the night of Wednesday, and the morning of Thursday, that, on the latter day, order was in a great measure restored; but the alarm of the inhabitants was so great that every door remained shut. So speedily and effectually, however, did the strict exercise of authority subdue the spirit of tumult that on Friday the shops once more were opened and business resumed its usual course."

So terminated the Gordon Riots. No figures are available showing the total cost of the damages done, or the total casualties suffered. A military return of the killed and wounded for whom they were responsible totalled 458. But this list is, of course, exclusive of those who perished by accident or by their own folly and infatuation. "Great numbers", we are told, "died from sheer inebriation, especially at the distilleries of the unfortunate Mr Langdale, from which the unrectified spirits ran down the middle of the streets, was taken up in pailfuls, and held to the mouths of the deluded multitude, many of whom dropt down dead on the spot, and were burned or buried in the ruins." To the death-roll falls to be added the toll which the Law now proceeded to take. Eighty-five were tried at the Old Bailey—thirty-five capitally convicted, forty-three acquitted, seventeen respited, and eighteen executed. At St. Margaret's Hill forty were tried under special commission, of whom about twenty were executed. Besides these, several of the rioters were afterwards from time to time apprehended, tried, and executed in various parts of the country. Amongst those convicted at the Old Bailey, but afterwards respited, was *the common hangman*,

Edward Dennis. His respite was probably due to the immediate occasion for his services.

The temper of the times, and the ignominious and repressed condition of the proletariat, must be understood in accounting for this great boiling over of popular passion. It heralded the coming of new democratic forces—the growth of radical opinions, agitation for parliamentary and municipal reform, sympathy with the French Revolution, the vogue of Tom Paine's *Rights of Man*—which characterised the last decade of the century, to be met, on the part of the authorities, with brutal repression. As a recent very moderate historian has said: "Only craven fear can explain the wanton travesties of justice and the monstrous sentences imposed in the trials of 'Friends of the People' and people of like mind. Late in 1793, Thomas Muir, a prominent lawyer with progressive views, was sentenced to transportation for fourteen years, while a Methodist clergyman called Palmer was given seven years; the penal system then in use was such as to ensure untold misery, privation, and exposure for the sufferers. Early in 1794 three further sentences of fourteen years' transportation were pronounced after farcical sedition trials, and, later in the same year, two death sentences were imposed (though a reprieve was granted in one case) for what was deemed treason. The legislature helped the courts in the vile work by refusing to discriminate between anarchist hooliganism and orderly demands for much-needed change. In 1794 the English Habeas Corpus Act and the Scottish Act of 1701 'for preventing Wrongous Imprisonment' were suspended to give officials a free hand in seizing suspects. Acts of 1795 defining treason and sedition gave the Government virtually unhampered control of public meetings. A small minority of the well-to-do began to feel that repression had gone too far, and when in 1796 his Whig sympathies caused the deposition of Henry Erskine from the deanship of the Faculty of Advocates (in theory an annual office, but practically bestowed for life) the opposition gained an eminent lawyer as a leader. Henceforth the Scottish Whigs, under Erskine, Francis Jeffrey, and some of the Popular Party in the Church, set to work to undermine Tory influence, attracting to their ranks more and more of the thoughtful and progressive members of all callings, but especially the legal. The fact that they had a considered policy of constitutional reform, where their opponents had none, told in their favour, but their day of triumph was still far off."

So far as Lord George Gordon is concerned, however, it is another eminent Scottish lawyer of progressive sympathies and the same surname who comes prominently into the picture—Thomas, afterwards Lord Erskine. The Privy Council, immediately after the cessation of the riots, had issued a warrant for Lord George's arrest for high treason, and he was forthwith imprisoned in the Tower of London. There was a delay for nearly eight months before his trial—5th February 1781. "During his confinement, Lord George was frequently visited by his brother the Duke, and other illustrious individuals, and every attention was paid to his comfort and convenience. He was accompanied from the Tower to Westminster Hall by the Duke and a great number of other noble relatives. His counsel were Mr (afterwards Lord) Kenyon, and Mr (afterwards Lord) Thomas Erskine. The charge against the prisoner was that of high treason, in attempting to raise and levy war and insurrection against the King, etc. His Lordship pleaded not guilty. The trial commenced at nine o'clock on the morning of Monday the 5th and at a quarter-past five next morning the jury returned an unqualified verdict of acquittal. Twenty-three witnesses were examined for the Crown, and sixteen for the prisoner. The evidence, as may be imagined, was extremely contradictory in its tendency, proceeding as it did from individuals whose impressions as to the cause and character of the fatal occurrences were so very dissimilar,—one party seeing in the conduct of Lord George merely that of an unprincipled, callous-hearted, and ambitious demagogue, reckless of the consequences to the well-being of society, provided he obtained his own private ends; while another looked upon him an an ill-used and unfortunate patriot, whose exertions to maintain the stability of the Protestant religion, and vindicate the rights and privileges of the people, had been defeated by the outrages of a reckless and brutal mob. By the latter party, all the evil consequences and disreputability of the tumults were charged upon the Government and civic authorities, on account of the lax state of the police and the utter want of a properly organised defensive power in the metropolis."

Great rejoicings took place on account of his Lordship's acquittal, among his partisans, particularly in Scotland. General illuminations were held in Edinburgh and Glasgow; congratulatory addresses were voted to him; and £485 subscribed to reimburse him for the expenses of his trial. He continued in high favour with the Protestant party and took part in most of the public discussions in Parliament as usual.

Thomas Erskine's great abilities and sympathies had already manifested themselves on the progressive side. He was called to the Bar in 1778 and at the very outset distinguished himself by a brilliant display of professional talent in the case of Captain Baillie, against whom the Attorney-General had moved for leave to file a criminal information in the court of King's Bench for a libel on the Earl of Sandwich. In the course of this, his first speech, Erskine displayed the same undaunted spirit which marked his whole career. He attacked the noble earl in a strain of severe invective. Lord Mansfield, observing the young counsel heated with his subject and growing personal on the first Lord of the Admiralty, told him that Lord Sandwich was not before the court. "I know", replied the fearless orator, "that he is not formally before the court; but for that very reason I will bring him before the court. He has placed these men in the front of the battle in hopes to escape under their shelter; but I will not join in battle with them; *their* vices, though screwed up to the highest pitch of human depravity, are not of dignity enough to vindicate the combat with *me*; I will drag *him* to light who is the dark mover behind this scene of iniquity. I assert that the Earl of Sandwich has but one road of escape out of this business without pollution and disgrace; and that is by publicly disavowing the acts of the prosecutors and restoring Captain Baillie to his command."

Erskine's next speech was for Mr Carnan, a bookseller, at the Bar of the House of Commons, against the monopoly of the two universities in printing almanacs. Lord North, then Prime Minister, and chancellor of Oxford, had introduced a bill into the House of Commons for revesting the universities in their monopoly which had fallen to the ground by certain judgements Carnan had obtained in the courts of law. The opposition to the Premier's measure was considered almost hopeless; but, to the honour of the House, the bill was rejected by a majority of 45 votes.

Erskine's speech on behalf of Lord George was, however, considered a still greater triumph. "The proceedings, as may be imagined, engrossed the undivided attention of the whole kingdom, but almost the sole point of interest connected with them now, after such a lapse of time, is the speech of the celebrated Honourable Thomas Erskine, which has been regarded as one of the very highest flights of overpowering eloquence with which that 'remarkable man from time to time astonished his audiences, and, indeed, the whole world'." Erskine's speech was considered less remarkable, perhaps, for dazzling eloquence than for the clear texture of the whole argument maintaining it. "One very remarkable passage in it has been considered by his political friends and admirers as the *ne plus ultra* of rhetorical tact and effective energy. In reviewing Lord George's conduct and deportment during the progress of the unhappy tumults, the orator abruptly broke out with the following emphatic interjection: 'I say, *by God*, that man is a *ruffian* who will dare to build upon such honest, artless conduct as an evidence of guilt'." The effect of this most unexpected and unparalleled figure of oratory is described by those who heard it to have been perfectly magical. The court, the jury, the bar, and the spectators were for a while spell-bound with astonishment and admiration.

Erskine got his silk gown in 1783 and was elected M.P. for Portsmouth the same year. Dr. Johnson himself, notwithstanding his hostility to the test laws, was highly pleased by the verdict obtained in Lord George's trial. "I am glad", he said, "that Lord George Gordon has escaped, rather than a precedent should be established of hanging a man for constructive treason."

Another great service of Erskine's was his defence of John Stockdale; the doctrine Erskine maintained and expounded in this important case is the foundation of that liberty which the press enjoys in this country. When the House of Commons ordered the impeachment of Warren Hastings, the articles were drawn up by Mr Burke, who infused into them all his usual fervour of thought and expression. The articles, so prepared, instead of being confined to the records of the House until they were carried up to the Lords for trial, were printed and allowed to be sold in every bookseller's shop in the kingdom, before the accused was placed upon his trial; and undoubtedly, from the style and manner of their composition, made a deep and general impression upon the public mind against Mr Hastings. To repel or neutralise the effect of the publication of the charges, Mr Logan, one of the ministers of Leith, wrote a pamphlet which Stockdale published, containing most severe and unguarded reflections upon the conduct of the managers of the impeachments, which the House of Commons deemed highly contemptuous and libellous. The publisher was accordingly tried, on an information filed by the Attorney-General. In the speech delivered by Mr Erskine on this occasion the very highest efforts of the orator and the rhetorician were united to all the coolness and precision of the *nisi prius* lawyer. To estimate the mightiness of that effort by which he defeated his powerful antagonists in this case, we must remember the imposing circumstances of Mr Hasting's trial—the "terrible, unceasing, exhaustless artillery of warm zeal, matchless vigour of understanding, consuming and devouring eloquence, united with the highest dignity"—to use the orator's own words—which was then daily pouring forth upon the man in whose defence Logan had written and Stockdale had published. It was "amidst the blaze of passion and prejudice" that Mr Erskine extorted that verdict which rescued his client from the punishment which a whole people seemed interested in awarding against the reviler of its collective majesty.

Erskine was exalted to the peerage in 1807 and accepted the seals as Lord High Chancellor, but resigned them on the dissolution of the short-lived administration of that period and retired on a pension of £4000 per annum. Up to his death he steadily devoted himself to his duties in Parliament and never ceased to support in his high position those progressive measures and principles he had advocated in his younger years. His pamphlet, *A View of the Causes and Consequences of the War with France*, published in support of Fox's principles, ran through no fewer than forty-eight editions.

Following his acquittal, Lord George found himself "sent to Coventry". "He was studiously shunned by all his legislative colleagues, and was in such disgrace at Court that we find him detailing to his Protestant correspondents in Edinburgh his reception at a royal levée, where the King coldly turned his back upon him, without seeming to recognise him." The authorities were determined to have their revenge upon him, and his increasingly bold and radical utterances and actions soon gave them the handle they wanted. In April 1787 two prosecutions were brought against him at the instance of the Crown; one for preparing and presenting a pretended petition to himself from certain prisoners confined in Newgate, praying him to intercede for them and prevent their being banished to Botany Bay; the other for a libel upon the Queen of France and the French ambassador. Erskine on this occasion was employed on the other side. Lord George defended himself, on the score of being too poor to employ counsel. "The Newgate petition, evidently his Lordship's production, was a mere farrago of absurdity, treason, and blasphemy, reflecting on the laws, railing at the Crown officers, and condemning his Majesty by large quotations from the book of Moses." Lord George was found guilty. "Upon the second charge, the gist of which was a design to create a misunderstanding between the two courts of France and England, he was also found guilty. His speech on this last occasion was so extravagant, and contained expressions so indecorous, that the Attorney-General told him 'he was a disgrace to the name of Briton'," but judges and lawyers even to-day are easily moved to such comments on matters which traverse their personal political prejudices and notions of propriety.

The writer I have been drawing upon in most of the quotations in this essay was distinctly hostile to Lord George, and accordingly his admission that "the sentence upon him was severe enough" is a sufficiently significant understatement. It was, as a matter of fact, nakedly revengeful and out of all proportion to the crimes of which he had been found guilty. On the first verdict he was sentenced to two years' imprisonment; on the second to a further imprisonment of three years, at the expiry of which he was to pay a fine of £500, find two securities in £2500 each for his good behaviour for fourteen years, and himself be bound in a recognisance of £10,000. Between the verdict and the passing of the sentence Lord George escaped to Holland, but he was not allowed to remain there long. Repatriated to England, he arrived at Harwich in the latter end of July, and went thence to Birmingham, where he lay low till December. He had in the meantime become a convert to the Jewish faith and was rigidly performing its prescribed rites and duties. Then the authorities got on his track. Questions had also arisen, it seems, as to his sanity and the advisability of his being at large. He was arrested, taken to London, and lodged in Newgate. "His appearance in court when brought up to receive the sentence he had previously eluded is described as being miserable in the extreme. He was wrapt up in an old greatcoat, his beard hanging down on his breast, whilst his studiously sanctimonious deportment and other traits of his conduct too evidently showed an aberration of intellect. He bowed in silence and with devout humility on hearing his sentence. Soon after his confinement he got printed and distributed a number of treasonable handbills, copies of which he sent to the Ministry with his name attached to them. These, like his 'prisoners' petition', were composed of extracts from Moses and the prophets, evidently bearing upon the unhappy condition of the King, who was then in a state of mental alienation. In the following July 1789, this singular and unhappy being addressed a letter or petition to the National Assembly of France, in which, after eulogising the progress of revolutionary principles, he requests of them to intervene on his behalf with the English Government to get him liberated. He was answered by that body that they did not feel themselves at liberty to interfere; but he was visited in prison by several of the most eminent revolutionists, who assured his lordship of their best efforts for his release. To the application of these individuals, however, Lord Grenville answered that their entreaties could not be complied with. After Lord Grenville's answer, Lord George remained quietly in prison, occasionally sending letters to the printer of the *Public Advertiser*, written in the same half-frenzied style as his former productions. In November 1793, after being confined ten months longer than the prescribed term of his imprisonment, for want of the necessary security for his release, he expired in Newgate of a fever, having been delirious for three days previous to his death."

SIR THOMAS URQUHART

The Knight of Cromarty

IT was long the opinion, repeatedly expressed by writers about him, that few details were available of the life of Urquhart, or, as one of them said, after putting all he had been able to glean into three short sentences, "meagre and few as these particulars are, they yet comprehend all that is left us regarding the history of a person who, to judge by the expressions which he employs when speaking of himself in his writings, expected to fill no inconsiderable space in the eyes of posterity". But this opinion as to the lack of biographical material was happily as wrong as the same writer's opinion that, "with a translation of Rabelais, remarkably well executed, begins and ends all possibility of conscientiously complimenting him on his literary attainments—all the rest of his productions, though in each occasional scintillations of genius may be discovered, are mere rhapsodies, incoherent, unintelligible, and extravagantly absurd".

A full-dress, and admirably written, biography of Sir Thomas by the Rev. John Willcock appeared in 1899, and it has since become known that materials exist for its not inconsiderable amplification. That, together with a much fuller study of Urquhart's writings, is a task well worth undertaking, especially since, in regard to the latter, modern taste is likely to make far more of them and enjoy them much better than that of our ancestors, who were unduly attached to what was plainly rational and had little or no appreciation of Urquhart's stylistic tricks. They were much too ready to dismiss him as a nonsensical braggart and arrant liar just because they could not appreciate a man using the mythopoeic faculty on the facts of his own life and the men and events of which he was writing.

But despite the extravagances of his style, subsequent research has shown that Urquhart told the truth to a far greater extent than was generally believed to be possible. It must also be remembered that Urquhart was utterly opposed to the side that won in his time and has since dominated Scotland. Practically all those who have written about it were not only on that side, opposed to his, but were constitutionally incapable of understanding him, since "only a mind like his own could trace the maze of its windings and turnings, and fathom the depths of its eccentricity. In his thoughts 'truth is constantly becoming interfused with fiction, possibility with certainty, and the hyperbolical extravagance of his style only keeps even pace with the prolific shootings of his imagination'." His vanity is perhaps, as Mr Willcock agrees, the most striking trait of his character, "but only a very hard-hearted moralist would call it a vice in his case, for it is as artless as it is boundless, and is combined with so much kindness of heart and generosity of feeling, that we are more entertained by it than indignant at it. No one who looks into his works can doubt the intensity of his patriotism. Indeed, his passionate longing after personal fame is in all cases combined with the wish to confer additional glory upon the land of his birth. His devotion to the Royalist cause is of the purest and most heroic type, and the general tone of his character, as revealed to us in his books, is elevated and noble. At the same time there is an element of the grotesque in it, so that in his disinterested and chivalrous disposition he reminds us of Don Quixote, while in his frequent allusions to struggles with pecuniary difficulties, as well as in his use of magniloquent language, he distinctly recalls Wilkins Micawber. A lively fancy, a strain of genuine erudition beneath his pedantry, and some sparks of insanity, are other elements in his fantastical character. . . . It is perhaps expected that one should, in a measure, apologise for the eccentricities of Urquhart's character and literary style by explaining that he was a humorist. But, unfortunately, humour is a quality in which Urquhart is lacking, unless we understand by the word mere fantastical quaintness of thought and speech. In one passage of his works he speaks with contempt of 'shallow-brained humorists', and we should wrong his ghost by putting him among those whom he abhorred. Not a single trace of that subtle, graceful play of fancy and of feeling which enters into our conception of humour is to be found in his works. His readers may smile as they turn over his pages, but he is always in deadly earnest."

It must not be forgotten, however, that Mr Willcock was a minister. The present writer does not find Urquhart's lack of humour in any way unfortunate. Humour has long been the curse of Scotland. It is a means of avoiding, of laughing away, all serious issues. It is generally assumed, and acted upon, that "to have no sense of humour" is a man's worst condemnation and immediately disposes of him as a mere crank. It is Urquhart's style that has always been the great offence and stumbling-block to the nit-wits. Everything must be dressed up "with divers quaint and pertinent similes" before it is fit to be introduced to the reader's notice. "History, philosophy, science, literature are ransacked for illustrations of the commonest subject." As Sir Theodore Martin says: "His fancy is ever on the alert, and you are constantly surprised by some incongruous image, begotten in its wanton dalliance with knowledge the most heterogeneous. He has always an eye to effect. His own learning must be brought into play, rhetorical tropes must flourish through his periods, 'suggesting to our minds two several things at once', and, of course, as diverse as possible, that 'the spirits of such as are studious in learning may be filled with a most wonderful delight'." This is not the sort of thing that appeals to the man in the street, and in these democratic days Urquhart is an insult to common sense. Carlyle was long gravely misunderstood for a similar reason. "Carlyle had his own vituperative form of expression; he was impatient and irritable; but it is abundantly clear now, upon the evidence of a cloud of witnesses, that his marriage was happy above the average. Mary Boyle, a most discerning woman, protested that 'the injudicious publication of such exaggerated expressions through a cold medium of printed words conveyed a most erroneous impression of the man himself'. . . . He would break off suddenly, and all the venom and bitterness be drowned in a burst of ringing laughter, and his handsome though naturally grim face ripple all over with good-humoured smiles, so that no one who saw or heard him could doubt the kindly nature and the tender heart."

Urquhart has been divided from the vast majority of Scots since his own day—and is divided to-day—by the barrier he indicates when he says (and I think rightly) that "ignorance, together with hypocrisy, usury, oppression, and iniquity took root in these parts [Scotland], when uprightness, plain-dealing, and charity, with Astroea, took their flight with Queen Mary of Scotland into England".

Here is a picture of a Scot. "Alan had a weird innate conviction that he was beyond ordinary judgment. Katherine could never quite see where it came in. Son of a Scottish baronet, and captain in a Highland regiment, did not seem to her stupendous. As for Alan himself, he was handsome in uniform, with his kilt swinging and his blue eye glaring. Even stark naked and without any trimmings, he had a bony, dauntless, overbearing manliness of his own. The one thing Katherine could *not quite* appreciate was his silent, indomitable assumption that he was actually first-born, a born lord. He was a clever man, too, ready to assume that General This or Colonel That might really be his superior. Until he actually came into contact with General This or Colonel That. Whereupon his overweening blue eye arched in his bony face, and a faint tinge of contempt infused itself into his homage. Lordly, or not, he wasn't much of a success in the worldly sense. . . . Sometimes he would stand and look at her in silent rage, wonder, and indignation. The wondering indignation had been *almost* too much for her. What did the man think he was?"

That (the quotation is from one of D. H. Lawrence's short stories) is precisely the sort of Scot Urquhart was; the sort that is in the minority but every one of whom is worth thousands of the other sort, the canny, respectable, hard-working, humorous sort. The Katherine of the short story succumbed to one of the other sort, and it was profound understanding of Lawrence's to write: "Gradually a curious sense of degradation started in her spirit. It was almost like having a disease. Everything turned into mud. She realised the difference between being married to a soldier, a ceaseless born fighter, a sword not to be sheathed, and this other man, this cunning civilian, this subtle equivocator, this adjuster of the scales of truth." That is just what has happened to Scotland; that is what the Union with England has resulted in—the general, almost the complete, substitution of that first sort of man for this second sort. "What do they want to do?" one is inclined to ask of all these hordes of Anglo-Scots, and to reply with Lawrence: "Undermine, undermine, undermine. Believe in nothing, care about nothing; but keep the surface easy, and have a good time. Let us undermine one another. There is nothing to believe in, so let us undermine everything. But look out! No scenes, no spoiling the game! Stick to the rules of the game. Be sporting, and don't do anything that would make a commotion! Keep the game going smooth and jolly, and bear your bit like a sport. Never by any chance injure your fellow man openly. But always injure him secretly. Make a fool of him and undermine his nature. Break him up by undermining him, if you can. It's good sport."

As Mr Willcock says: "Few persons who take an interest in general literature are wholly unacquainted with the name of Sir Thomas Urquhart, as that of the translator of a great French classic. Only the more erudite can tell how the name of another literary man, Pierre Antoine Motteux, comes to be associated with his in connection with the translation in question, and are aware that the Scottish knight is the author of original compositions in such diverse departments as poetry, trigonometry, genealogy, and biography, and that he played a prominent part in the public life of his time. . . . I think it would be a pity if his romantic, fantastical figure were to pass into oblivion." All the more so, since, as a recent writer on Urquhart, Mr Francis Watson, has said: "If the seventeenth century could have brought itself to believe that any good thing could come out of Scotland, *The Jewel* might have been recognised as the product of one of the most astonishing minds of the northern Renaissance. In his epistle, 'to the honoured, noble translatour of Rabelais', De la Salle wrote that—

> . . . Now we see
> All wit in Gascone and in Cromartie,
> Besides that *Rabelais* is conveigh'd to us,
> And that our Scotland is not barbarous.

But the legend of Scottish Barbarism dies hard, and we still seem content to accept Urquhart's Rabelais as an unaccountable miracle."

Urquhart was born in 1611, and entered the University of Aberdeen in 1622. Whatever doubts may be entertained as to Urquhart's claim that the connection of his family with the north-west of Scotland went back as far as 554 B.C., when an ancestor of his named Beltistos crossed over from Ireland and built a castle near Inverness, the family was certainly of considerable antiquity and for many generations one of the most distinguished in that part of the country. Nisbet, the great authority on heraldry, says that "they enjoyed not only the honourable office of hereditary Sheriff-Principal of the Shire of Cromarty, but the great part, if not the whole, of the said shire did belong to them, either in property or superiority, and they possessed a considerable estate besides in the Shire of Aberdeen". The admiralty of the seas from Caithness to Inverness also belonged to them. Although his father, also Sir Thomas, received his estates "without any burden of debt, how little soever, or provision of brother, sister, or any other of his kindred or alliance wherewith to affect it'', his affairs got into serious disorder through mismanagement and neglect and the later years of his life were troubled by pecuniary difficulties. His son says of him: "Of all men living he was the justest, equallest, and most honest in his dealings, and his humour was, rather than to break his word, to lose all he had, and stand to his most undeliberate promises whatever they might cost; which too strict adherence to the austerest principles of veracity proved oftentimes damageable to him in his negotiations with many cunning sharks, who knew with what profitable odds they could screw themselves in upon the windings of so good a nature. . . . By the unfaithfulness, on the one side, of some of his menial servants, in filching from him much of his personal estate, and falsehood of several chamberlains and bailiffs to whom he had entrusted the managing of his rents, in the unconscionable discharge of their receipts, by giving up one account thrice, and of such accounts many; and, on the other part, by the frequency of disadvantageous bargains, which the slyness of the subtle merchants did involve him in, his loss came unawares upon him, and irresistibly, like an armed man; too great trust to the one, and facility in behalf of the other, occasioning so grievous a misfortune, which nevertheless did not proceed from want of knowledge or ability in natural parts, for in the business of other men he would have given a very sound advice, and was surpassing dexterous in arbitraments, upon any reference submitted to him, but that he thought it did derogate from the nobility of his house and reputation of his person to look to petty things in matters of his own affairs."

In 1637 he had to appeal to his sovereign against the urgency of his creditors, and a Letter of Protection was issued in his favour. It ran as follows: "Letter of Protection granted by King Charles the First, under his great seal, to Sir Thomas Urquhart of Cromarty, from all diligence at the instance of his creditors, for the space of one year, thereby giving him a *persona standi in judicio* notwithstanding he may be at the horn and taking him under his royal protection during the time. Dated at St. James's, 20th March, 1637." The paradoxical effect of this was that the creditors might "put him to the horn", *i.e.* according to the usual legal form, order him in the King's name to pay his debts on penalty of being outlawed as a traitor, while the King himself authorised him to take no notice of the proceedings.

Meanwhile the son, our Sir Thomas, was travelling on the Continent. "The kind of figure cut by a young *English* gentleman of that period upon the Continent we know from the testimony of Portia, for it can scarcely be that much change had taken place in the interval of a generation, between her time and the end of the first quarter of the seventeenth century. He was generally unversed in the languages of the countries he visited, and, from his lack of Latin, French, or Italian, was apt to fail in understanding the natives, or in making himself understood by them. He might be handsome in figure, but conversation with him was reduced to the level of a dumb-show. His dress was often very odd and his manners eccentric, as though he had bought his doublet in Italy, his round hose in France, his bonnet in Germany, and his behaviour—everywhere. A strong contrast to him in the matter of language was the young Scotsman of the period, if Sir Thomas Urquhart is to be taken as at all the average specimen of his nation. He says that when he travelled through France, Spain, and Italy, he spoke the languages to such perfection that he might easily have passed himself off as a native of any one of these countries. Some advised him to do so, but his patriotic feelings were too strong to allow him to follow such a course; 'he plainly told them (without making bones thereof) that truly he thought he had as much honour by his own country, which did contrevalue the riches and fertility of those nations, by the valour, learning, and honesty, wherein it did parallel, if not surpass, them'. It is somewhat difficult for the mind to grasp the idea of a Scotsman in those days, when so many of the things which we now associate with the nationality were not in existence—when his Church was Episcopalian in constitution, the Shorter Catechism not yet written by Englishmen for his use, Burns unborn, and distilled spirits not extensively used as a beverage. . . . The characteristics by which a Scot abroad in those days was recognised were, not shrewdness in making bargains, economical habits, indomitable perseverance, and unsleeping caution but the pride and high-spiritedness which made him keen in detecting and swift in avenging slights that might be cast upon the country from which he came. So deep was the impression made by these peculiarities upon foreign nations that they became proverbial. 'He is a Scot, he has pepper in his nose' (*Scotus est, piper in naso:* mediaeval proverb) said they, somewhat familiarly yet with a touch of fear, when they noticed the flashing eye, and the hand instinctively seeking the sword-hilt. 'High-spirited as a Scot' (*Fier comme un Écossais:* French proverb) they exclaimed with admiration when among themselves some soul was moved to unwonted courage."

"My heart", says Sir Thomas himself, "gave me the courage for adventuring in a foreign climate, thrice to enter the lists against men of three several nations, to vindicate my native country from the calumnies wherewith they had aspersed it; wherein it pleased God so to conduct my fortune that, after I had disarmed them, they in such sort acknowledged their error, and the obligation they did owe me for sparing their lives, which justly by the law of arms I might have taken, that, in lieu of three enemies that formerly they were I acquired three constant friends both to myself and my compatriots, whereof by several gallant testimonies they gave evident proof, to the improvement of my country's credit in many occasions."

Part of Urquhart's time abroad was devoted to the fascinating occupation of book-hunting, and he took great pleasure in the spoils thus won. When they were set in order on shelves in the library of the castle of Cromartie, he looked upon them with the joy which only book-collectors know. "They were", he says, "like to a complete nosegay of flowers which in my travels I had gathered out of the gardens of above sixteen several kingdoms."

Returning to Scotland, Urquhart took an active part as a Royalist in the troubles of the times. He tells us that, early in 1639, "having obtained, though with a great deal of difficulty, fifteen hundred subscriptions to a bond conceived and drawn up in opposition to the vulgar covenant; he selected from amongst them so many as he thought fittest for taking in hand the dissolving of their committees and unlawful meetings". "About ten o'clock on 13th May, they started for Turriff, marching in 'a very quiet and sober manner', and by daybreak managed to steal upon the village by an unguarded path. The sound of trumpets and of drums aroused the unsuspecting Covenanters to the fact that they had been fairly surprised. 'Some were sleeping, others drinking and smoking tobacco, others walking up and down.' A few volleys of musketry, and a few shots discharged from the cannon, served to disperse them, and the village was taken possession of by the attacking force. It was but a slight skirmish, in which three men were killed, two of the Covenanters and one of the Royalists, but it was the first of the battles in the great Civil War, which raged for so many years and deluged with blood so many fruitful plains in each of the three kingdoms. On this account 'the Trot of Turriff', as it was called, should not be forgotten." A little later "a small number of prominent Royalists, of whom Sir Thomas was one, resolved to leave Scotland where the cause to which they were devoted was at such a low ebb". They embarked at Aberdeen and sailed to England to offer their services to Charles I. "Urquhart", says Dr. Irving, "was within two days landed at Berwick, where he found the Marquis of Hamilton and delivered to him a letter from the leaders of the Northern Royalists. He had likewise undertaken to be the bearer of despatches to the King, containing the signatures of the same chieftains; and, having proceeded to the royal quarters, he obtained an audience of His Majesty and explained to him their past exertions and future plans for his service. He appears to have been satisfied with his own reception, and the written answer 'gave great contentment to all the gentlemen of the north that stood for the king'."

In the meantime old Sir Thomas's affairs have been going from bad to worse, till at last the sound of one of his creditors' voices was in his ears as "the hissing of a basilisk". "The disorderly troubles of the land", says his son of him, "being then far advanced, though otherways he disliked them, were a kind of refreshment to him and intermitting relaxation from a more stinging disquietness. For that our intestinal troubles and distempers, by silencing the laws for a while, gave some repose to those that longed for a breathing time, and by huddling up the terms of Whitsuntide and Martinmas, which in Scotland are the destinated times for payments of debts, promiscuously with the other seasons of the year, were as an oxymeljulep wherewith to indormiat them in a bitter-sweet security." However, old Sir Thomas died in April 1642, and our author took up the burdens of his ancestral estate and commenced a long and bitter warfare against the "usurious cormorants", as he called the creditors.

He returned in 1645 to live at Cromartie. His rental still amounted to £1000 sterling a year, which represents £7000 in our time, but a debt of twelve or thirteen years' income was a very serious burden upon such an estate. "There can be little doubt that the entanglement to which the financial affairs of the house of Urquhart were involved became none the less confused and confusing when the gallant knight applied himself to unravel it", says Mr Willcock. "That was scarcely a task for which he was fitted. Much more appropriate would it have been for him to draw the sword, like Alexander, and cut the Gordian knot. . . . There can be no doubt that he 'made an effort' more than once. In vain did he have recourse to 'pecunial charms, and holy water out of Plutus' cellar'. The charms were indeed potent, but they were not applied long enough; the holy water was composed of the right ingredients, but there was too little of it in the cellars at Cromartie. He could not, with all his struggles, succeed in curing what the Limousin scholar in Rabelais calls 'the penury of pecune in the marsupie' (*i.e.* the want of money in the purse)—that complaint which is so mortifying to the pride of any gentleman, but which is specially exasperating to a Highland gentleman. His cares and distresses, or, as he calls them, his 'solicitudinary and luctiferous discouragements', were enough 'to appal the most undaunted spirits, and kill a very Paphlagonian partridge, that is said to have two hearts'.

"Probably Sir Thomas was harshly dealt with by his father's creditors. They had to do with a man who was unpractical, and fantastical in the highest degree, and morbidly sensitive in all matters that seemed to lower his dignity or to cast a slur upon his honour. His brains seethed with plans for the improvement of agriculture, trade, and education, but none of these did the importunity of his creditors permit him to carry into effect. 'Truly I may say', he complains, 'that above ten thousand several times I have by these flagitators been interrupted for money, which never came to my use, directly or indirectly, one way or other, at home or abroad, at any one time whereof I was busied with speculations of greater consequence than all they were worth in the world; from which, had I not been violently plucked away by their importunity, I could have emitted to public view above five hundred several treatises on inventions never before thought upon by any.' Before his imagination there floated the dream of what he might have been, and his mind alternated between passionate remonstrances against his unfortunate circumstances and delusive hopes and anticipations. The editor of the Maitland Club edition of Urquhart's works truly remarks that there is a melancholy earnestness, almost approaching insanity, in his wild speculations on what he might have done for himself and his country, but for the weight of worldly encumbrances. 'Even so', he says, 'may it be said of myself, that when I was most seriously inbusied about the raising of my own and my countrie's reputation to the supremest reach of my endeavours, then did my father's creditors, like as many millstones hanging at my heels, pull down the vigour of my fancy and violently hold that under which otherwise would have ascended above the sublimest regions of vulgar conception.' So convinced was he that the schemes and inventions with which his thoughts were occupied were of immense value that he declared that he ought to have the benefit of that Act of James III (36th statute of his fifth Parliament) which provides that the debtor's movable goods be first 'valued and discussed before his lands be apprised'. He claimed this as a right from the State; 'and if', he says, 'conform to the aforesaid Act, this be granted, I do promise shortly to display before the world ware of greater value than ever from the East Indias was brought in ships to Europe'. But unfortunately the Philistines were too strong for him. . . . Among other wrongs and losses inflicted upon him was the sequestration of his library, which he had collected with such pains. Sir Thomas says that he sought eagerly to be allowed to purchase back the precious volumes, but was hindered by the spitefulness and indifference of those to whom he made application, and was ultimately able to secure only a few of them. . . . It must have been very hard for the proud-hearted chieftain to see his farms devastated, his tenants maltreated, his library thrown to the winds, a garrison placed in his house, and troops of horse quartered upon his lands without any allowance, in addition to all the misery and impoverishment which his father's wastefulness and neglect had brought upon him."

Urquhart in his *Logopandecteision* gives a splendid picture of his arch-enemy, Robert Lesley of Findrassie, the most relentless of his creditors. "Several gentlemen of good account", he says, "and other of his familiar acquaintance having many times very seriously expostulated with him why he did so implacably demean himself towards me, and with such irreconcilability of rancour that nothing could seem to please him that was consistent with my weal, his answers most readily were these: 'I have (see ye?) many daughters (see ye?) to provide portions for (see ye?) and that (see ye now?) cannot be done (see ye?) without money; the interest (see ye?) of what I lent (see ye?) had it been termly payed (see ye?) would have afforded me (see ye now?) several stocks for new interests; I have (see ye?) apprized lands (see ye?) for these sums (see ye?) borrowed from me (see ye now?), and (see ye?) the legal time being expired (see ye now?), is it not just (see ye?) and equitable (see ye?) that I have possession (see ye?) of these my lands (see ye?) according to my undoubted right (see ye now?)?' With these overwords of 'see ye' and 'see ye now', as if they had been no less material than the Psalmist's *Selah* and *Higgaion Selah*, did he usually nauseate the ears of his hearers when his tongue was in the career of uttering anything concerning me; who always thought that he had very good reason to make use of such like expressions, 'do you see' and 'do you see now' because there being but little candour in his meaning whatever he did or spoke was under some colour."

Urquhart's relations with the ministers of the churches of which he was patron were also of a painful character. The grounds of misunderstanding and dispute were numerous. In addition to political and ecclesiastical differences of opinion between him and the ministers of the three parishes (of which he was the sole heritor), there were disputes about augmentation of stipends, the abolition of his heritable right to the patronage of their churches, the legal proceedings taken by the incumbents to compel him to agree to arrangements decided upon by the Presbytery with regard to stipends and the upkeep of buildings, and there were also personal quarrels with the ministers themselves.

Urquhart gives a marvellously vivid and vigorous account of one of these: who "for no other cause but that he [Urquhart] would not authorise the standing of a certain pew in the church of Cromarty, put in without his consent by a professed enemy of his house, who had plotted the ruin thereof and one that had no land in the parish, did so rail against him and his family in the pulpit at several times, both before his face and in his absence, and with such opprobrious terms, more like a scolding knife-seller's wife than good minister, squirting the poison of detraction and abominable falsehood in the ears of his tenantry, who were the only auditors, did most ingrately and despitefully so calumniate and revile their master, his own patron and benefactor, that the scandalous and reproachful words striving which of them should first discharge against him its steel-pointed dart did oftentimes, like clusters of hemlock or wormwood dipt in vinegar, stick in his throat; he being almost ready to choke with the aconital bitterness and venom thereof, till the razor of extreme passion by cutting them into articulate sounds, and very rage itself, in the highest degree, by procuring a vomit, had made him spew them out of his mouth into rude, undigested lumps, like so many toads and vipers that had burst their gall. . . . The best is, when by some moderate gentlemen it was expostulated why against their master, patron, and benefactor they should have dealt with such severity and rigour, contrary to all reason and equity, their answer was, They were enforced and necessitated so to do by the synodal and presbyterial conventions of the Kirk, under pain of deprivation and expulsion from their benefices: I will not say 'an evil egg of an evil crow', but may safely think that a well-sanctified mother will not have a so ill-instructed brat, and that *injuria humana* cannot be the lawful daughter of a *jure divino* parent."

Although Sir Theodore Martin says that Urquhart's statements with regard to his misfortunes should not be taken too literally, any more than the announcements of his wonderful inventions and designs, the fact of the matter is that in both these, and all other, connections Urquhart told a great deal more truth (no matter how richly he dressed it up) than was generally believed; and the grievances he complained of were certainly not imaginary. "It is beyond dispute that he suffered heavily in his property in consequence of his adherence to the Royalist cause. In 1663 his brother, Sir Alexander, presented a petition asking compensation for the losses suffered in the time of his father and brother. The commissioners appointed to examine into these claims reported that, before 1650, the damage inflicted upon the Urquhart property amounted to £20,303 Scots, and, during 1651–52, to £39,203 Scots—in all £59,506 Scots, which is almost £5000 sterling."

After the death of the King, Urquhart again appeared in arms, having joined a considerable party, of which the other leaders were Thomas Mackenzie of Pluscardine, brother to the Earl of Seaforth, Colonel Hugh Fraser, and John Munro of Lumlair. They took possession of Inverness and dismantled the fortifications. On 2nd March 1649 the Estates of Parliament declared Sir Thomas a rebel and a traitor, characterising him and his associates as "wicked and malignant persons intending so far as in them lies, for their own base ends, to lay the foundation of a new and unnatural war within the bowels of this their native country". He, and others, were also threatened with excommunication, but he made a satisfactory appearance before the Commission of the General Assembly in Edinburgh on 22nd June 1650, and was spared that penalty and pardoned for his share in the Northern insurrection. In 1651 he took up arms for the third time and marched into England with the Scottish forces under David Lesley. In due course Urquhart found himself in quarters at Worcester. His luggage, which was stored in an attic in his billet there, consisted, besides "scarlet cloaks, buff suits, and arms of all kinds", of seven large "portmantles", three of which were filled with unpublished works in manuscript, and other valuable documents The battle of Worcester was fought on 3rd September, and Urquhart, as also, it seems, more than one of his brothers, was taken prisoner. The greatest misfortune that befel him was the sad fate that overtook his precious manuscripts. He related the story in his own inimitable way:

"No sooner had the total rout of the regal party at Worcester given way to the taking of that city, and surrendering up of all the prisoners to the custody of the marshal-general and his deputies, but the liberty, customary at such occasions to be connived at in favour of a victorious army, emboldened some of the new-levied forces of the adjacent counties to confirm their conquest by the spoil of the captives. For the better achievement of which design, not reckoning those great many others that in all the other corners of the town were ferreting every room for plunder, a string or two of exquisite snaps and clean shaves, if ever there were any, rushed into Master Spilsbury's house [Urquhart's billet], broke into an upper chamber, where finding (besides scarlet cloaks, buff suits, arms of all sorts, and other such rich chaffer) at such an exigent escheatable to the prevalent soldier [*i.e.* at such an extremity liable to be forfeited to the victorious soldier], seven large portmantles full of precious commodity; in three whereof, after a most exact search for gold, silver, apparel, linen, or any whatever adornments of the body, or pocket implements, as was seized upon in the other four, not hitting on any things but manuscripts in folio, to the quantity of six score and eight quires and a half, divided into six hundred and forty-two quinternions and upwards, the quinternion consisting of five sheets, and the quire of five and twenty; besides some writings of suits in law, and bonds, in both worth above three thousand pounds English, they in a trice carried all whatever else was in the room away save those papers, which they then threw down on the floor as unfit for their use; yet immediately thereafter, when upon carts the aforesaid baggage was put to be transported to the country, and that by the example of many hundreds of both horse and foot, which they had loaded with spoil, they were assaulted with the temptation of a new booty, they apprehending how useful the paper might be unto them, went back for it, and bore it straight away; which done, to every one of those their comrades whom they met with in the streets they gave as much thereof for packeting up of raisins, figs, dates, almonds, caraway, and other such like dry confections and other ware, as was requisite; who, doing the same themselves, did together with others kindle pipes of tobacco with a great part thereof, and threw out all the remainder upon the streets. . . . Of these dispersedly-rejected bundles of paper, some were gathered up by grocers, druggists, chandlers, pie-makers, or such as stood in need of any cartapaciatory utensil, and put in present service, to the utter undoing of all the writing thereof, both in its matter and order. One quinternion, nevertheless, two days after the fight on the Friday morning, together with two other loose sheets more, by virtue of a drizelling rain, which had made it stick fast to the ground, where there was a heap of seven and twenty dead men lying upon one another, was by the command of one Master Braughton taken up by a servant of his; who, after he had (in the best manner he could) cleansed it from the mire and mud of the kennel, did forthwith present it to the perusal of his master; in whose hands it no sooner came, but instantly perceiving by the periodical couching of the discourse, marginal figures, and breaks here and there, according to the variety of the subject that the whole purpose was destinated for the press, and by the author put into a garb befitting either the stationer's or printer's acceptance, yet because it seemed imperfect and to have relation to subsequent tractates, he made all the enquiry he could for trial whether there were any more such quinternions or not; by means whereof he got full information that above three thousands sheets of the like paper, written after that fashion and with the same hand, were utterly lost and embezzled, after the manner aforesaid; and was so fully assured of the misfortune that to gather up spilt water, comprehend the winds within his fist, and recover those papers, he thought would be a work of one and the same labour."

Urquhart, to whom the few papers Braughton found were restored, was not unduly distressed at his loss, stating that if he got but encouragement and time, freedom, and the enjoyment of his ancestral estates, he could reproduce the writings that had been on these lost papers again all right. Indeed the manner in which he subsequently made good and published some of these lost works witnesses to a speed in composition which might well leave him relatively undismayed by such a calamity. He refers to his book *The Jewel*: "Laying aside all other businesses", he says, "and cooping myself up daily for some hours together, betwixt the case and the printing-press, I usually afforded the setter copy at the rate of above a whole printed sheet in the day; which, although by reason of the smallness of a Pica letter, and close couching thereof, it did amount to three full sheets of my writing; the aforesaid setter, nevertheless (so nimble a workman he was), could in the space of twenty-four hours make dispatch of the whole, and be ready for another sheet. He and I striving thus who should compose fastest, he with his hand and I with my brain; and his uncasing of the letters and placing them in the composing instrument, standing for my conception; and his plenishing of the gally and imposing of the form, encountering with the supposed equi-value of my writing, we would almost every foot or so jump together in this joint expedition, and so nearly overtake other in our intended course, that I was oftentimes (to keep him doing) glad to tear off parcels of ten or twelve lines apiece, and give him them, till more were ready; unto which he would so suddenly put an order that almost still, before the ink of the written letters were dry, their representatives were (out of their respective boxes) ranked in the composing-stick; by means of which great haste, I writing but upon the loose sheets of carding-quires, which, as I minced and tore them, looking like pieces of waste paper, troublesome to get rallied, after such dispersive scatteredness, I had not the leisure to read what I had written, till it came to a proof, and sometimes to a full revise. So that by virtue of this unanimous contest, and joint emulation betwixt the theoretic and practical part, which of us should overhil other in celerity, we in the space of fourteen working days completed this whole book (such as it is) from the first notion of the brain to the last motion of the press; and that without any other help on my side, either of quick or dead (for books I had none, nor possibly would I have made use of any, although I could have commanded them), than what (by the favour of God) my own judgment and fancy did suggest unto me."

Urquhart was confined in the Tower of London, where he seems to have got on well with his captors and been treated with leniency. He writes with affectionate respect of several officers of the Parliamentary party and acknowledges courtesies extended towards him by Cromwell himself. He was later removed to Windsor Castle and not long afterwards paroled *de die in diem*. Among his friends at this time was the celebrated Roger Williams, the apostle of civil and religious liberty, founder of the settlement of Providence, Rhode Island, and missionary to the Indians. Williams was on intimate terms with Cromwell, Milton, and other leading Puritans, and able to render great service to his friend Urquhart, who pays a warm tribute to him in the Epilogue to his *Logopandecteision*.

Urquhart now set himself to make up for lost time in the matter of literary productivity, and published five books in 1652–3. The first of these was his famous *Peculiar Promptuary of Time* in which he set himself to show the Protector and the English Parliament that the family of Urquhart could be traced back, link by link, to Adam, and to suggest how unfortunate it would be if the ruling power extinguished a race which had successfully resisted the scythe of Time and was capable of rendering great service to the State. This *Hantoxpondoxanon* or *Pedigree* shows him as 153rd in descent from Adam, while on the maternal side, his mother was 146th in descent from Eve. The line runs through the Sethite and not the Cainite branch of the human race, and, among the sons of Noah, it passes through Japhet. "The story", says Mr Willcock, "is told of a marginal note being found in the history of some ancient Highland family, to the effect that 'about this time the Flood took place'."

Something like this is to be found in the document before us, for under the date 2893 B.C. Sir Thomas adds to a mention of his ancestor Noah, a remark to the effect that "the Universal Deluge occurred in the six hundredth year complete of his age". Mr Willcock also adds the following footnote: "Poor Sir Thomas thought that he was going back to the beginning when he traced his descent up to Adam, or, to be more exact, to the red earth of which the 'protoplast' was made. The late Charles Darwin carried back the pedigree of man a prodigious length, though he lowered its quality. There can be little doubt that our author would have disdained to accept what used to be called 'the lower animals' as, in any sense, ancestors of mankind, or, at any rate, of the dignified family of Urquhart." He, indeed, never "lowers the quality"; the record is one of descent from generation to generation through men of most distinguished fame, and women of exceptional beauty and brilliance. "Sir Thomas does not let us off easily. After subjecting our credulity to a severe strain by one kind of statement, he unexpectedly increases the tension by another. Thus he says that an ancestor in the fifteenth century, Thomas Urquhart, had by his wife Helen Abernethie, daughter of Lord Salton, five and twenty sons, who grew up to manhood, and eleven daughters, all of whom found husbands. It would only have been kind of him to have reduced these numbers a little. But on one point he has spared us; we are not asked to believe that there were others who died in infancy."

In a postscript to this amazing production Sir Thomas explains that he has just given his readers a sketch of the history of his family, but hopes to furnish them with a complete narrative as soon as he obtains his release from his parole and is at liberty to attend to this and to other matters of great importance. The thought of the delightful book in store for mankind is so attractive to him that he cannot help dilating upon it. "In the great chronicle of the House of Urquhart", he continues, "the aforementioned Sir Thomas Urquhart purposeth, by God's assistance, to make mention of the illustrious families from thence descended, which as yet are in esteem in the countries of Germany, Bohemia, Italy, France, Spain, England, Scotland, Ireland, and several other nations of a warmer climate, adjacent to that famous territory of Greece, the lovely mother of this most ancient and honourable stem." He also intends not to omit the name of any family with which at any time the aforesaid house has contracted alliance. "And finally," he says, "for confirmation of the truth in deriving his extraction from the Ionian race of the Prince of Achaia, and in the deduction of all the considerable particulars of the whole story, the author is resolved to produce testimonies of Arabic, Greek, Latin, and other writers of such authentic approvation that we may boldly from thence infer consequences of no less infallible verity than any that is not grounded on faith by means of a Divine illumination as is the story of the Bible, or on reason by virtue of the unavoidable inference of a necessary concluding demonstration as that of the Elements of Euclid." Alas, this great and conclusive work was never forthcoming.

I only know of one Scottish parallel to Urquhart's inordinate love of family and it took a very different direction. It was the provision in the will of John Stuart McCaig, banker and art critic, for a Tower situated on the Battery Hill above Oban, with trust funds "for the purpose of erecting monuments and statues for myself, brothers, and sisters" in the niches thereof, the making of these statues to be given to Scottish sculptors from time to time as the necessary funds accumulate for that purpose". "In order to avoid the possibility of vagueness of any kind I have to describe and explain that I particularly want the trustees to erect on the top of the wall of the tower, statues in large figures of all my five brothers, and of myself, namely Duncan, John, Dugald, Donald, and Peter, and of my father, Malcolm, and of my mother Margaret, and of my sisters Jean, Catherine, Margaret, and Ann, and that these statues be modelled upon photographs, and where these may not be available, that the statues may have a family likeness to my own photograph, or any other member of my aforesaid family, and that these statues will cost not less than one thousand pounds sterling." The idea was that these statues should continue to be produced in perpetuity by successive generations of Scottish sculptors. One has a vision of scores of each ultimately crowding the top of the tower wall. One of the members of the family thus to be commemorated had died in infancy, but this was, of course, no reason why she should not be sculpt, as she might have become. McCaig died in 1902. He left ample funds, possessing heritable property with a yearly rental of between £2000 and £3000, and movable estate to the value of about £10,000. Unfortunately his testamentary disposition was set aside by the law courts and so the serried battalions of McCaigs in stone with which he designed to gratify the eyes of posterity to the end of time have not materialised.

Among Urquhart's other books there was *The Jewel* and *Logopandecteision*, or *The Universal Language*. The former is a collection of bits and pieces of various kinds, the best of which is Urquhart's famous account of his wonderful fellow countryman, the Admirable Crichton. He gives full rein here to his boundless love of Scotland while deploring the sad state of contemporary affairs. After suggesting various ways in which the tone of society in Scotland might be raised and sweetened—one being the establishment of "a free school and standing library in every parish"—he argues in favour of complete union between Scotland and England. The subject is introduced by lengthy quotations from speeches by Bacon delivered by him in Parliament as far back as 1608, in which the advantages of such an arrangement are urged. I cannot resist quoting his denunciation of those who by their covetousness had cast a slur on the Scottish name.

"Another thing there is", he says, "that fixeth a grievous scandal upon that nation in matter of philargyrie, or love of money, and it is this: There hath been in London, and repairing to it, for these many years together, a knot of Scottish bankers, collybists, or coin-couses, of traffickers in merchandise to and again, and of men of other profession, who by hook and crook, *fas et nefas*; slight and might (all being as fish their net could catch), having feathered their nests to some purpose, look so idolatrously upon their Dagon of wealth, and so closely (like the earth's dull centre), hug all unto themselves, that for no respect of virtue, honour, kindred, patriotism, or whatever else (be it never so recommendable) will they depart from so much as one single penny, whose emission doth not, without hazard of loss, in a very short time superlucrate, beyond all conscience, an additional increase to the heap of that stock which they so much adore; which churlish and tenacious humour hath made many that were not acquainted with any else of that country, to imagine all their compatriots infected with the same leprosy of a wretched peevishness, whereof those *quomodocunquizing* clusterfists and rapacious varlets have given of late such cannibal-like proofs, by their inhumanity and obdurate carriage towards some (whose shoe-strings they are not worthy to untie), that were it not that a more able pen than mine will assuredly not fail to jerk them on all sides, in case, by their better demeanour for the future, they endeavour not to wipe off the blot wherewith their native country, by their sordid avarice and miserable baseness, hath been so foully stained, I would at this very instant blaze them out in their names and surnames, notwithstanding the vizard of Presbyterian zeal wherewith they mask themselves, that like so many wolves, foxes, or Athenian Timons, they might in all times coming be debarred the benefit of any honest conversation."

The man who wrote that was no fool and had a very proper spirit. His pen would to-day be a valuable accession to the propaganda of his countryman, Major C. H. Douglas.

In the peroration of *The Jewel* Urquhart apologises for the comparative simplicity or baldness some may find in his style therein. "I could truly", he says, "have enlarged this discourse with a choicer variety of phrase, and made it overflow the field of the reader's understanding, with an inundation of greater eloquence; and that one way, tropologetically, by metonymical, ironical, metaphorical, and synecdochical instruments of elocution, in all their several kinds, artificially effected, according to the nature of the subject, with emphatical expressions in things of greater concernment, with catachrestical in matters of meaner moment; attended on each side respectively with an epiplectic and exegetic modification; with hyperbolical, either epitatically or hypocoristically, as the purpose required to be elated or extenuated, with qualifying metaphors, and accompanied by apostrophes; and lastly, with allegories of all sorts, whether apologal, affabulatory, parabolary, aenigmatic, or paraemial. And on the other part, schematologetically adorning the proposed theme with the most especial and chief flowers of the garden of rhetoric and omitting no figure either of diction or sentence, that might contribute to the ear's enchantment, or persuasion of the hearer. I could have introduced, in case of obscurity, synonymal, exargastic, and palilogetic elucidations; for sweetness of phrase, antimetathetic commutations of epithets; for the vehement excitation of a matter, exclamation in the front and epiphonemas in the rear. I could have used, for the promptlier stirring up of passion, apostrophal and prosopopoeial diversions; and, for the appeasing and settling of them, some epanorthotic revocations, and aposiopetic restraints. I could have inserted dialogisms, displaying their interrogatory part with communicatively psymatic and sustentative flourishes; or proleptically, with the refutative schemes of anticipation and subjection, and that part which concerns the responsary, with the figures of permission and concession. Speeches extending a matter beyond what it is, auxetically, digressively, transitiously, by ratiocination, aetiology, circumlocution, and other ways, I could have made use of; as likewise with words diminishing the worth of a thing, tapinotically, periphrastically, by rejection, translation and other means, I could have served myself."

As Mr Willcock suggests, had that nightmare of another Scotsman, Ruskin, who once had a vision of 10,000 school inspectors assembled on Cader Idris, been realisable, and could they have been treated as a class in elementary English, that passage might well have been read out to them as an exercise in dictation!

As to the *Logopandecteision*, "the idea of a universal language was not originated by Urquhart for it is said that something of the kind had been planned a generation earlier by the celebrated William Bedell (1570–1642), the Bishop of Kilmore and Ardagh, who is better known for promoting the translation of the Bible into the Irish tongue. We are told by Burnet, who wrote his life that he had in his diocese a clergyman named Johnston, a man of ability, but, unfortunately of 'mercurial wit'. In order to give him adequate employment, and to keep him, we suppose, out of mischief, Bedell planned out a scheme of a universal character, which should be understood by all nations as readily as the Arabic numerals or the figures in geometry, and started Johnston upon the task of completing it. He made, we are told, considerable progress with the scheme, but his labours were interrupted, and the results of them destroyed, by the frightful rebellion of 1641. . . . There is no evidence that Sir Thomas Urquhart ever really made a grammar or vocabulary of the new language. Indeed, he writes about it in such a manner as to lead one to think that he had made no way in the real working out of the scheme, but merely dreamed of what he was going to do. In the new tongue which was to supersede all others there were to be twelve parts of speech, all words would have at least ten synonyms, nouns and pronouns would have eleven cases and four numbers—singular, dual, plural, and redual—and verbs would have four voices, seven moods, and eleven tenses. 'In this tongue', says the author, 'there are eleven genders', wherein, he truthfully adds, 'it exceedeth all other languages'. 'Every word in this language', we are told [how it would have suited McGonagall!], 'signifieth as well backward as forward, and however you invert the letters, still shall you fall upon significant words, whereby a wonderful facility is obtained in making of anagrams. . . . Of all languages this is the most compendious in compliment and consequently fittest for courtiers and ladies. . . . As its interjections are more numerous, so are they more emphatical in their respective expression of passions, than that part of speech in any other language whatsoever.' 'This language', he says, 'affordeth so concise words for numbering, that the number for setting down, whereof would require in vulgar arithmetic more figures in a row than there might be grains of sand containable from the centre of the earth to the highest heavens, is in it expressed by two letters.' "

Hugh Miller, the geologist, speaks in high terms of Urquhart's linguistic invention. "The new chemical vocabulary," he says, "with all its philosophical ingenuity, is constructed on principles exactly similar to those which he [Urquhart] divulged more than a hundred years prior to its invention." Commenting on this, Mr Willcock says: "It is true that anyone who knows the principle of the nomenclature of salts, to which, we suppose, Hugh Miller refers, can tell a good deal about a salt from the name of it, say, nitrate of potassium KNO^2, but it would be impossible to invent a systematic nomenclature of which this would not be true". With regard to Urquhart's proposed eleven genders, Mr Willcock says: "Fault has been found with our English language for being somewhat defective in accentuating these distinctions; and an attempt to correct this shortcoming, to a certain extent, has been made by Southey in *The Doctor*. He proposed to anglicise the orthography of the female garment 'which is indeed the sister to the shirt', and then to utilise the hint offered in its new form; thus *Hemise* and *Shemise*. In letter-writing every person knows that male and female letters have a distinct character; they should therefore, he thought, be generally distinguished thus, *Hepistle* and *Shepistle*." And so on, with *Penmanship* and *Penwomanship*; *Heresy* and *Sheresy*; *Hecups* and *Shecups*, "which upon the principle of making our language truly British is better than the more classical form of *Hiccups* and *Hoeccups*, while, in its objective use, the word becomes *Hiscups* and *Hercups*".

Urquhart's literary fame rests securely upon his translation into English of the first three books of Rabelais. Of these the first and second appeared in two separate volumes in 1653, and the third was published by Pierre Antoine Motteux in 1693, long after Sir Thomas's death. Little need be said of this masterpiece here. As Tytler says: "It is impossible to look into it without admiring the ease, freshness, and originality which the translator has so happily communicated to his performance. All those singular qualifications which unfitted Sir Thomas to succeed in serious composition—his extravagance, his drollery, his unbridled imagination, his burlesque and endless epithets—are in the task of translating Rabelais transplanted into their true field of action and revel through his pages with a licence and buoyancy which is quite unbridled, yet quite allowable. Indeed, Urquhart and Rabelais appear, in many points, to have been congenial spirits, and the translator seems to have been born for his author."

"The buoyancy and unembarrassed sweep of its general

character," says Sir Theodore Martin, "which gives his Rabelais more the look of an original than of a translation, its rich and well-compacted diction, the many happy turns of phrase that are quite his own, have fairly earned for it the high estimation in which it has long been held. His task was one of extreme difficulty, and there have perhaps been few men besides himself who could have brought to it the world of omnigenous knowledge which it required. It was apparently Urquhart's ambition to realise in his own person the ideal of human accomplishment, to be at once

> Complete in feature and in mind,
> With all good grace to grace a gentleman.

He had left no source of information unexplored, few aspects of life unobserved, and, in the translation of Rabelais, he found full exercise for his multiform attainments. Ably as the work has been completed by Motteux, one cannot but regret that the worthy Knight of Cromarty had not spared him the task."

It is indeed an achievement which completely redeemed all the seemingly unprofitable foibles and extravagances of Urquhart's life. I will only quote one other tribute to it—a recent one by Mr Francis Watson. "The excellence and defects of Urquhart's masterpiece, 'the exuberant diversitie of his jovialissime entertainment', and the mishandling of the original which results from that exuberance, cannot", he says, "here be discussed at large. It is sufficient to declare that in spite of its inaccuracies, in spite of its length of two hundred thousand words as compared with the one hundred and thirty thousand words of Rabelais, Urquhart's translation of the first three books must still be considered the best rendering into any language of the work of the Reverent Rabbles (as Sir John Harrington affectionately called him). A single passage from the thirteenth chapter of the 'Third Book' will not only suggest the freedom with which Urquhart expanded the text, but will prove also that his fertility was not entirely polysyllabic. In this passage

Rabelais provides nine characteristic noises of animals. Here is Urquhart with seventy-one:

" 'The Philosopher . . . was, notwithstanding his uttermost endeavour to free himself from all untoward Noises, surrounded and environed about so with the barking of Currs, bawling of Mastiffs, bleating of Sheep, prating of Parrots, tattling of Jackdaws, grunting of Swine, girning of Boars, yelping of Foxes, mewing of Cats, cheeping of Mice, squeaking of Weasils, croaking of Frogs, crowing of Cocks, kekling of Hens, calling of Partridges, chanting of Swans, chattering of Jays, peeping of Chickens, singing of Larks, creaking of Geese, chirping of Swallows, clucking of Moorfowls, cucking of Cuckoos, bumbling of Bees, rammage of Hawks, chirming of Linnets, croaking of Ravens, screeching of Owls, wicking of Pigs, gushing of Hogs, curring of Pigeons, grumbling of Cushet-doves, howling of Panthers, curkling of Quails, chirping of Sparrows, crackling of Crows, nuzzing of Camels, wheening of Whelps, buzzling of Dromedaries, mumbling of Rabbits, cricking of Ferrets, humming of Wasps, misling of Tygers, bruzzing of Bears, sussing of Kitnings, clamouring of Scarfs, whimpering of Fullmarts, boing of Buffalos, warbling of Nightingales, quavering of Mavises, drintling of Turkeys, coniating of Storks, frantling of Peacocks, clattering of Magpies, murmuring of Stock-Doves, crouting of Cormorants, cighing of Locusts, charming of Beagles, guarring of Puppies, snarling of Wessens, rantling of Rats, guerieting of Apes, snuttering of Monkies, pioling of Pelicans, quecking of Ducks, yelling of Wolves, roaring of Lions, neighing of Horses, crying of Elephants, hissing of Serpents, and wailing of Turtles, that he was much more troubled than if he had been in the middle of the Crowd at the Fair at Fontenoy or Niort.' "

Urquhart died in Rabelaisan fashion—*car le rire est le propre de l'homme*. Exiled in France, secure from Presbyterians and creditors, he took such a fit of laughing when he heard of the Restoration of Charles II that he expired therewith. Dullards have doubted the truth of this story;

but, as Mr Willcock says, "we have to keep in mind that Sir Thomas was not alone in his folly, if folly it were; for a great wave of exultation swept over the three kingdoms at that time. Our author had, like many of his fellow Royalists, staked and lost everything he possessed in the defence of the House of Stuart, and one can have little difficulty in understanding how the announcement of the triumph of the cause, which was so dear to him, should have agitated him profoundly."

It was a very fitting end to his extraordinary life.

THE GREAT McGONAGALL

CONTRARY to the general opinion—in Scotland at all events, for I am not sure that he is much known in the English-speaking world outside Scotland—William McGonagall was not a bad poet; still less a good bad poet. He was not a poet at all, and that he has become synonymous with bad poetry in Scotland is only a natural consequence of Scottish insensitivity to the qualities alike of good poetry and of bad. There is so much that is bad in all the poetry that Scots people know and admire that it is not surprising that for their pet example of a good bad poet they should have had to go outside the range of poetry, good, bad, or indifferent, altogether. McGonagall is in a very special category, and has it entirely to himself. There are no other writings known to me that resemble his. So far as the whole tribe of poets is concerned, from the veritable lords of language to the worst doggerel-mongers, he stands alone, "neither fish, flesh, nor good red-herring," and certainly his "works" will be searched in vain for any of those ludicrous triumphs of anti-climax, those devastating incongruities, which constitute the weird and wonderful qualities of bad verse. This, of course, is recognised by experts in this peculiar department of literature. Hence, although it may be true enough of McGonagall that, in his own way,

> O'er all the Bards together put,
> From Friockheim to Japan,
> He towers above, beyond dispute,
> Creation's greatest man,

he, rightly, does not figure in such an anthology as *The Stuffed Owl.* As Wordsworth says:

> Yet, helped by Genius—untired Comforter,
> The presence even of a stuffed owl for her
> Can cheat the time. . . .

But McGonagall had no such help, and the last thing his incredible sincerity sought to do, or succeeded in doing, even to the tiniest extent, was to cheat the time.

It is laid down in the above-mentioned anthology that "good Bad Verse is grammatical, it is constructed according to the rubrics, its rhythms, rimes, and metres are impeccable. Generally the most distinguished poets—from Cowley to Tennyson—provide the nicest pieces in this anthology. The first quality of Bad Verse which the compilers have aimed at illustrating is bathos; other sure marks are all those things connoted by poverty of the imagination, sentimentality, banality, anaemia, obstipation, or constipation of the poetic faculty . . . and what Mr Polly called 'rockcockyo'." McGonagall stands outside all these requirements. His productions know nothing of grammar, the rubrics and the accepted devices of versification. Bathos is a sudden descent from some height —a manœuvre of mood of which McGonagall's dead levelness of utterance is quite incapable. Poverty of the imagination is a different thing altogether, and produces quite different effects, from that utter absence of anything in the nature of imagination at all in which he stands sole and supreme. His invariable flatness is far below mere banality; sentimentality and "rockcockyo" of any sort are entirely foreign to his stupendous straightforward seriousness alike of intention and expression; and anaemia is a term that suggests a human character of which his inspired work is completely devoid. So we find nothing at all in any of the Scottish examples given in this Anthology which resembles McGonagall's effects or suggests his singular signature. John Armstrong may write:

> For from the colliquation of soft joys
> How changed you rise, the ghost of what you was,

or describe Cheshire cheese as

> That which Cestria sends, tenacious paste
> Of solid milk . . .

or tell, in his *Advice to the Stout*, how

. . . The irresoluble oil
So gentle late and blandishing, in floods
Of rancid bile o'erflows.

Boswell may report the explosion of mirth which greeted the reading aloud at Reynolds' house of the apostrophe,

Now, Muse, let's sing of rats,

with which the poet, James Grainger, pompously began a fresh paragraph. Grainger, too, it was who, in the lines which begin, "And pity the poor planter", describes the dangers of blight to which the crops are subject and ends his passage thus:

The greenest garlands to adorn their brows
First pallid, sickly, dry, and withered show;
Unseemly stains succeed; which, nearer viewed,
By microscopic arts, small eggs appear,
Dire fraught with reptile life; alas, too soon
They burst their filmy gaol, and crawl abroad,
Bugs of uncommon shape. . . .

And Grainger's was the *Call to the Muse*:

Of composts shall the Muse disdain to sing?
Nor soil her heavenly plumes? The sacred Muse
Nought sordid deems, but what's base; nought fair
Unless true Virtue stamp it with her seal.
Then, planter, wouldst thou double thine estate,
Never, ah, never, be ashamed to tread
Thy dung-heaps.

Then there is Robert Pollok, author of *The Course of Time*, who now and again vouchsafes choice fragments such as the following:

And as the anatomist, with all his band
Of rude disciples, o'er the subject hung,
And impolitely hewed his way, through bones
And muscles of the sacred human form,
Exposing barbarously to wanton gaze
The mysteries of nature, joint embraced
His kindred joint, the wounded flesh grew up,
And suddenly the injured man awoke
Among their hands, and stood arrayed complete
In immortality—forgiving scarce
The insult offered to his clay in death.

Burns might have been much better represented than

he is in this collection, where all that is given is *Verses on the Death of Sir James Hunter Blair*, but the anthologists justly observe that "though the genius of Robert Burns is but grudgingly admitted by his countrymen, whose passion for their national poets Dunbar and James I tend perhaps to blind them to his undoubted merits, it must be allowed that Burns was a poet far above the average, a keen Freemason, a delightful table-companion, and a father whose habit of christening his daughters, legitimate and otherwise, by the name of Elizabeth, shows some appreciation of official or Whig history". And they add, very appropriately, that "a modern critic has well observed that when Burns unwisely discards the vernacular his efforts resemble 'nothing so much as a bather whose clothes have been stolen' ".

Scottish poetry is undoubtedly relatively very poor in the particular kinds of effects these anthologists are concerned with—largely because the poetic pretensions of Scotland have never soared so high, or been therefore susceptible of such falls, as those of England. My countrymen cannot vie with their Southern neighbours in the production of such gems as

> He cancelled the ravaging plague
> With the roll of his fat off the cliff;

or Chatterton's

> The blood-stained tomb where Smith and Comfort lie;

or Wordsworth's

> Spade, with which Wilkinson hath tilled his lands;

or Scott of Amwell's

> Methinks of friendship's frequent fate
> I hear my Frogley's voice complain.

Even in this department, however, the Scottish production is far richer than is commonly realised. We have, for example, those lines in James Hogg's *The Wife of Crowle*, when the ghost

> Has offered his hand with expression so bland,

and the same poet's quatrain in *Young Kennedy*:

> Who wept for the worthy MacDougal?—Not one.
> His darling Matilda, who, two months agone,
> Would have mourned for her father in sorrow extreme,
> Indulged in a painful delectable dream.

Scotland's Cornelius Whur, however—its prince of bad poets—is the eminent divine and religious writer, Zachary Boyd (1590–1653). Boyd was a scholar of very considerable learning; he composed in Latin and his qualifications in that language may be deemed respectable; his works also bear the evidence of his having been possessed of a critical knowledge of the Greek, Hebrew, and other languages. "He has", says one writer, "great fertility of explication, amounting often to diffuseness, and, in many cases, it would have been well had he known where to have paused." This is a very considerable understatement. He continually lapses into the ludicrous. He celebrated the fight at Newburnford, 28th August 1640, by which the Scottish Covenanting Army gained possession of Newcastle, in a poem of sixteen octavo pages. It opens with a panegyric on the victorious Lesley, and then proceeds to describe the battle:

> The Scots cannons powder and ball did spew,
> Which with terror the Canterburians slew.
> Balls rushed at random, which most fearfully
> Menaced to break the portals of the sky.
> In this conflict, which was both swift and surly,
> Bones, blood, and brains went in a hurly-burly.
> All was made hodge-podge. . . .

The pistol bullets were almost as bad as the cannon balls. They

> In squadrons came, like fire and thunder,
> Men's hearts and heads both for to pierce and plunder,
> Their errand was (when it was understood)
> To bathe men's bosoms in a scarlet flood.

In *The Flowers of Zion* he has a long grotesque description of Jonah's situation and soliloquy in the whale's belly:

What house is this, where's neither coal nor candle,
Where I nothing but guts of fishes handle?
. . . I sit still in such a straitened roome
Among such grease as would a thousand smother. . . .
In all the earth like unto me is none,
Far from all living I here lie alone,
Where I entombed in melancholy sink,
Choked, suffocated. . . .

In the vast mass of Boyd's unpublished manuscripts there must be many wonderful gems of absurdity. There is, for one thing, his preposterous ichthyology of which Mr John Buchan gives us a taste (from the MS. of Boyd's *The English Academie*) in his anthology *The Northern Muse*:

There is such great varietie
Of fishes of all kind
That it were great impietie
God's hand there not to find.

The Puffen Torteuse, and Thorneback,
The Scillop and the Goujeon,
The Shrimpe, the Spit-fish, and the Sprat,
The Stock-fish, and the Sturgeon . . .

The Periwinkle and Twinfish—
It's hard to count them all;
Some are for oyle, some for the dish;
The greatest is the Whale.

This, however, though somewhat akin, has a pedantic quality, an insistence on trifling detail, which McGonagall would have disdained. His very different angle of approach to such a subject is shown in his stanzas on *The Famous Tay Whale*:

'Twas in the month of December, and in the year of 1883,
That a monster whale came to Dundee,
Resolved for a few days to sport and play
And devour the small fishes in the silvery Tay.

He describes the efforts made to harpoon the whale, and how it was finally towed ashore at Stonehaven, and ends:

And my opinion is that God sent the whale in time of need,
No matter what other people may think or what is their creed;
I know fishermen in general are often very poor,
And God in His goodness sent it to drive poverty from their door.

So Mr John Wood has bought it for two hundred and twenty-six
pound
And has brought it to Dundee all safe and all sound;
Which measures 40 feet in length from the snout to the tail,
So I advise the people far and near to see it without fail.

Then hurrah for the mighty monster whale,
Which has got 17 feet 4 inches, from tip to tip, of a tail;
Which can be seen for a sixpence or a shilling,
That is to say, if the people are all willing.

What this amounts to, of course, is simply what quite uneducated and stupid people—the two adjectives by no means necessarily go together, for many uneducated people have great vitality and a raciness of utterance altogether lacking here—would produce if asked to recount something they had read in a newspaper. It is almost exactly of material of this kind that the consciousness of current events consists so far as most people are concerned. In their retailings of, or comments upon, such matters, the *hoi polloi* would also reflect their personal feelings, as is done here, by the tritest of emotional exclamations. If this is not quite all they are capable of "carrying away" of what they hear, see, and read, it is, at any rate, a very fair specimen of their powers of articulation.

The deviations from this stuff of common consciousness, or rather common conversation, are two. In the first place, there is the organisation of the material not only into some regular succession of sentences but into verses if only of the crudest kind. This is to be explained partly by the fact that McGonagall was trying to write up to a very vaguely conceived, or misconceived, level; he was trying to be "litt'ry". A similar laboriously unnatural organisation manifests itself very often when uneducated people try "to talk polite" rather than in their natural, much racier, if quite ungrammatical and disjointed way—and partly by the fact that a kind of rude rhyming is a very common knack and comes much more easily to many such people than any similar attempt to "rise above themselves" in prose would do.

In the second place, there is the insistence on giving the

exact figures. This was a special characteristic of McGonagall's. It is just possible that it was due at the outset to a vague Biblical reminiscence, but his constant use of it is due to his incorrigible laziness. In these circumstances the precise numbers were a veritable stand-by to him. They fascinated him; there was something so incontestable, so convincing about them; there was no getting past them—they clinched the whole matter. If his work gave him a real thrill at all it was when he came to such figures. Apart from that, however, his use of them was due to his laziness because he found them where he found his themes—in newspaper reports, which he did little but hammer out till he got rhymes at the end of his sprawling lines. What set McGonagall off on this tack was a combination of three factors—his laziness, his peasant conceit (carried, of course, to an absolutely abnormal length), and the fact that he lived in Dundee. Dundee was then and has since been the great home and fostering centre of the cheapest popular literature in Scotland, and huge fortunes have been built up there on precisely the chief ingredients of McGonagall's art—mindlessness, snobbery, and the inverted snobbery of a false cult of proletarian writers. So far as literature has been concerned, the idea of Burns as a "ploughman poet" has been fatal. Scotland has suffered since from an endless succession of railwayman poets, policeman poets, and the like. The movement was in full swing when McGonagall was caught up in it. It culminated in the collection and publication by a gentleman who lived near Dundee of the work of scores of utterly worthless rhymers, in no fewer than sixteen volumes, with a table showing the occupations of the contributors. It is not surprising that McGonagall thought—or was easily persuaded by one of his friends or more likely one of his tormentors—that he could do as well as any of these. Having once performed the miraculous feat of knocking a bit of journalese into rough rhyming verses, he naturally conceived an inordinate admiration for his own powers—and so far as any question of comparative worth arose it naturally seemed to his type of mind, with its almost inconceivably complete absence of intellectual background, that this was only a question of one man's opinion against another's, and McGonagall was not the man to cry stinking fish. He was, indeed, genuinely incapable of realising or being persuaded that his poems were not at least as good as any ever written—with the possible exception of Shakespeare's—and he did not hesitate to proclaim the fact. It may have been his persistence in this, the realisation that he really believed it and was prepared, if need be, to become a martyr for genius's sake, that led to his subsequent shameful baiting. For though the great majority of his contemporary Scottish rhymsters were exceedingly vain, and believed, no matter how belauded their contemptible productions might be, that far greater praise was their real due and would be accorded by posterity, it was their fashion to pretend to be humble. There was no pretence about McGonagall—a fact which in no way runs counter to his cunning understanding that most of those who praised him so egregiously did not believe what they said, though for the sake of a few coppers it paid him to accept their bogus attentions and finally allow them to "give him the bird" to their hearts' content. Where McGonagall differed from all these other working-men poets was that he knew nothing of poetry—nothing even of the execrable models they copied, nothing of the whole debased tradition of popular poetry in which they operated. He was quite incapable of all their stock *clichés*, their little flights of fancy, any indication whatever of play of spirit, anything like their range of subject-matter, and, above all, of any humour. He, in fact, heartily despised them and all the common attributes and graces of their verses, which he regarded as trivial and unworthy of his portentous Muse. But he stuck fast by the fundamental ingredients of the great Dundee recipe for sound family literature—a love of battles and an incontinent adoration of kings, queens, members of the royal family, the nobility, and the leading officers of the army and the navy; in short, the recipe which has made modern Scotland what it is. Knowing his own perfect loyalty and integrity in these great matters, the "slings and arrows of outrageous fortune" to which he was continuously subjected were incredible to him. He deserved better—in fact, there was nothing that he did not deserve. He was sustained through all his miserable career by this unwavering consciousness of his high deserts and enabled to regard all his calamities as a series of monstrous and inexplicable injustices. His "poems" were, in truth, little worse than those of the vast majority of Scottish poets whom the very type of people who baited him regarded with affectionate interest and approval; his "poems" were, in truth, little worse than those the vast majority of the Scottish people, now as then, regard as very poetry—but, in both cases, the little and yet how much it is! If, however, "extremes meet", there is no little justification for McGonagall linking his name with Shakespeare's, and indeed the course of literary history shows countless such linkings with that great name.

The connection between versification and mendicancy is a very old one. The writers of the old broadsides required a livelier turn of language, some faculty of satire or invective, and a sense of news values, all of which McGonagall conspicuously lacked. Neither had he the social address which was such an asset to Duncan Graham, the Skellat Bellman of Glasgow, for example. His affiliations are rather with the melancholy individuals, purporting to be ex-soldiers, who hawk terribly bad sets of verses from door to door to-day. I have no idea how this line pays these gentlemen, but a slightly higher type of tramp poet, selling little pamphlets of verse, seems to do fairly well, judging by several of these men I have known personally, who, little though they made by it, at least wrung a livelihood out of it and in so doing made a great deal more than all but one or two of the genuine and really gifted poets of our time. Even in Scotland to-day some of these tramp poets are faring none too badly.

McGonagall would have been exceedingly glad to have had a tenth of what they earn.

Others before McGonagall, much abler men, have tried in vain in Scotland to make a living by peddling their verses. Alexander Wilson, who subsequently became the great American ornithologist, for instance. "His muse was so busy that, in 1789, he began to think of publishing. As he could get no bookseller, however, to risk the necessary outlay, he was compelled to advance what little gains he had stored up, and getting a bundle of prospectuses thrown off, he set out with his pack for the double purpose of selling muslins and procuring subscribers for his poems. In the latter object he was grievously disappointed; but Wilson was not a man to travel from Dan to Beersheba and say all is barren, even although foiled in the immediate purpose of his heart. Upon his return home, he obtained the publication of his poems by Mr John Neilson, printer in Paisley, when he again set out on his former route, carrying with him a plentiful supply of copies for the benefit of those who might prefer poetry to packware. His expectations were soon resolved in the present instance. The amount of his success may be gathered from a passage in one of his letters from Edinburgh, wherein he says: "I have this day measured the height of a hundred stairs, and explored the recesses of twice that number of miserable habitations; and what have I gained by it? only two shillings of worldly pelf." In short, poetry and peddlery proved equally unsuccessful in his hands; he had neither impudence, flattery, nor importunity enough to pass off either the one or the other upon the public, and he returned, mortified and disappointed, to Lochwinnoch, where necessity compelled him to resume the shuttle.

McGonagall had also been a weaver, but once he abandoned that trade to follow the Muse he never "resumed the shuttle". There was no turning back for this indomitable spirit, who might, in all seriousness, have declared in Henley's words:

In the fell clutch of circumstance
I have not winced nor cried aloud.
Under the bludgeonings of chance
My head is bloody, but unbow'd.

His head was often enough literally bloody. At first—living in one of the vilest slums of Dundee—he secured a regular clientele for his penny poems, but he also fancied himself as a tragic actor. His appearances in various public halls in the city led to his being pelted with refuse of all kinds and generally mishandled, and the police warned the lessees that he must be given no further engagements. McGonagall justly enough protested against this, declaring that he was the innocent party and yet he was being punished and deprived of a source of livelihood. The police would not listen to his complaints, however. His appearances on the streets next became signals for all manner of baiting and hooliganism. It became impossible for him to try to sell his broadsides at street corners or in the shops, or even to go round his regular clientele. He was made the prey of practical jokes and hoaxes of all sorts and sent off on wild-goose chases to London and to America. Forced to leave Dundee, he lived for a little in Perth; but Perth was too small to yield even the minimum number of poem-purchasers at a penny a time to keep him (and his wife) in the barest necessities. So he went to Edinburgh (where he died), and there, and in Glasgow, was subjected to extreme ill-usage and baited unmercifully by students and others who organised mock dinners at which he was crowned as the world's greatest poet and decorated with bogus honours. The small collections taken up at these affairs, as the price of his ignominy, and frequently of his acquiescence in physical assault and battery, were his main—almost his only—source of income. He became a national joke. His claims to be superior to every other poet, with the sole exception of Shakespeare, were in all the papers—with samples of his indescribable doggerel. Ludicrous incidents were invented—like his attempted interview with Queen Victoria at

Balmoral; and most of his alleged sayings and poems (certainly all of these which show the slightest wit or advance his claims in a super-Shavian fashion) were invented by his baiters.

The way in which McGonagall's effusions were thrown off in penny broadsides makes anything like a collection of authentic examples at this time of day impossible. But the genuine McGonagall article is fairly easily distinguishable from the far too farcically funny efforts fathered upon him. There is nothing superficially funny about his authentic productions at all—they are all dead serious.

Through it all McGonagall remained a perfect Micawber, always looking for something to turn up, and believing that at any moment he would be translated to his rightful place in the enjoyment of world-wide fame. The only little tokens he ever got which he could construe as the smallest advance instalments of the meed of praise that was his due were the formal acknowledgements he got from various distinguished people to whom (as is the custom of Scottish poetasters) he sent copies of his productions. These acknowledgments enabled him to have an elaborate headpiece set at the top of his broadsides—with the Royal Arms, the Lion and Unicorn, and V.R. in heavy type; extracts from the letters flanking the poem which occupied the centre of the page; and, under his own name beneath the title of the latest effort, the magical phrases "Patronised by Their Majesties, Lord Wolseley of Cairo, H.R.H. the Duke of Cambridge, the Right Hon. W. E. Gladstone, and General Graham, etc."

As his latest editor, Mr Lowden Macartney, says: "He was a strange, weird, drab figure, and suggested more than anything else a broken-down actor. He wore his hair long and sheltered it with a wide-rimmed hat. His clothes were always shabby, and even in summer he refused to discard his overcoat. Dignity and long skirts are considered inseparable, and a poet is ruined if he is not dignified. He had a solemn, sallow face, with heavy features and eyes of the sort termed fish-like."

Nothing in the history of modern Scotland is more discreditable than the treatment accorded—and allowed by the authorities to be accorded—to McGonagall. It is without a single redeeming feature. Certainly the type of "humour" it gave rise to does nothing to redeem the brutal baiting to which he was subjected; it is more deplorable than McGonagall's poems in every way and has been one of the most widespread and powerful influences operating in Scotland, for upwards of a century, amongst all classes of the population. It is a wholly vicious and unintelligent facetiousness—the flower of which is the "Scotch coamic" and the typical "Scotch joke". It is displayed at its very worst, perhaps, in the bogus autobiography of McGonagall, entitled *The Book of the Lamentations of the Poet McGonagall*, and sold at a shilling a copy. This is now exceedingly rare, although it was published as recently as 1905—and naturally, of course, in Dundee. Its only really valuable feature is its magnificent frontispiece photograph of McGonagall, an appalling portrait, a fish-belly face, as of something half-human struggling out of the aboriginal slime. All the incurable illiteracy, the inaccessibility to the least enlightenment, and the unquenchable hope of the man are to be seen in the eyes. It is, indeed, a face to make one despair of humanity. What passes almost universally for wit in Scotland is splashed all over these unspeakably nauseating pages. The book is "Dedicated to Himself, knowing none Greater". The chapters are headed by fake quotations, like this, from the *Delhi Thug*:

> Rejoice, Edina, shout and sing,
> And bless your lucky fates;
> McGonagall, the lyric king,
> Was born within your gates.

We are given harrowing pictures of the ill-used bard "cleansing my garments from rotten eggs, ostensibly administered as an antidote to rotten egotism". Writing of the Grassmarket in Edinburgh, we find him quoting Mark Twain's statement about a city in Italy, "The streets are narrow and the smells are abominable, yet, on reflection, I am glad to say they are narrow—if they had been wider they would have held more smell, and killed all the people''. An alleged gift to be sent to the famous poet by the King of Burmah leads McGonagall's wife to complain of the idea of sending "an elephant to a man that couldna feed a canary"; and there is any amount of this sort of thing (an alleged dialogue between McGonagall and one of his patrons, following a misunderstanding)—"I am prepared to apologise, poet," he frankly rejoined; "when I called you by that dreadful name, believe me, I meant the opposite of the reverse". "Thank you," I replied, "I can see now that it was only the want of ignorance on my part, and I am fully satisfied with your apology"—and holds out his hand, only to get a copper tack rammed into it. These are the excruciatingly amusing things which delighted McGonagall's baiters.

"Look here, poet," a shopkeeper in Perth is reported saying to him, "I do not wish to flatter any man to his face, it is against my creed; but common honesty and a sense of fair play compels me to say that your poems are unique. In Scott, Byron, or Burns, for instance, if you omit a line, ten to one you lose the sense. With you it is totally different. I have read a whole production of yours, omitting each alternate line, and getting quite as much sense and literary power out of it as ever. Nay, more, if you read the fourth line first, and work back, the effect is quite as wonderful. The other night my wife pointed out to me that, in experimenting with a recent issue, she managed to derive even more benefit from it by reading the last line first, the first line next, the penultimate line third, the second line fourth, and so on till its natural conclusion by exhaustion. With this one I have bought just now we are to try another experiment to-night. We mean to clip each word separately, shake them all up in a bag, and paste them together on a clean sheet of paper as they come, and will let you know the result. If it is as I anticipate, I would strongly advise you to take out a patent, and float it in £1 shares—'The Patent Reversible Poetry Company Ltd.'—in which I would be glad to invest as a shareholder."

"I thanked the gentleman cordially," McGonagall is given as replying, "but told him that such commercial enterprises were not at all in my line, but that I would gladly supply the raw material and sell him the patent rights for a consideration if the result of his next trial justified his anticipations. At our next interview he told me that 'the test was too severe even for my effusions, so that meantime at least the matter would go no further'. At the same time he answered me that both he and his good lady fully agreed that the individual words were fully up to the Shakespearean standard, the only difference discernible in the completed article consisting merely in the matter of their arrangement."

A few pages further on, the autobiographer recurs to the matter: "And now, gentle reader, I will give you an object lesson regarding the peculiarities of my poetry, so eloquently referred to in a previous part of this chapter by my Perth shopkeeper friend and his lady. I refer, of course, to the reversible, interchangeable, double-breasted, universal-jointed nature of my composition. This is the distinguishing mark of my work, to copy which is moral felony. Like the rock we used to buy at the fairs, break it where you will, the hall-mark of excellence stares you in the face. Read the lines in any order you like; begin at the top, middle, or bottom, and continue in any direction you choose, and you receive the same benefit."

The song given in the spurious autobiography, "I'm the rattling boy from Dublin town," with its catchy refrain

Wack fal the dooral, ooral, ido,
Wack fal the dooral, ooral, aà,
Wack fal the dooral, ooral, ido,
Wack fal the dooral, ooral, aà,

is not an authentic McGonagall item. He worked in a different vein altogether. His true sort is to be found in the verses on *The Attempted Assassination of the Queen*:

God prosper long our noble Queen,
And long may she reign.
Maclean he tried to shoot her,
But it was all in vain.

For God he turned the Ball aside,
Maclean aimed at her head,
And he felt very angry
Because he didn't shoot her dead.

Maclean must be a madman,
Which is obvious to be seen,
Or else he wouldn't have tried to shoot
Our most beloved Queen;

or, again, in his *Address to the New Tay Bridge*:

Beautiful new railway bridge of the silvery Tay,
With your strong brick piers and buttresses in so grand array,
And your thirteen central girders, which seems to my eye
Strong enough all windy storms to defy.
And as I gaze upon thee my heart feels gay,
Because thou art the greatest railway bridge of the present day,
And can be seen for miles away,
From north, south, east, or west, of the Tay;

or, once more, in his *Descriptive Jottings of London*:

As I stood upon London Bridge and viewed the mighty throng
Of thousands of people in cabs and buses rapidly whirling along,
All furiously driving to and fro,
Up one street and down another as quick as they could go.
Then I was struck with the discordant sounds of human voices there
Which seemed to me like wild geese cackling in the air;
And the River Thames is a most beautiful sight,
To see the steamers sailing upon it by day and by night.

All these are typical McGonagallese. As Mr Macartney remarks: "One of the things that go to make a man great is uniqueness. He must in some way be totally unlike anybody else in the world. McGonagall did most certainly possess this qualification. Not only did he excel in the peculiar form of writing with which he clothed his ideas when offering them for the edification of an astonished, if somewhat irreverent, public, but while others might write a little like him, no one has ever succeeded in successfully copying his style. In that respect he remained the master, unapproached and unapproachable. Another individual can thrust aside any rule or regulation calculated to hamper his movements; and here McGonagall excelled every other singer of sweet song. Literary composition is an art, and, like other arts, is governed by certain rules and limitations—we might even say conventions. So great indeed was our 'poet' that he deigned to observe only a few—and that the simplest of these. In rhymed verse a certain amount of harmony is considered necessary. It is one of the elements totally lacking in the writings of this wonderful man. Rhythm and measure, also, have been considered from time immemorial as essential to the making of good verse, but rhythm and measure were cast aside when our bard took up his pen. . . . In the words of his own favourite poet, we may say

> Take him for all in all,
> We shall not look upon his like again."

In view of current developments in Scotland it is interesting to note that McGonagall was opposed to Home Rule. He sang:

> The man that gets drunk is little else than a fool
> And is in the habit, no doubt, of advocating Home Rule.
> But the best of Home Rule for him, as far as I can understand,
> Is the abolition of strong drink from the land.
>
> And the men that get drunk, in general, wants Home Rule,
> But such men, I think, should keep their heads cool,
> And try to learn more sense, I most earnestly do pray,
> And help to get strong drink abolished without delay.

Mr William Power in his book *My Scotland* tells how he attended one of McGonagall's performances in the Albion Halls in Glasgow many years ago. "He was an old man, but, with his athletic though slightly stooping figure and his dark hair, he did not look more than forty-five; and he appeared to have been shaved the night before. He wore a Highland dress of Rob Roy tartan and boy's size. After reciting some of his own poems, to an accompaniment of whistles and cat-calls, the Bard armed himself with a most dangerous-looking broadsword, and strode up and down the platform, declaiming 'Clarence's Dream' and 'Give me another horse—Bind up my wounds'. His voice rose to a howl. He thrust and slashed at imaginary foes. A shower of apples and oranges fell on the platform. Almost before they touched it, they were met by the fell edge of McGonagall's claymore and cut to pieces. The Bard was beaded with perspiration and orange juice. The audience yelled with delight; McGonagall yelled louder still, with a fury which I fancy was not wholly feigned. It was like a squalid travesty of the wildest scenes of *Don Quixote* and *Orlando Furioso*. I left the hall early, saddened and disgusted.

"The mental condition of the Melancholy Dane", Mr Power concluded, "is not more debatable than that of McGonagall. Was his madness real or feigned? I imagine that at first it had been no more than harmless conceit; that it was a rather deliberate pose for a time, when the poet found it paid; and that finally he became, like the 'Sobieski Stuarts', the victim of his own inventions. He was a decent-living old man, with a kindly dignity that, while it need not have forbidden the genial raillery that his pretensions and compositions provoked, ought to have prevented the cruel baiting to which he was subjected by coarse ignoramuses. McGonagall deserved well of his day and generation, and Time has dealt handsomely with him. He added to the gaiety of at least one nation, and, as the Ossian of the ineffably absurd, he has entered upon immortality."

JAMES HOGG

THE ETTRICK SHEPHERD

THE restless, cavalier, intellectual free-lance type of Scot presents himself at every period of our history as our best-defined and most persistently recurring national type. Many of them are like embodiments of characteristic phases of our national history—full of those strange, smoky antinomies, of hellfire and starlight and broad tallowy farce that clash so wildly in the dramas of successive ages in Scotland. They are to be found in all ranks of society. James VI of Scotland and I of England was one of them—"a shambling, comic figure in the sad and stately procession of the Stewarts", who nevertheless "held his own through almost the longest and loneliest, and certainly not the least dangerous, of the stormy range of the Stewart minorities, and died peaceably in his bed after a reign reasonably successful in itself, astoundingly so when one looks at the conditions in both kingdoms". His latest biographer, Mr Charles Williams, in one of the most interesting of those recent revaluations that are part of the post-war escape from the neat complacent tradition of Macaulay, paints him admirably in terms which, as my preceding chapters have shown, are applicable to a very large degree to a whole host of distinguished Scots.

King James, he says, "loved ease and peace, but if he were stirred he was capable of carrying himself with dignity, at the head of his troops or alone. He loved loose freedoms and gross pleasures, yet he never lost himself in them. He loved arguments and theological hair-splitting, yet he had at any moment that sense of actuality which is rare in such theoretical minds. He loved idleness and pleasure, but when he was rebuked for it he answered by saying that he did more work in an hour than others in a day. . . . And as in labour so in temper. He was good-humoured and kindly and loved it in others, but if his spiritual nerves were touched . . . he was capable of spasms of vengeful cruelty, and of disguising them from himself."

In the vast majority of Scots there has been exceedingly little or no intellectual element. With them we relapse upon high animal spirits for a distinguishing feature, and the *vis comica* of our breed. Here "the broad tallowy farce" —the "loose freedoms and gross pleasures"—predominate, where, indeed, they are not all. We come nearer here to the Harry Lauder tradition, or rather to the tradition of which the Harry Lauder tradition is a debased relic. But it is necessary to "distinguish and divide". The indubitable Scot of this sort can be presented in a couple of typical pictures.

Leyden was an intellectual, but he had this other side of him unsubdued, and it welled up irresistibly through all his scholarly interests. So we find Sir John Malcolm telling of his encounters with Leyden in India. "His love of the place of his nativity was a passion in which he had always a pride, and which in India he cherished with the fondest enthusiasm. I once went to see him when he was very ill, and had been confined to his bed for many days. There were several gentlemen in the room. He inquired if I had any news. I told him I had a letter from Eskdale. 'And what are they about in the Borders?' he asked. A curious circumstance, I replied, is stated in my letter; and I read him a passage which described the conduct of our volunteers on a fire being kindled by mistake at one of the beacons. This letter mentioned that the moment the blaze, which was the signal of invasion, was seen, the mountaineers hastened to their rendezvous, and those of Liddesdale swam the Liddel Water to reach it. They were assembled (though several of their houses were at a distance of six or seven miles) in two hours, and at break of day the party marched into the town of Hawick (at a distance of twenty miles from the place of assembly) to the Border tune of '*Wha daur meddle wi' me?*' Leyden's countenance became animated as I proceeded with this detail, and at its close he sprang from his sick-bed, and, with much strange melody, and still stranger gesticulations, sang aloud, '*Wha daur meddle wi' me? Wha daur meddle wi' me?*' Several of those who witnessed this scene looked at him as one who was raving in the delirium of a fever."

My second example is from the biographic sketch of Neil Gow written by Dr. McKnight, himself a skilful violinist and who frequently heard Neil play, to illustrate the peculiar character of his style: "There is perhaps no species whatever of music executed on the violin, in which the characteristic expression depends more on the power of the *bow*, particularly in what is called the *upward*, or returning *stroke*, than the Highland reel. Here accordingly was Gow's forte. His bow-hand, as a suitable instrument of his genius, was uncommonly powerful; and when the note produced by the *up-bow* was often feeble and indistinct in other hands, it was struck in his playing with a strength and certainty which never failed to surprise and delight the skilful hearer. As an example may be mentioned his manner of striking the tenor C in '*Athol House*'. To this extraordinary power of the bow, in the hand of great original genius, must be ascribed the singular felicity of expression which he gave to all his music, and the native Highland *goût* of certain tunes, such as '*Tullochgorum*', in which his taste and style of bowing could never be exactly reached by any other performer. We may add, the effect of the *sudden shout*, with which he frequently accompanied his playing of the quick tunes, and which seemed instantly to *electrify* the dancers; inspiring them with new life and energy, and rousing the spirits of the most inanimate."

This regardless uproariousness, this irrepressible vim and gusto, is a prime characteristic of the Scottish people, and it is to be hoped that it may never be bred out or subdued. It is a mistake to attribute it too much to drunkenness. The Scots have always been great drinkers, but there are grounds for believing that the alleged boozing capacities of past generations (which so greatly outrun any possibility of competition by the most determined of living topers) are greatly exaggerated, and in one case I have hit upon definite testimony to that effect; doubtless the same thing is true of many.

"The convivialities of Robert Fergusson, the poet, have been generally described as bordering on excess, and as characterising himself in particular, amidst a population generally sober. The sober truth is that the poor poet indulged exactly in the same way, and in general to the same extent, as other young men of that day. The want of public amusements, the less general taste for reading, and the limited accommodations of private houses in those days, led partly to a practice, which prevailed among all orders of people in Edinburgh, of frequenting taverns in the evening, for the sake of relaxation and exercise of the intellect. The favourite haunt of Robert Fergusson, and many other persons of his own standing, was Lucky Middlemass's tavern in the Cowgate which he celebrates in his poem on *Cauler Oysters*. One of the individuals who almost nightly enjoyed his company there, communicated to the present writer, in 1827, the following particulars respecting the extent and nature of their convivialities: 'The entertainment almost invariably consisted of a few boards of raw oysters, porter, gin, and occasionally a rizzared [dried] haddock, which was neither more nor less than what formed the evening enjoyments of most of the citizens of Edinburgh. The best gin was then sold at about five shillings a gallon, and accordingly the gill at Lucky Middlemass's cost only threepence. The whole debauch of the young men seldom came to more than sixpence or sevenpence. Fergusson always seemed unwilling to spend any more. They generally met at eight o'clock, and rose to depart at ten; but Fergusson was sometimes prevailed upon to outsit his friends, by other persons who came in late and for the sake of his company entreated him to join them in further potations. The humour of his conversation, which was in itself the highest treat, frequently turned upon the odd and obnoxious characters who then abounded in the town. In the case, however, of the latter, he never permitted his satire to become in the least rancorous. He generally contented himself with conceiving them in ludicrous or awkward situations, such, for instance, as their going home at night, and having their clothes bleached by an impure ablution from the garrets—a very common occurrence at that time, and the mention of which was sufficient to awaken the sympathies of all present."

Fergusson, however his drinking habits may have been exaggerated and his tragic fate blamed upon them, was a "broth of a boy"—a splendid mimic, a most diverting conversationalist, and full of wild pranks and practical jokes. Inspired by a rare poetic genius in the authentic Scots tradition, he was nevertheless full of the reckless humour and abandon with which I am now concerned. So was Burns—"rantin', rovin' Rabbie". So was Hogg, whom "Christopher North" and his colleagues, with Hogg's acquiescence and active assistance (though he occasionally felt things were being carried too far), represented in the famous *Noctes* as far more of a drunkard and buffoon than he really was, but who, nevertheless, was a heavy enough drinker and full enough of buffoonery. The *vis comica* rose in him like milk coming to the boil.

In his history of *Scottish Vernacular Literature* Mr T. F. Henderson says: "Carlyle has asserted that had Burns been 'a regular, well-trained intellectual workman' he might 'have changed the whole course of British literature'; but this, of course, Burns was very far from being. Time, opportunity, and environment were alike wanting to it; his poetry was the product of moments of leisure snatched from hours of grinding toil amid the companionships of simple rustics. Moreover, at a very early period he had got mentally habituated to the old Scots vernacular staves, especially those which had been revived by Ramsay and Fergusson; and this early bias was not helpful, but the opposite, to success in English verse. These metrical forms had become effete in England—

effete because of changes in the idiosyncrasy of the language, and advancement in the art of poetical expression since the days of the old vernacular 'makaris'. For Scottish vernacular they were still the most suitable, if not the only possible, forms; but the constant practice of them tended, if anything, to dull the ear for the appreciation of the fuller and richer and more subtle and varied melody of modern English verse, or at least introduced a disturbing influence which embarrassed endeavours after accomplishment in its special achievements."

The assumption here seems to be that it is unfortunate that Burns was tainted in this way with the crude Scots tradition—that he might have risen to greater heights drawing upon the "well of English, pure and undefiled". The truth is rather the other way about. It is unfortunate that Burns troubled about English at all—it is unfortunate that he did not recapture Scots more completely and exploit its potentialities more fully. If the older Scots metrical forms have become effete, English poetry in their absence has become dangerously super-refined and anaemic. The whole course of British literature does not necessarily depend upon anything that is done in English; if the force of the distinctive Scots tradition could be caught again and used in all its integrity it would have a terrific effect. Burns, Hogg, and the others have been only half-and-half users of it—none of them commanded the power that comes from being "a' ae oo". Like Ephraim they were all "joined to strange Gods". The Scots are much slower, unfortunately, at recognising this than the English are. They are still far too much taken up with "learning English". English critics point out the consequences. Professor Ifor Evans, who is only one of many I could quote, says, for example, R. L. Stevenson "is more outspoken in his Scots than in his English poems; it is as if the satiric tradition of Scottish poetry allowed him to speak his mind"; and, again, George MacDonald, "like Stevenson, seems, in his own tongue, to penetrate to some parts of his nature, humorous, satiric, which he can never release in English. His Jacobite ancestry seems to take possession of him in such a full-blooded ballad as *The Yerl of Waterydeck*, while there is a roguish humour which did not appear in the English verses in *The Waesome Carl*. . . . One wishes that the Jacobite ancestor could have dominated him more often and allowed him, in writing more Scottish ballads, to have grown into a greater poet." And it is not for nothing that James Hogg's latest, and ablest, biographer, Miss Edith Batho, insists on the Ettrick Shepherd's distressing fluctuation between English and Scots, and the falsities, feeblenesses, and absurdities of his dealings with the former, while the more he adhered to the latter the racier and better his work was. And at its best it was very, very good indeed.

Pointing to his ridiculous use of the word in his phrase "*unguent* hard to be swallowed" of *The Confessions of a Justified Sinner* and another example of the same sort of thing in *Disagreeables*,

> I wish all blustering chaps were dead,
> That's the true *bathos* to have done with them,

Miss Batho says: "He did not know the meaning of unguent or bathos, but they were good words. This affection for good words, regardless of their accepted meaning, had sometimes disastrous consequences. . . . But even when apparently writing English, Hogg heard Scots in his mind. His rhymes in his later poems, where he is usually fairly accurate, often will not fit in English but will in Scots. Here and there he attempts to reproduce the Highlands or the North of England speech, with only fair success. But when he takes to his Scots without disguise, he shows a humorous appreciation and right use of words, which may be illustrated by a passage in *The Brownie of Bodsbeck*. John Jay, the Shepherd, is being examined by Claverhouse about the soldiers who have been found murdered in the linn:

> "How did it appear to you that they had been slain? Were they cut with swords, or pierced with bullets?"

"I canna say, but they war sair hashed."

"How do you mean when you say they were hashed?"

"Champit like; a' broozled and jurmummled, as it were."

"Do you mean that they were cut, or cloven, or minced?"

"Na, na,—no' that ava'. But they had gotten some sair doofs. They had been terribly paikit and daddit wi' something."

"I do not in the least conceive what you mean."

"That's extr'ord'nar, man—can ye no' understand folk's mother-tongue? I'll mak it plain to ye. Ye see, whan a thing comes on ye that gate, that's a dadd—sit still now. Then a paik, that's a swap or a skelp like—when a thing comes on ye that way, that's a paik. But a doof's warst ava'—it's——"

"Prithee, hold; I now understand it all perfectly well."

Unfortunately Hogg had all too seldom the courage—and practically never the full courage—of his native speech. If he had not been cursed with the conceit of "writing polite", if he had not been consumed with the infernal inferiority complex of Post-Union Scotland, he would have been a much greater writer. It is true of him, as of many other Scottish writers, that we could gladly have dispensed with all he wrote in English for a few more things equal to his best in unadulterated Scots. The former were weak and artificial; the latter alone were "the real Mackay". He was poorly educated and hopelessly un-self-critical, and frequently ashamed of his best things, or unaware of their relatively high merit, while paltry and affected pieces in English made him feel that he was really essaying great flights. They were lamentable fugues from his essential self which alone mattered, flights from the veridical Scots utterance, of which he was so superbly capable, into stilted and worthless English.

What modern Scotland has lacked is this integrity—what the Chinese philosopher Mencius calls *Hsing*. "*Hsing*", as Professor Richards says, "is that in man which, though slight, makes him different from the animals; it is common to all men, and indeed is that which, as regards the mind, men have in common—their common humanity in things of the mind parallel to their common size, roughly, in feet, and their common tastes in meats, music, and beauty. *Hsing*, moreover, is complex, a complex of impulsions. If it is allowed by circumstances to follow, and develop according to its constituent impulsions then it is good, does good, and can be conceived good. These impulsions can be interfered with by bad conditions. Famine, for example, can entrap and drown the mind and thus distort them. So can bad government. The impulsions tend to be frustrated and curtailed by daily affairs. Rest and especially the breath of dawn and the night-breath restore them. The differences in men's humanity are, at least in part, due to these varying conditions. Even the sage is not different from the ordinary man in his native endowments. These impulsions show themselves in a minimal degree in such universal promptings as pity, shame, reverence, and sense of right and wrong, which are not due to inculcation or example or social pressure in the first place, but are native to man. These promptings are the minimal manifestations, the first and lowliest signs of the virtues which under favourable conditions they develop into. Those who make the most of their capacities (common to all men) 'who seek then get it' and do not 'give up so lose it' become virtuous and, in the highest examples, sages. All men by universal inheritance like the virtues. But the sage—who not only realises in the sense of fulfils his mind (gives the utmost development to his nature) but realises, in the other sense, what he is doing and becomes a teacher and an example, has a further function. As Yi Ya the epicure was the first to grasp what all mouths agree in liking, so the sage is the first to grasp what all *human* minds agree in. He is the sage because he is the most human of men." Hogg in our phrase "failed to find himself" or only found himself intermittently and incompletely and spent too much of his time denying himself and trying for ignoble reasons to be something else. Whenever he used English virtue went out of him, he did not direct his energies into their proper development. He lacked that other quality Mencius calls *Jen*—"the heart of man", "being a man", which is "like archery because when we miss the mark we come back for self-examination".

Mencius also says its actuality "lies in serving the parents" (in this connection Hogg's native tongue) and "with effort to strive for mutuality and so act in the nearest way to seek it". Hogg's eyes, alas, were not on his own kind but on the *literati* of Edinburgh and London. He was diverted by false ambitions. If an additional definition of *hsing* is that in us by which our virtues are what we can trust in, Hogg was deplorably lacking in it. Happily Hogg had frequently a good grip on Truth, not as a matter of correspondence between our observations and something they observe, the order of Nature or of events, as we might say, but as a matter of coherence or consistency among the items belonging to the system or hypothesis which is being developed. His most extravagant or incredible fabrications were true in the setting which he gave them—were artistically true, and that was all that mattered. Even his mendacities in social intercourse were true to his character, whereas his deviations into truth in the conventional sense generally struck a false and feeble note and lacked the congruity, as well as the splendid stamina, of his most palpable inventions.

"It is easy to find faults in the Shepherd himself and in his work", says Miss Batho. "He was shrewd enough to guard against the grosser physical temptations, he was good-humoured—except when an offence to his vanity called forth a kind of spitefulness—and a good husband and father, as well as a dutiful son, but in other ways he was not to be trusted. His friends helped him untiringly, but the greatest kindness they could have done him would have been to help him free from any but a shepherd's responsibilities. He might have written less if he had remained the shepherd which he always called himself, but I doubt whether his best things would have been lost: *Kilmeny*, *The Confessions of a Justified Sinner*, and the songs all belong to that side of him. There was never a writer who showed fewer signs of growth in his craft;

you can find no essential difference of spirit or technique between *The Mountain Bard* and *A Queer Book*, or the early ghost stories and the *Justified Sinner*. He lived as he wrote in a casual, rather breathless fashion; he was a man less fitted than most for the world's business, and if he could have been kept out of it we might have been able to regard him with some of the affectionate veneration of his daughter. As things are he is a figure comic even in his iniquities."

This is well said. Hogg became a great popular character, a national joke; he indulged his egregious exhibitionism to the full, and, however much they helped him and were genuinely his friends, "Christopher North", Lockhart, and the others all had, *au fond*, a snobbish attitude to him. And, what is far more important, they had no notion that he was a writer of infinitely greater consequence than themselves; and that all their affiliations were of precisely the wrong sort for him—he belonged to a different tradition altogether. Scotland has paid, and is still paying, all too dearly for this sort of thing. A recent writer on Neil Munro stresses another tragic instance of it: "Part of the sometimes irritating air of preciousness is no doubt due to certain self-consciousness, but most of it comes from the fact that he was *thinking* much of his work in Gaelic; it is the translation of an unwritten original. . . . And there is only too often the real defect that he slips between the two tongues into a restless, self-conscious affectation, that blots in places even the best of his work, gives his enthusiasms, especially over landscape (where in fact the translation from Gaelic *would* be most cramping) an air of falsetto when they are in fact sincere."

To this, in Hogg's case, was added peasant conceit and the propensity of showing-off, and, worst of all, that craving of the Lowland Scot to "get on", "to rise in the world", to show that he is as good as his "betters" merely by becoming one of them. The Highlanders with their classical tradition are far freer of this sort of thing. All the pith and value went out of "Surfaceman's" work (not that it ever had very much) when he became Librarian at Edinburgh University. "As a railway worker he looks from his portraits rather like William Morris, but in his Edinburgh days he develops a genteel, frock-coated benevolence. His poetry belongs mainly to his surfaceman period; in the academic atmosphere, away from the railroad scenes, he lost his poetic power." Yet this emasculation and falsification of the Scottish people is exactly what our educational system is primarily dedicated to. Compare with cases like those of Hogg and "Surfaceman" and Neil Munro, the case of Duncan MacIntyre—Donacha Ban—the great Gaelic poet: "a singular specimen of original and brilliant talent, altogether unfavoured by direct instruction, and going contentedly side by side for a long life with a character of the most simple and unworldly kind—his whole life passed in the humblest obscurity, undisturbed by so much as a wish for anything better." His poetry was none the worse of that.

Hogg, sharing with Scott "the faculty of rising to strange heights in dealing with the supernatural", came at last to such feeble prettinesses as:

> Thus ends my yearly offering bland,
> The Laureat's Lay of the Fairy Land.

But how splendid he was, either in prose or verse, when he struck his true vein. The story of the Laird of Ettrickshaw, for instance:

> It was the Laird o' Ettrickshaw; he that biggit his house amang the widow's corn, and never had a day to do weel in it. It isna yet a full age sin' the foundation-stone was laid, an' for a' the grandeur that was about it, there's nae man at this day can tell where the foundation has been, if he didna ken before.

With the help of "hurkle-backit Charley Johnston" the Laird used to dispose of his illegitimate children and their mothers. Then he was haunted and took to drinking:

> He durst never mair sleep by himself while he lived: but that wasna lang, for he took to drinking, and drank, and sware, and blasphemed, and said dreadfu' things that folk didna understand. At

length, he drank sae muckle a'e night out o' desperation that the blue lowe came burning out at his mouth, and he died on his ain hearthstone, at a time o' life when he should scarcely have been at his prime.

But it wasna sae wi' Charley. He wore out a lang and hardened life; and at the last, when death came, he couldna die. For a day and two nights they watched him, thinking every moment would be the last, but always a few minutes after the breath had left his lips, the feeble cries of infants arose from behind the bed, and wakened him up again. The family were horrified; but his sons and daughters were men and women, and for their ain sakes they durstna let ane come to hear his confessions. At last, on the third day at two in the morning, he died clean away. They watched an hour in great dread, and then streekit him, and put the dead-claes on him, but they hadna weel done before there were cries, as if a woman had been drowning, came from behind the bed, and the voice cried, "O, Charley, spare my life. Spare my life. For your own soul's sake and mine, spare my life." On which the corpse sat up in the bed, pawled wi' its hands, and stared round wi' its dead face. The family could stand it nae langer, but fled the house, and rade and ran for ministers, but before any of them got there, Charley was gane. They sought a' the house and in behind the bed, and could find naething; but that same day he was found about a mile frae his ain house, up in the howe o' the Baileylee-linn, a' torn frae limb to limb, an' the dead-claes beside him. There was two corbies seen flying o'er the muir that day, carrying some thing atween them, an' folk suspectit it was Charley's soul, for it was heard makin' a loud maen as they flew o'er Alemoor.

Hogg abounded in grisly superstitions and ghost stories of this kind and now and again achieved a veritable supernatural thrill of a finer and rarer kind; but how little transposed material of this kind was from the very colour and substance of a great deal of Scottish life, how much it was just the general mode of seeing and feeling things, may be grasped by comparing it with a matter-of-fact first-hand account of one of the incidents in the great floods in Moray in August 1829. One of the victims was an old bedridden widow, Mrs Speediman, who lived with an elderly niece, Isabella Morrison. As the rescue party drew near their dwelling they saw that one of the walls was gone and that the roof was only kept up by resting on a wooden boarded bed

"Here those in the boat beheld a most harrowing spectacle. Up to the neck in water sat the niece, scarcely sensible and supporting what was now the dead body of the aunt, with the livid and distorted countenance of the old woman raised up before her. The story will be best told in her own words, though at the risk of some prolixity.

"It was about eight o'clock, an' my aunty in her bed, fan I says till her, 'Aunty, the waters cumin' aboot's', and I had hardly spoken fan they war at my back. 'Gang to my kist', says she to me, 'and tak' oot some things are to be pit aboot me fan I'm dead.' I'd hardly takken oot the claes fan the kist was floated bodalie through the hoose. 'Gie me a haud o' your hand, Bell,' says my aunty, 'and I'll try an' help ye into the bed.' And sae I gat in. I think we war strugglin' i' the bed for aboot twa hours and the water floatit up the cauf-bed, and she lyin' on't. Syne I tried to keep her up, an' I took a haud o' her shift to try to keep her life in. But the waters war aye growin'. At last I got her up wi' a'e haun' to my breest, and hed a haud o' the post o' the bed wi' the ither. An' there waz ae jaw o' the water that cam' up to my breest, an' anither jaw cam' and poppit my aunty oot o' my airms. 'Oh, Bell, I'm gane,' says she; and the waters just chokit her. It waz a dreadfu' sight to see her. That *waz* the fight and struggle she had for life. Willin' waz she to save that. And her haun', your honour! How she fought wi' that haun'! It wud hae drawn tears o' pity frae a heathen. An' then I had a dreadfu' spekalation for my ain life, and I canna tell the conseederable moments I was doon in the water, an' my aunty abeen me. The strength o' the waters at last brak' the bed, an' I got to the top o't; an' a dreadfu' jaw knockit my head to the bed-post; I waz for some time oot o' my senses. It was surely the death-grip I had o' the post; an' surely it waz the Lord that waukened me, for the dead sleep had cum'd on me, an' I wud ha'e faun and been droon't in the waters. After I cam' to mysel' a wee, I feelt something at my fit, and I says to mysel', this is my aunty's head that the waters hae toorn aff. I feelt wi' my haun', and tuk haud o't wi' fear an' trumlin'; an' thankfu' was I fan I faund it to be naething but a droon't hen. . . . I suppose it waz twelve o'clock o' the day before I saw my aunty again, after we had gane doun thegither, an' the draedfu' ocean aboot huz, just like a roarin' sea. She was left on a bank o' san', leanin' on her side, and her mouth was fou' o' san'."

Hogg might have written that. Scotland was—and still is—full of that sort of stuff. It is a pity to let it go and be fobbed off with elegant literature—snobbish imitations of the English—instead. Hogg was always at his best when he was just reproducing the actual speech and notions of the countryside and of his own boon-companions in the taverns. He was not only a master of the supernatural and the gruesome, but of all reckless humour, exercising, as Miss Batho puts it, "his peculiar notions, or rather no notions, as to the proper limits of a joke". One of Hogg's relations was that James Laidlaw whose prayer for Cow Wat the Shepherd gave in a letter printed in *Blackwood's*. The story runs as follows:

> I remember, and always will, a night that I had with him about seventeen years ago. He and one Walter Bryden, better known by the appellation of Cow Wat, Thomas Hogg, the celebrated Ettrick tailor, and myself, were all drinking in a little change house one evening. After the whisky had fairly begun to operate Laidlaw and Cow Wat went to loggerheads about Hell, about which their tenets of belief totally differed. The dispute was carried on with such acrimony on both sides that Wat had several times heaved up his great cudgel, and threatened to knock his opponent down. Laidlaw, perceiving that the tailor and I were convulsed with laughter, joined us for some time with all his heart; but all at once he began to look grave, and the tear stood in his eye. "Aye, ye may laugh," said he; "great gomerals. It's weel kend that ye're just twae that laugh at everything that's good. Ye hae mair need to pray for the poor auld heretic than laugh at him, when ye see that he's on the braid way that leads to destruction. I'm really sorry for the poor auld scoundrel after a', and troth I think we sude join and pray for him. For my part I sall lend my mite." With that he laid off his old slouched hat,

and kneeled down on the floor, leaning forward on a chair, where he prayed a long prayer for Cow Wat, as he familiarly termed him, when representing his forlorn case to his Maker. I do not know what I would give now to have a copy of that prayer, for I never heard anythink like it. It was so cutting that before the end Wat rose up, foaming with rage, heaved his stick, and cried, "I tell ye, gie ower, Jamie Laidlaw. I winna be prayed for in that gate." If there were different places and degrees of punishment, he said, as the auld hoary reprobate maintained—that was to say, three or four hells—then he prayed that poor Cow Wat might be preferred to the easiest one. "We couldna expect nae better a place", he said, "for sic a man, and indeed we would be ashamed to ask it. But on the ither hand," continued he, "if it be true that the object of our petition cheated James Cunningham and Sandy o' Bowerhope out o' from two to three hunder pounds o' lamb-siller, why, we can hardly ask sic a situation for him; and if it be further true that he left his ain wife, Nanny Stothart, and took up wi' another (whom he named, name and surname), really we have hardly the face to ask any mitigation for him at a'." The tailor and I, and another one, I have forgot who it was, but I think it was probably Adie o' Aberlosk, were obliged to hold Wat by main force on his chair till the prayer was finished.

Similar in kind, and among the very best of their kind, but too long to reproduce here, are *David Tait's Prayer*, and Lucky Shaw's story of the escape of the people of Auchtermuchty, but how near all these were to reality may be seen by comparing the prayer for Cow Wat with one of the genuine prayers given in *The Shepherd's Calendar*:

For thy mercy's sake—for the sake o' thy poor sinfu' servants that are now addressing thee in their ain shilly-shally way, and for the sake o' mair than we dare well name to thee, hae mercy on Rob. Ye ken yoursel he is a wild mischievous callant, and thinks nae mair o' committing sin than a dog does o' licking a dish; but put thy hook in his nose, and thy bridle in his gab, and gar him come back to thee wi' a jerk that he'll no' forget the langest day he has to live.

Dinna forget poor Jamie, wha's far away frae amang us the night. Keep thy arm o' power about him, and oh, I wish ye wad endow him wi' a like spunk and smeddum to act for himsel. For if ye dinna, he'll be but a bauchle in this world, and a backsitter in the neist.

We're a' like hawks, we're a' like snails, we're a' like slogie riddles.

Like hawks to do evil, like snails to do good, and like slogie riddles, that let through a' the good and keep the bad.

Hogg never "got away with it" better than he did in that glorious comic ballad of witchcraft, *The Witch of Fife*. As Miss Batho says, it was not consistently comic at first, but ended lamentably with the death of the witch's auld guidman. Scott, however, begged him off, and the Shepherd added the last thirteen riotous stanzas. Here are the last seven of them (I have modernised the spelling of some of the words):

The auld guidman he gave a bob
In the midst o' the burning lowe;
And the shackles that bound him to the ring,
They fell from his arms like tow.

He drew his breath, and he said the word,
And he said it with muckle glee,
Then set his foot on the burning pile
And away to the air flew he.

Till once he cleared the swirling reek
He looked both feared and sad;
But when he won to the light blue air
He laughed as he'd been mad.

His arms were spread and his head was high
And his feet stuck out behind
And the tails o' the old man's coat
Were waffling in the wind.

And aye he nikkered and aye he flew,
For he thought the ploy so rare;
It was like the voice of the gander blue
When he flies through the air.

He looked back to the Carlisle men
As he bored the norland sky;
He nodded his head, and gave a girn,
But he never said goodbye.

Then vanished far in the sky's blue vale,
No more the English saw,
But the old man's laugh came on the gale
With a long and a loud guffaw.

Hogg was just such an old man himself and in his best

flights he soars into heights of reckless fun in which he is soon lost to English eyes.

Hogg, as Miss Batho says, "stood between two worlds, a belated minstrel, making his living, for the greater part of his life by journalism. He was an almost uneducated peasant, not, like Burns, in the true line of Scottish poets, but far more original and racy and, in a sense, cultured than the purely peasant poets with whom it might seem natural to compare him, and the second-rate literary men with whom some of his work would associate him. He knew nearly all his great and most of his lesser contemporaries, and was liked and laughed at by all of them. Scott comes with justice first on the list, unfailing in kindness and generosity from their earliest meeting; Wordsworth displays a degree of humorous appreciation of character of which he might not have been suspected, and is moved by the Shepherd's death to write one of his tenderest poems—his lament for the makers; Byron writes him friendly letters. He moves through the literary and polite society of his day, sometimes outraging conventions but more often escaping happily from unseen difficulties by his observance of what is, after all, the fundamental rule of good breeding, that of having only one set of manners for all companies." He is constantly trying things that call for far more knowledge and a different equipment altogether than he possesses. He writes fake antiques, and parodies, and plagiarises. He is not to be trusted in all sorts of connections.

His frequent self-contradictoriness is well seen in such a letter as that in which, pressing Blackwood to accept *John Paterson's Mare*, he says: "I cannot conceive why your editors rejected it; for I am sure that a more harmless good-natured allegory was never written. It is besides quite unintelligible without a key, which should never be given. I think it will be next to the *Chaldee* in popularity, as it is fully as injurious." He was persistently caricatured in the *Noctes*, made far more profane and witty and bibulous than he really was, and, with very rare qualms or spasms of virtuous indignation, he rejoiced in the process, and assisted it, seeing it did him no harm and fed the great legend of the Ettrick Shepherd as a public character. "I dashed on", says Hogg of one of his romances, "and mixed up with what might have been made one of the best historical tales our country ever produced, such a mass of diablerie as retarded the main story, and rendered the whole perfectly ludicrous."

That was, in fact, his usual practice all his life. The memorable words in which he describes a seraph in his story *On the Separate Existence of the Soul* are not a bad description of himself in his more fantastic moods: "The radiant being had neither wings nor female habiliments, but appeared much rather like a prince newly arisen from his bed, and arrayed in a tinsel nightgown and slippers".

The lengths to which the leg-pulling log-rolling used to go in *Blackwood's* is well illustrated by the review in 1821, of the revised Memoir which preceded the third edition of *The Mountain Bard*. This review begins with a complaint against Hogg's presumption in publishing autobiographies at all, and especially in such numbers; then deals unkindly with various writings and statements of the Shepherd; and finally comes to his chief offence, the claim to the authorship of the Chaldee MS., of whose origin the reviewer professes to give the true account:

"The Chaldee Manuscript. Why, no more did he write the Chaldee Manuscript than the five books of Moses. . . . You, yourself Kit, were learned respecting that article; and myself, Blackwood, and a reverend gentleman of this city, alone know the perpetrator. The unfortunate gentleman is now dead, but delicacy to his friends makes me withhold his name from the public. It was the same person who murdered Begbie. Like Mr Bowles and Ali Pacha, he was a mild man, of unassuming manners—a scholar and a gentleman. It is quite a vulgar error to suppose him a ruffian. He was sensibility itself, and would not hurt a fly. But it was a disease with him, 'to excite popular emotion'. Though he had an amiable wife and a vast family, he never was happy, unless he saw the world gaping like a stuck pig. With respect to his murdering Begbie, as it is called, he knew the poor man well, and had frequently given him both small sums of money and articles of wearing apparel. But all at once it entered his brain that, by putting him to death in a sharp, and clever, and mysterious manner, and seeming also to rob him of an immense number of banknotes, the city of Edinburgh would be thrown into a ferment of consternation and there would be no end of the 'public emotion', to use his own constant phrase on occasions of this nature. The scheme succeeded to a miracle. He stabbed Begbie to the heart, robbed the dead body in a moment, and escaped. But he never used a single stiver of the money, and was always kind to the widow of the poor man, who was rather a gainer by her husband's death. I have reason to believe that he ultimately regretted the act; but there can be no doubt that his enjoyment was great for many years, hearing the murder canvassed in his own presence, and the many absurd theories broached on the subject, which he could have overthrown by a single word. Mr —— wrote the Chaldee Manuscript precisely on the same principle on which he murdered Begbie; and he used frequently to be tickled at hearing the author termed an assassin. 'Very true, very true,' he used to say on such occasions, shrugging his shoulders with delight, 'he is an assassin, sir; he murdered Begbie';—and this sober truth would pass at the time for a mere *jeu d'esprit*, for my friend was a humorist, and was in the habit of saying good things. The Chaldee was the last work, of the kind of which I have been speaking, that he lived to finish. He confessed it and the murder, the day before he died, to the gentleman specified, and was sufficiently penitent, yet with that inconsistency not unusual in dying men, almost his last words were (indistinctly mumbled to himself), 'It ought not to have been left out of the other editions'. After this plain statement Hogg must look extremely foolish. We shall next have him claiming the murder likewise, I suppose; but he is totally incapable of either."

At the end of this amazing article there is a note by "Christopher North", explaining that it is only an example of the puff collusive, and even insinuating that the unfortunate Shepherd may have written it himself.

Hogg loved to be lionised, although on such occasions he was generally only a pantomime lion, whose skin was apt to fall off at the critical moment and reveal the man on all-fours who had been playing the part of the king of beasts. Usually when Hogg went to Edinburgh, on his last night before returning to Yarrow he would give a party. Robert Chambers was present at one at least of these feasts and has left a lively description of it:

"In the course of the forenoon, he [Hogg] would make a round of calls, and mention in the most incidental possible way, that two or three of his acquaintances were to meet that night in the Candlemaker Row at nine, and that the addition of this particular friend whom he was addressing, together with any of *his* friends he chose to bring along with him, would by no means be objected to. It may readily be imagined that, if he gave this kind of invitation to some ten or twelve individuals, the total number of his visitors would not probably be few. In reality it used to bring something like a Highland host upon him. Each of the men he had spoken to came, like a chief, with a long train of friends, most of them unknown to the hero of the evening, but all of them eager to spend a night with the Ettrick Shepherd. He himself stood up at the corner of one of Watson's biggest bedrooms to receive the company as it poured in. Each man, as he brought in his train, would endeavour to introduce each to him separately, but would be cut short by the lion with his bluff good-natured declaration: 'Ou ay, we'll be a' weel acquent by and by'. The first two clans would perhaps find chairs, the next would get the bed to sit upon; all after that had to stand. This room being speedily filled, those who came subsequently would be shown into another bedroom. When it was filled too, another would be thrown open, and still the cry was: 'They come'. At length, about ten o'clock, when nearly the whole house seemed 'panged' with people, as he would have himself expressed it, supper would be announced. . . . All the warning Mr Watson had got from Mr Hogg about this affair was a hint, in passing that morning, that *twae-three* lads had been speaking of supping there that night. Watson, however, knew of old what was meant by *twae-three*, and had laid out his largest room with a double range of tables, sufficient to accommodate some sixty or seventy people. . . . At length all is arranged; and then, what a strangely miscellaneous company is found to have been gathered together. Meal-dealers are there from the Grassmarket, genteel and slender young men from the Parliament House, printers from the Cowgate, and booksellers from the New Town. Between a couple of young advocates sits a decent grocer from Bristo Street; and amidst a host of shop-lads from the Luckenbooths is perched a stiffish young probationer, who scarcely knows whether he should be here or not and has much dread that the company will sit late. Jolly, honest-like bakers, in pepper-and-salt coats, give great uneasiness to squads of black coats in juxtaposition to them, and several dainty-looking youths, in white neck-cloths and black silk eye-glass ribbons, are evidently much discomposed by a rough tyke of a horse-dealer who has got in amongst them and keeps calling out all kinds of coarse jokes to a crony about thirteen men off on the same side of the table. Many of Mr Hogg's Selkirkshire store-farming friends are there, with their well-oxygenated complexions and Dandie-Dinmont-like bulk of figure; and in addition to all comers, Mr Watson himself and nearly the whole of the people residing in his home at the time. If a representative assembly had been made up from all classes of the community it could not have been more miscellaneous than this company, assembled by a man to whom in the simplicity of his heart all company seemed alike acceptable."

Then follows the account of the supper itself, which, though it might be noisy and prolonged to four or five o'clock in the morning, was innocent mirth and had no bad consequences. Hogg was in his element at a gathering of this sort. But he was not always equally fortunate. On one of his visits to Edinburgh in 1803 he called on Scott to ask his advice about the publication of a book and was invited to dinner in Castle Street. Lockhart tells the story:

"When Hogg entered the drawing-room, Mrs Scott, being at the time in a delicate state of health, was reclining on a sofa. The Shepherd, after being presented and making his best bow, forthwith took possession of another sofa placed opposite to hers and stretched himself thereupon at all his length; for, as he said afterwards, 'I thought I could never do wrong to copy the lady of the house'. As his dress at this period was precisely that in which any ordinary herdsman attends cattle to the market, and as his hands, moreover, bore most legible marks of a recent sheep-smearing, the lady of the house did not observe with perfect equanimity the novel usage to which her chintz was exposed. The Shepherd, however, remarked nothing of all this—dined heartily and drank freely, and by jest, anecdote, and song afforded plentiful merriment to the more civilised part of the company. As the liquor operated, his familiarity increased and strengthened; from 'Mr Scott' he advanced to 'Shirra', and thence to 'Scott', 'Walter', and 'Wattie'—until, at supper, he fairly convulsed the whole party by addressing Mrs Scott as 'Charlotte'."

"CHRISTOPHER NORTH"

Professor John Wilson

"CHRISTOPHER NORTH" (Professor John Wilson), 1785–1854, might well have joined in—ought, indeed, to have led—the chorus for which Mr T. S. Eliot so perfectly supplied the words:

> We are the hollow men,
> We are the stuffed men,
> Leaning together,
> Headpiece filled with straw.

It is well known to-day that exceedingly few people think; that only an infinitesimal proportion of humanity have ever accomplished that exceedingly painful and unnatural feat; and that what passes for thinking with all the others is only rationalisation, and what they are pleased to imagine their own opinions are anything but theirs. And all but the smallest percentage of statements are not really intended to be examined for their sense. They represent merely the performance of a set of social gestures. Their accommodation to this—if we attempt to investigate the sense of the words—turns them into so many exploits in Lancelot Gobbo confusions. The main purpose of all verbiage is simply to batter the hearer into a pulpy state of vague acquiescence in which a sense of mutual enlightenment can at least exist as an illusion. The most important words in the language—"living experience", "passion", "beauty"—are the most effective for this purpose, and the clergy and the politicians in particular make great play with them. To such an extent has this gone that words have practically ceased to have any meaning; no wonder that Wyndham Lewis contends that a stiffening of satire or straight-speaking is needful in anything that wishes to survive the subtle misconstruings of the defensive reader or hearer. The fluent eye of the reader is so apt to glide deceitfully over the page—or the adept ear of the hearer to act in an equivalent fashion—that the words have no time to make much more than an approximate impression at best. But most of the words are *clichés*, headlines, a verbomania in which the expression of thought in any real sense of the term has practically ceased to be an element at all.

Scotland, in particular, is dominated in every direction by an abracadabra impervious to all sense—overridden by meaningless phrases. This is not surprising. "Christopher North" was only the most extraordinary exponent of this sort of thing carried to the furthest degree, but it has long been not only general in Scotland but actually recognised and defended. It has been written, for example—and a similar tribute could be paid to the vast majority of Scottish "philosophers", divines, and public speakers generally—of the celebrated Dr. Thomas Brown, co-professor with Dugald Stewart in Edinburgh University, that "the fine poetical imagination of Dr. Brown, the quickness of his apprehension, and the acuteness and ingenuity of his argument, were qualities but little suited to that patient and continuous research which the phenomena of the mind so peculiarly demand. He accordingly composed his lectures with the same rapidity that he would have done a poem, and chiefly from the resources of his own highly gifted but excited mind. Difficulties which had appalled the stoutest hearts yielded to his bold analysis, and, despising the formalities of a siege, he entered the temple of pneumatology by storm. When Mr Stewart was apprised that his own favourite and best-founded opinions were controverted from the very chair which he had scarcely quitted; that the doctrines of his reverend friend and master Dr. Reid were assailed with severe and not very respectful animadversions; and that views of a doubtful tendency were freely expounded by his ingenious colleague, his feelings were strongly roused."

No doubt; but it was only one brand of Mumbo-Jumbo objecting to a slightly different mixture of substantially the same principal ingredients. Dugald Stewart himself "accepted on Thursday and commenced the course of metaphysics the following Monday, and continued during the whole of the season to think out and arrange in his head in the morning (while walking backwards and forwards in a small garden attached to his father's house in the college) the matter of the lecture of the day. The ideas with which he had thus stored his mind he poured forth extempore in the course of the forenoon, with an eloquence and a felicity of illustration surpassing in energy and vivacity (as those who have heard him have remarked) the more logical and better digested expositions of his philosophical views which he used to deliver in his mature years." The latter did not really differ in kind from the former, however; the say-away, the off-lay, the "intoxication of his own verbosity", was always what mattered most.

As Miss Elsie Swann says in her Life of "Christopher North": "In nineteenth-century Edinburgh the very crown and summit of a University career was represented by Moral Philosophy, the supreme expression of a nation that resorted to metaphysical terms for its intimate and personal life. The Chair of Moral Philosophy was the most lofty the University afforded, and the Professor of Moral Philosophy the most august in the academical world. He represented the ultimate apotheosis of Scottish scholarship, and as such was the cynosure of intellectual eyes. Lockhart, in his character of the fictitious Welsh doctor, Peter Morris, retails the academic hierarchy of this time, when the students were 'giddy urchins' of fourteen or even younger, who laid claim to very little Latin and less Greek. The first two years at the University were spent in attaining to a sketchy classical education under the harassed Professor of 'Humanity', Mr Christie, and Mr Dunbar, Professor of Greek; each of whom had to deal with a class of some two hundred lively youngsters, 'who, although addressed by the name of "Gentlemen", were at least as full of boyish romping as at any previous period of their lives'. Although Professor Dunbar was much above the common run of Northern scholars (the letters after his name were English), it availed him little in his duties, which consisted of laying the very lowest part of the foundation upon which a superstructure of erudition was probably never reared; for before the boys had Latin enough to read any Latin author with facility or Greek enough to understand any one line in any one Greek book, they were handed over to the Professor of Logic, Rhetoric and Belles-Lettres, whose duty was to 'inform the minds of his pupils with some first faint ideas of the Scottish systems of metaphysics and morals—to explain to them the rudiments of the vocabulary of Reid and Stewart, and to fit them, in some measure, for plunging next year into the midst of all the light and all the darkness scattered over the favourite science of this country by the Professor of Moral Philosophy'. There was, however, little solidarity in the study of philosophy, little core of impersonal truth, for philosophy was an essentially personal teaching, and the students of it were as a weathercock that turned wheresoever the teachers listed to blow. Moral Philosophy was distinguished by an exuberant enthusiasm for the different generations of Professors, and a whole-hearted advocacy and adoption of their particular interpretations. . . . The ludicrous pendulum of Scottish philosophical opinion was tartly commented on by one styling himself a Modern Greek, in his survey of the Modern Athens [Edinburgh] of the early nineteenth century. He further declared that the oscillations of the pendulum, though not fewer in number, gradually became more and more insignificant in range. 'Under Robertson they all knew history, and with Blair every sentence was taken from the storehouse of the Belles-Lettres, and measured by the gauge of Rhetoric. When Reid and Dugald Stewart turned the tables upon the sceptics, the Athenians were entirely composed of intellectual and of active powers, and they were drawn and held by the sweetest chords of association. With Playfair, they attempted to go quietly to the very depth of philosophic systems, and, anon, they started to the moon with Dr. Brewster.' . . . Stewart ever treated his metaphysical matter as a poet, and eschewed the coarse unwieldiness of mere uncompromising reason. He carefully avoided anything connected with his subject that might have made the philosophy of morals repulsive; according to Lord Cockburn, one of his students, who declared him to be 'without genius or even originality of talent', yet felt towards him the prevailing enthusiasm. According to discriminating critics, Stewart's greatly exaggerated reputation rested upon his effective use of the commonplace and his mastery of detail. His wide reading provided him with illustrative quotations from literature, and his moral theories were supported by an elaborate sentimental rhetoric—methods continued by his successors, Brown and Wilson. He expatiated upon popular aspects of moral themes, and, avoiding technicalities, bolstered up his sentimental and unscholarly dissertations by the maintenance of great formal dignity of speech and manners. He was no classical scholar or modern linguist, and most of his philosophical ideas were secondary and derived from modern translations. De Quincey pointed out scornfully that Stewart studies the Kantian philosophy through the French of Marie, Baron Degérando, whose *Histoire Comparée des systèmes de philosophie* was published in 1803; and Lockhart in *Peter's Letters* affirms that 'this great and enlightened man has been throughout contented to derive his ideas of the Greek philosophers from very secondary sources', and proceeds: 'If such be his ignorance . . . what may we not suppose to be the Cimmerian obscurity which hangs over his worshippers and disciples?' . . . The darkness with them is a 'total eclipse'. But in spite of these shortcomings in the eyes of scholars Dugald Stewart was regarded with an almost universal frenzy of admiration that had no justification in his philosophical genius. In the opinion of metaphysicians such as Sir William Hamilton and Professor Ferrier, he was trite, commonplace, limited, utterly unequal to clear and powerful thought; but these inferiorities were as nothing against his sentimental eloquence and his fluent rhetoric, for these reached at once the Achilles' heel in the invincibility of the Scottish moral frame. We have it on Lord Cockburn's authority that Dugald Stewart varied his elegant expatiation on the more elementary aspects of moral philosophy with equally elegant expectoration, for being asthmatical he frequently indulged in this relief; but it was generally held in the Modern Athens that there was more true eloquence in the way he cleared his throat and spat than in the most studied perorations of lesser men. As a lecturer Dugald Stewart was magnificent. It is important to realise the effectiveness of Stewart's eloquent sentimentality, his many tasteful literary allusions, his fastidious abhorrence of brain-taxing subtleties and crude reason, for in him is the first full flowering of the Tradition. His successor, Dr. Thomas Brown, was a true pupil of Stewart's—though perhaps more abstruse, but with a flow of beautiful language 'in those parts of his subject which admitted of being tastefully handled'—and it was very much his practice to introduce quotations from the poets, so furnishing 'a pleasing relaxation to the mind of the hearer in the midst of the toils of abstract thought'. Obviously what was needed as a corrective to the honeyed sweetness and rather superficial brilliance of these two moral philosophers was the sound scholarship and unassuming worth of a Sir William Hamilton. What actually happened was that the tradition established by Stewart found a notable and legitimate heir, and the same banner of sentimental rhetoric 'marked with most flimsy mottoes' was borne forward by Wilson."

Wilson secured the Chair of Moral Philosophy in Edinburgh University in 1820 and retained it until 1851. It was thirty-one years of the most arrant humbug. Exceedingly few Scottish professors then or since, including the present day, have had any genius or originality of talent whatever, but there is, so far as has yet been divulged, no imposition to beat Wilson's. He had a stiff fight for the Chair—every possible wire had to be pulled—he was strongly opposed on political grounds and also on his unsuitability of character, for his reputation so far had been that of a practical joker and swashbuckling critic and lampooner. He had no ideas on the subject he was about to profess at all, and never acquired, or tried to acquire, any, being content to remain from start to finish entirely dependent on an obscure friend who kept him "on the rails". He could supply all the rhetoric that was required, and the personality, the presence; but he had to be given the bones to clothe with his eloquence. He could not trust himself to express any opinions on moral philosophy matters off his own initiative. He had to be told what to say—given the gist of the argument; then he could go ahead—he knew how to say it. The utter immorality of the whole business, especially in conjunction with a Chair of Moral Philosophy, is piquant in the extreme; and the abjectness of his dependence is probably without a parallel. His friend behind the scenes was a Mr Alexander Blair.

"Wilson", says Miss Swann, "never fully formulated his moral philosophy, for the Professor's ideas were always a little vague, and somewhat cloudy through lack of disciplined thought. His own doctrines were never quite fixed, and he stated publicly to the class at the close of his last session that he had all along been conscious there was some gap in it. He read widely, but in a haphazard and desultory way that never digested the reading so that it became an organic whole in his being; consequently he could not only contribute nothing new to philosophy, but because he would not take the intellectual effort of absorbing his material had much ado to keep going as a lecturer. He shuffled along in a hand-to-mouth existence, fed with assiduous small scraps from Blair, in letters that arrived frequently. With a few crude notes of his own on the backs and on the envelopes, and chiefly with his gift of impassioned rhetoric, Wilson contrived to fill out the daily lecture, and enflesh the few philosophical bones at his disposal with the juicy meat of his eloquence. The hungry sheep looked up and they were duly fed; but the more intelligent discovered later that there was surprisingly little sustenance in the fare provided by the persuasive shepherd. Hence one disillusioned member of the flock (Sir Archibald Alison) remarked that Wilson's eloquence was of a very brilliant kind, but his speeches sounded better at the time than they appeared on reflection. Through the force of his high-flown diction, his retentive memory, his knowledge of the classics and of English literature, and his superficial excursions into moral philosophy, Wilson managed to keep afloat; but he must inevitably have foundered and sunk with all hands had not Blair manned the lifeboat with commendable frequency. What Blair thought about the situation cannot be known, but he seemed always prepared to supply Wilson with lectures and speeches, and apparently had no objection to having his brain picked so persistently and exhaustively. Perhaps it flattered this quiet, unassuming, little Doctor Blair to prop up the massive, gesticulating carcase of Wilson; perhaps it also amused him. Certainly but for the stuffing that Alexander Blair put into him John Wilson would have been but a hollow man. Therefore, taking him on his own merits, he *was* a hollow man, and he knew it better than anyone else. The knowledge made him awkward and *gauche* with Thomas Carlyle, because he sensed that Carlyle had looked within and seen his hollowness; as, of course, Carlyle had, with a most rare perception. Wilson, however, felt safe before the rest of the world, who accepted him at his face-value—provided that Blair stood behind him, and plied him with the means to keep up appearances."

It was a canny Glasgow student who shrewdly observed of Wilson: "I think that man is a fool; and that if he wasna sic a *big fool* he would be laughed at".

Miss Swann quotes a famous passage from Wilson's masterpiece, the lecture on the Love of Power, which "depended on a series of highly-wrought and poetical illustrations of the workings of this passion, arriving at a sensational climax in the description of 'the Stoics of the wood, the men without a tear'. This magnificent flight of oratory was not unknown to fame, and duly as it came round, on the last day of November, the class-room was crowded with an appreciative audience, not only of students from all departments, but professors and lecturers and strangers of note, all in a joyous state of anticipation. Conspicuous among them, in the middle of the front bench, sat the erudite Sir William Hamilton, eager with expectation. With even firmer step and more heroic aspect than usual, Wilson advanced to the desk and when the pleased rustle was stilled among his audience, began a hasty recapitulation that soon led into the main theme—the Love of Power. Through various references to its manifestations expressed in an elaborate poetical diction, with the Miltonic observation that to be weak is miserable, doing or suffering, the lecturer began to expatiate on the debased and humiliating state of men who debased themselves under disadvantages, and so reached the grand climax of the Grilling of the Noble Savage. Wilson proceeded somewhat as follows:

" 'Let us picture to our mind's eye a pampered Sybarite, nursed in all the wantonness of high-fed luxury, dallying on a downy sofa, amid all the gorgeousness of ornamental tapestry, listening to the soft sound of sweetest music playing in his ears . . . whose rest would be broken, whose happiness would be spoiled, by the doubling of the highly scented rose-leaf that lies beneath him on his silken couch. Let us by the magic powers of imagination transport this man to the gloomy depths of an American forest, where the dazzling glare of a bright fire instantly meets the eye. If he does not forthwith ignominiously expire at the first view, suppose him to survey the characters who compose or fill up the busy scene around it. The barbarous savages of one tribe have taken captive the chief of another engaged in deadly hostilities with them. They have not impaled him alive. That would be to consign him too speedily to unhearing death. But they have tied him fast with bands made of the long and lithe forest grass which yields not quickly to the fire. They have placed him beside the pole which they kindle with fiendish satisfaction, and feed with cautious hand, well knowing the point or pitch to raise it to, which tortures but not speedily consumes. They have exhausted all their energy in uttering a most diabolical yell, on witnessing their victim first feel the horrid proofs of their resentment, and now, seated on the grass around, they look on in silence. The chief stands firm with unflinching nerve; his long eye-lashes are scorched off, but his proud eye disdains to wink; his dark raven locks have all perished but there is not a wrinkle seen on his forehead. From the crown of his head to the sole of his foot his skin is one continued blister, but the courage of his soul remains unshaken and quails not before the tormenting pain. The Sybarite has expired at the mere sight; his craven heart has ceased to beat. The Indian hero stands firm. There is even a smile on his sadly marked cheek, and it is not the smile which is extorted by excruciating pain, and forms the fit accompaniment of a groan, but he smiles with joy as he chants his death-song. The chief is inflamed with a glorious rapture that exalts him beyond the sensation of pain and conquers agony.'

"This noble lecture had an electrifying effect on its audience; dead silence held the class, only to be shattered by vociferous applause that could not be restrained. Expecially after the glorious consummation of the North American Indian's discomforts in feeling the 'horrid proofs' of his foes' resentment, the cheers were repeated till the class-room rang, and Sir William Hamilton, almost hysterical with enthusiasm, sprang to his feet and clapped his hands with delight. There is, of course, no hint as to what aspect of this luscious eloquence so transported with joy the learned metaphysician; though he shared outwardly the appreciation and approval of the students, he may have had his own secret springs of enjoyment."

Wilson had a wonderful voice, as he chanted rather than read or spoke his lectures, swelling out wonderfully in passages of eloquence, but always with a certain sepulchral quality—"a moaning sough as of a wind from the tombs, partly blowing along, partly muffling the purely intellectual meaning". He had ludicrous mannerisms, intrusions of adventitious bathos, like a regular trick of drawing a finger down the side of his nose at the high points of his discourse. And he had a wild grandeur of personal appearance that often reminded his admirers of the First Man—of the fierce splendour of an untamed epoch, "when wild in woods the noble savage ran", and perhaps it was on this account that he displayed a luxuriant untrimmed savagery of wantoning hair and whiskers.

And all the time—all these thirty years—he was writing to Blair: "But for you, I could not flounder on even as I do"; "I am nearly *lectureless* on the subjects into which I have been precipitated, and sometimes enter the room in blind despair"; "Time hurries on with frightful rapidity, and *nothing can I think of*"; "Could you write me a letter or two on Order in the Physical and in the Moral World? And on your ultimate belief in the Doctrine of Cause and Effect?"—and so on, and on, and on. No wonder he had to subscribe himself at times: "Ever affectionately yours, with a weak numb hand and an aching heart and a head *whizzing* always"—very different from the "Christopher North" of the *Chaldee Manuscript*, "the beautiful Leopard . . . whose going forth was comely as the greyhound, and his eyes like the lightning of fiery flame".

THE STRANGE CASE OF WILLIAM BERRY

"THE Utopian notions, which so often mislead men of weak minds had no such effect", his biographer tells us, upon Sir James Mackintosh, the distinguished historian and statesman, enamoured though he was of political freedom. "He saw the necessity of sobering down all such fanciful theories to the level of real life, and of pruning and adapting them to the passions and weaknesses of human nature. He was above all impressed with the necessity of circumscribing his ideas of political freedom, which had before run wild, by the great outlines of the British constitution. In his own impressive and figurative language, he desired that the light which might break in on Great Britain should be 'through well-contrived and well-disposed windows, and not through flaws and breaches, the yawning chasms of our ruin'."

This is a very common attitude of liberal-minded men, but it fails to reckon with the fact that it is in no such way that the light has ever manifested itself but only through just such flaws and breaches. In particular it fails to reckon with the character of Scotland—a country whose record is fairly portrayed in what the reviewer, supposed to be Sir Walter Scott, in the *Quarterly Review* said of Robert Pitcairn's *Criminal Trials and other Proceedings before the High Court of Justiciary*.

"In truth no reader of these volumes—whatever his previous acquaintance with Scottish History may have been—will contemplate without absolute wonder the view of society which they unveil; or find it easy to comprehend how a system, subject to such severe concussions in every part, contrived, nevertheless, to hold itself together. The whole nation would seem to have spent their time, as one malefactor expressed it, 'in drinking deep and taking deadly revenge for slight offences'."

There is—opinions may differ as to whether fortunately or unfortunately—less deep drinking to-day, but in other respects the condition of society does not seem to the present writer to have improved. In so far as the promotion of higher culture is concerned, the hard fact with which we have to reckon is that the communications of genius have still to contend with a state of affairs not dissimilar to that protrayed in the *Noctes Ambrosianae* when the "adorable Shepherd" lets his alcoholic fancy recollect a visit to the slums of Glasgow:

"But was ye ever in the Guse-dubs o' Glasgow? Save us a'!—what clarty closes, narrowin' awa' and darkenin' doun—some stracht and some serpentine—into green middens o' baith liquid and solid matter, soomin' wi' dead cats and auld shoon, and rags o' petticoats that had been worn till they fell off and wad wear nae langer; and then ayont the midden, or, say, rather, surrounding the great central stagnant flood o' fulzie, the windows o' a coort, for a coort they ca't, some wi' panes o' glass and panes o' paper time aboot, some wi' what had ance been a hat in *this* hole and what had been a pair o' breeks in *that* hole, and some without lozens a'thegither; and then siccan faces o' lads that had enlisted, and were keeping themselves drunk night and day on the bounty-money, before ordered to join the regiment in the West Indies and die o' the yallow fever. And what fearsome faces o' limmers, like she-demons, dragging them down into debauchery, and hauding them there, as in a vice, when they had gotten them down—and, wad ye believe't, swearin' and damnin' ane anither's een, and then lauchin', and trying' to look lo'esome, and jeerin' like Jezabels."

That is the chaotic and discouraging milieu through which Scottish abilities have always sought to distribute their effulgence. It is not therefore any matter for surprise that it has been singularly spasmodic, broken, and erratic in its illuminating effects, or that it should be true of the vast majority of the talented men concerned that they have resembled James Gibbs, the architect of St. Martin's in the Fields, the Radcliffe Library at Oxford, and the senate house at Cambridge. Of him it was said that: "where the architect has been tasteful and correct, he only shows that mere mechanical knowledge which may avoid faults, without furnishing beauties, and where he has been picturesque and not void of grandeur, the whole is the effect of chance and blunder"—and so unequal that he ranges from the lofty pomp of the Radcliffe and the chaste proportions of St. Martin's to architectural mongrels of the most unspeakable description.

In such circumstances the type of artist Scotland has produced has not infrequently resembled that Andrew Macdonald, whose "literary talents seem to have been of that unfortunate description which attract notice, without yielding profit, which produce a show of blossom but no fruit, and which, when trusted to by their sanguine possessor as a means of insuring a subsistence, are certain to be found wholly inadequate to that end, and equally certain to leave their deceived and disappointed victim to neglect and misery"—that Andrew Macdonald of whom D'Israeli in his *Calamities of Authors* gives us an unforgettable glimpse:

"It was one evening I saw a tall, famished, melancholy man enter a bookseller's shop, his hat flapped over his eyes and his whole frame evidently feeble from exhaustion and utter misery. The bookseller inquired how he proceeded with his tragedy? 'Do not talk to me about my tragedy. I have indeed more tragedy than I can bear at home', was his reply, and his voice faltered as he spoke. This man was 'Matthew Bramble' [his pseudonym]—Macdonald, the author of the tragedy of Vimonda, at that moment the writer of comic poetry." He fell a victim at the age of thirty-three to sickness, disappointment, and misfortune. It is no joke being a Scottish genius, and an extraordinarily large proportion of our brightest spirits have gone the same way as Macdonald to untimely graves.

Others have resisted, or never felt, the temptation to make money by their gifts. Some have never even attempted "to bring their pigs to market", but have been content to allow themselves to be pulled this way and that by the frantic band.

So widely entertained is the conception of the Scot as cautious, practical, and above all intent on "the bawbees", that it is worth stressing that, on the contrary, an analysis of the lives of eminent Scots in all branches of arts and affairs, rather tends to characterise them as reckless, improvident, scatter-brained, and subject to the most extravagant generosities and the wildest whims. One of our scientists in particular, instead of profiting by his invention to enrich himself, set an example which is particularly worth recalling to-day and which it is one of the greatest tragedies of mankind that it should not be generally followed. This was the father of David Gregory, Professor of Astronomy at Oxford—the Rev. John Gregory, minister of Drumoak in the county of Aberdeen. Of him we read that he "removed with his family to Aberdeen and in the time of Queen Anne's war employed his thoughts upon an improvement in artillery, in order to make the shot of great guns more destructive to the enemy and executed a model of the engine he had conceived. I have conversed", says Dr. Reid, who tells the story, "with a clockmaker in Aberdeen who was employed in making this model; but having made many different pieces by direction, without knowing their intention or how they were to be put together, he could give no account of the whole. After making some experiments with this model, which satisfied him, the old gentleman was so sanguine in the hope of being useful to the allies in the war against France that he set about preparing a field equipage with a view to make a campaign in Flanders, and in the meantime sent his model to his son, the Savilian professor, that he might have his and Sir Isaac Newton's opinion of it. His son showed it to Newton, without letting him know that his own father was the inventor. Sir Isaac was much displeased with it, saying that if it had tended as much to the preservation of mankind as to their destruction the inventor would have deserved a great reward; but as it was contrived solely for destruction, and would soon be known to the enemy, he rather deserved to be punished; and urged the Professor very strongly to destroy it and, if possible, to suppress the invention. It is probable the Professor followed this advice, for at his death, which happened soon after, the model was not to be found."

This is in my opinion one of the greatest stories in the history of Scotland, and one which should be known to every Scottish child. There is another and an even greater one—unparalleled, I think, in the history of the world; and found in a still more unlikely direction so far as Scotland is concerned. The Allied and the German troops might fraternise spontaneously for a little time between their trenches in Flanders at Christmas-time (thanks to the action of a Scottish padre), but it is a still stranger thing to find the love of art triumphing over military discipline on active service.

This occurred at the battle of Inverurie in 1745, when Lord Louis Gordon's pipers kept silent because Duncan Ban MacCrimmon, the great piper, had been taken prisoner by him. It has been truly said that "this was the greatest tribute ever paid to genius".

> No Scottish Army or English, no army in the world,
> Would do that to-day, nor ever again,
> For they do not know and there is no means of telling them
> That Kings and Generals are only shadows of time,
> But time has no dominion over genius.

These are two supreme and glorious incidents, but to those who hold to the generally accepted fiction of the mean and money-grabbing Scot the history of our scientists and artists proffers many a striking instance of sheer disinterestedness and utter heedlessness of profit-making. There was, for example, the unfortunate Archibald Cochrane, ninth Earl of Dundonald, who initiated the use of tar to prevent vessels being rotted by the sea—the general adoption of copper-sheathing soon afterwards rendered the idea abortive—and concerned himself effectively with other uses of coal-tar and coal-varnish, with the manufacture of salt, with the connections between agriculture and chemistry, and with improvements in spinning machinery. He died in poverty at Paris in 1831, but the following remarks were made about him in the annual address of the Registrars of the Literary Fund Society in 1823:

"A man born in the high class of the old British peerage has devoted his acute and investigating mind solely to the prosecution of science; and his powers have prevailed in the pursuit. The discoveries effected by his scientific research, with its direction altogether to utility, have been in many instances beneficial to the community, in many have been the source of wealth to individuals. To himself alone they have been unprofitable; for *with a superior disdain, or (if you please) a culpable disregard of the goods of fortune, he has scattered around him the produce of his intellect with a lavish and wild hand.* If we may use the consecrated words of an apostle, 'though poor, he hath made many rich', and, though in the immediate neighbourhood of wealth, he has been doomed to suffer, through a long series of laborious years, the severities of want. In his advanced age he found an estimable woman, in poverty it is true, like himself, but of unspotted character, and of high, though untitled, family, to participate the calamity of his fortunes; and with her virtues and prudence, assisted by a small pension which she obtained from the benevolence of the Crown, she threw a gleam of light over the dark decline of his day. She was soon, however, torn from him by death, and, with an infant whom she bequeathed to him, he was abandoned to destitution and distress (for the pension was extinguished with her life). To this man, thus favoured by nature, and thus persecuted by fortune, we have been happy to offer some little alleviation of his sorrows; and to prevent him from battling his last under the oppressive sense of the ingratitude of his species."

I could multiply Scottish instances, in greater or less degree, of like unself-seeking devotion. Another to set beside Dundonald, though as fortunate as the latter was unfortunate, was Dr. Andrew Duncan (1773–1832), Professor of Medical Jurisprudence and Police in Edinburgh University. "Great energy and activity of mind, a universality of genius that made every subject, from the most abstruse to the most trivial, alike familiar to him, and a devoted love of science, which often led him to prefer its advancement to the establishment of his own fame, were his distinguishing traits. So well was he known and appreciated on the Continent that he received, unsolicited on his part, honorary degrees and other distinctions from the most famous universities; and few foreigners of distinction visited Edinburgh without bringing introductions to him. He had the honour of being in the habit of correspondence with many of the most distinguished persons in Europe, whether celebrated for high rank or superior mental endowments. He had a great taste for the fine arts in general and for music in particular; and from his extensive knowledge of languages was well versed in the literature of many nations. His manners were free from pedantry or affectation, and were remarkable for that unobtrusiveness which is often the peculiar characteristic of superior genius."

Right off the reel I can think of several scores of Scotsmen from the fifteenth century down to living men—all with a certain velocity of talents, wide-ranging interests, more concerned about other things than their personal advancement, witty, good "mixers"—who call for descriptions in terms that just fall between those applied to Professor Duncan in the foregoing passage, and those used to characterise Ben Jonson in contrast to the decorous, sedate Drummond of Hawthornden (also, of course, a very common type of Scotsman). "Jonson's unbridled exuberance of fancy, bordering occasionally upon irreverence, appears to have been a flight beyond what was calculated to please the pure mind of the retired and philosophic Drummond. 'Ben Jonson', says he, 'was a great lover and praiser of himself, a contemner and scorner of others, given rather to lose a friend than a jest; jealous of every word and action of those about him, especially after drink, which is one of the elements in which he lived; a dissembler of the great parts which reign in him; a bragger of some good that he wanted; thinketh nothing well done but what either he himself or some of his friends hath said or done; he is passionately kind and angry, careless either to gain or keep. . . . He was for any religion, being versed in both."

It is true, as Mr Moray MacLaren says, that "Scotland, that strange, infuriating, enchanting country that has almost ceased to be a country, has, with its ingrained Puritanism of the last three hundred years, proved to be an easy prey for the levelling and dulling tendency of modern pleasure. Our Americanism is peculiarly unpleasant Americanism, our middle class is peculiarly middle, our dancing peculiarly dull, our civic nosyparkerism peculiarly nosy . . . and so it could go on. But, at the same time, one of the most tantalising things about this most lovable ghost of a country is that it has a habit of justifying itself just when you least expect it. There are in Scotland remains of the old life which are so vivid that for a moment the observer is tricked or charmed into forgetting the slow death all around him, and sees in the vigour on which he has stumbled signs of a vitality which may reanimate Scotland once again."

The prevailing impression, however, is one of utter stupidity and sordidness—buddyism, Philistinism, dour, determined mindlessness. It is a horrible atmosphere for artists to live in, and while many incorrigible Bohemians have been brave enough to follow their art despite starvation and ghastly hardship, it is not surprising that others in a country where art and letters pay so poorly, and where 99 per cent of the people are so horribly anti-aesthetic, have dealt very differently with their talents—if few of them have reacted just in the manner of that great wit, Dr. John Arbuthnott. "Arbuthnott cared little to establish his personality in literature apart from the spirit of a group of humorists. We can accept the anecdote which best illustrates his temper in this point: 'No Adventure of any Consequence ever occurred on which the Doctor did not write a pleasant Essay in a great folio Paper-book, which used to lie in his Parlour; of these however he was so negligent that while he was writing them at one End he suffered his Children to tear them out at the other, for their Paper Kites.' Arbuthnott did not trouble to gather up his pleasant essays, or to detach what was his from the group production of the triumvirate to whom he was drawn. Swift and Pope looked upon him as the principal biographer of 'Martinus Scriblerus'; yet Martin came forth among their Miscellanies and would not lose his company. The *History of John Bull* was Arbuthnott's own, yet so delivered to the world that Swift long had the credit of it; on the other hand, *Robinson Crusoe* was on occasion attributed to Arbuthnott, and is indignantly noticed by his early biographer as one of 'several Brats illegitimately fathered upon him'."

There is not much of the conventional, greedy, thrustful Scot in this; and the case is no isolated one—indeed, the same disposition largely accounts for the very casual custodianship and frequent loss of valuable Scottish manuscripts of all kinds, the way in which so much of our literature has totally disappeared and much of the best of what remains to us of it only preserved by accident rather than design, and the unparalleled indifference of our people to the proper care and preservation of our national records.

Just as some of our most brilliant men can manifest a negligent attitude like Arbuthnott's to the children of their brains and any consideration of fame, so, on the other hand, now and again one of the Philistines breaks out in an unusual quarter. Sober-minded Scotland was greatly concerned a year or two ago lest a project mooted in America (and delayed from coming to anything by the slump) to establish a Gaelic University should not be run on sufficiently common-sense and utilitarian lines, instead of being devoted to hare-brained and useless matters like Gaelic literature and pipe music. But it is interesting to remember that it was a prince of utilitarian educationalists who long previously—and in my opinion very justly and wisely—advocated the closing-down of Glasgow University and the devotion of the funds thus freed to the exclusive purpose of a College of Bagpipe Playing in the Hebrides.

This was the eccentric Professor of Natural Philosophy in Glasgow University, John Anderson, whose benefaction made possible the beginning of technical education in the over-ambitious "Andersonian University", now the great Royal Technical School. Failing to suppress the older University in the manner indicated, it is a pity, I think, that he did not suppress his own and devote the funds to the more interesting project. As a suitable companion and counterpart to the story of the Rev. John Gregory's invention—and suppression—of a superior gun, it is worth recalling here that Anderson, too, among his multifarious interests, prosecuted a taste for the military art and invented a species of gun, the recoil of which was stopped by the condensation of common air within the body of the carriage. Having in vain endeavoured to attract the attention of the British Government to this invention, he went to Paris in 1791, carrying with him a model, which he presented to the National Convention. The governing party in France at once perceived the benefit which would be derived from this invention, and ordered Mr Anderson's model to be hung up in their hall with the following inscription over it—"The Gift of Science to Liberty". Whilst he was in France, he got a six-pounder made from his model, with which he made numerous experiments in the neighbourhood of Paris, at which his countryman, the famous Paul Jones, amongst others, was present, and gave his decided approbation to the gun as likely to prove highly useful in landing troops from boats, or firing from the round tops or poops of ships of war. Mr Anderson, at this period, took a keen interest in the transactions which passed before his eyes. He was present when Louis XVI was brought back from Varennes, and, on 14th July, on the top of the altar of liberty, and in the presence of half a million of Frenchmen sang *Te Deum* with the Bishop of Paris when the King took the oath to the Constitution, amen being said to the ceremony by the discharge of five hundred pieces of artillery. As the Emperor of Germany had drawn a military cordon around the frontiers of France, to prevent the introduction of French newspapers into Germany, he suggested the expedient of making small balloons of paper, varnished with boiled oil, and filled with inflammable air, to which newspapers and manifestos might be tied. This was accordingly practised, and when the wind was favourable for Germany they were sent off and descending in that country were, with their appendages, picked up by the people. They carried a small flag or streamer, bearing a motto of which the following is a translation:

> "O'er hills and dales, and lines of hostile troops, I float majestic
> Bearing the laws of God and Nature to oppressed men
> And bidding them with arms their rights maintain."

Before coming to the unique case of William Berry, let us glance at one or two other Scottish artists. Patrick Gibson, for example (1782–1829): "While advancing in the practical part of his profession, Mr Gibson, from his taste for general study, paid a greater share of attention to the branches of knowledge connected with it than most artists have it in their power to bestow. He studied mathematics with particular care, and attained an acquaintance with perspective, and with the theory of art in general, which was in his own lifetime quite unexampled in Scottish—perhaps in British—art. . . . He possessed great talents in conversation and could suit himself in such a manner to every kind of company that old and young, cheerful and grave, were alike pleased. He had an immense fund of humour; and what gave it perhaps its best charm was the apparently unintentional manner in which he gave it vent and the fixed serenity of countenance he was able to preserve while all were laughing around him. There are few men in whom the elements of genius are so admirably blended with those of true goodness and all that can render a man beloved as they were in Patrick Gibson."

This taste for general study, these conversational powers, and happy sociability are common Scottish traits, and the difficulty of inhibition, of self-limitation, of screwing oneself down to a particular line of accomplishment, accounts to a great degree for the relative paucity of Scottish arts and letters. Gibson, *inter alia*, did a lot of critical writing. "His most remarkable critical effort was an anonymous *jeu d'esprit*, published in 1822, in reference to the exhibition of the works of living artists then open, under the care of the Royal Institution for the Encouragement of the Fine Arts in Scotland. It assumed the form of a report, by a society of Cognoscenti, upon these works of art, and treated the merits of the Scottish painters, Mr Gibson himself included, with great candour and impartiality. The style of this pamphlet, though in no case unjustly severe, was so different from the indulgent remarks of periodical writers, whose names are generally known, and whose acquaintance with the artists too often forbids rigid truth, that it occasioned a high degree of indignation among the author's brethren, and induced them to take some steps that only tended to expose themselves to ridicule. Suspecting that the traitor was a member of their own body, they commenced the subscription of a paper, disclaiming the authorship, and this, being carried to many different artists for their adherence, was refused by no one till it came to Mr Gibson, who excused himself on general principles from subscribing such a paper and dismissed the intruders with a protest against his being supposed on that account to be the author. The real cause which moved Mr Gibson to put forth this half-jesting, half-earnest criticism upon his brethren was an ungenerous attack upon his own works which had appeared in a newspaper the previous year and which, though he did not pretend to trace it to the hand of any of his fellow labourers, was enjoyed, as he thought, in too malicious a manner by some to whom he had formerly shown much kindness."

There was another Scottish artist of brilliant parts who was well on the way to establishing a high reputation when he paid a visit to Italy and was so struck by some of the paintings he saw there that ever afterwards he suffered from the stultification of an inordinate perfectionism—not able to rival the masterpieces he so admired nor, on their account, to have any patience with his own abilities which tended in a different direction altogether.

I might also mention the sad case of John Donaldson (1737–1801). His father was a poor but worthy glover in Edinburgh, remarkable for the peculiar cast of his mind, which led him to discuss metaphysics as he cut out gloves on his board. The son inherited the same peculiarity, but to an excess which proved greatly more injurious to him. His father did not allow his metaphysics to interfere with his trade; but young Donaldson, disregarding all the ordinary means of forwarding his own particular interests, devoted himself with disinterested philanthropy to the promotion of various fanciful projects for ameliorating the condition of his fellow-creatures. The result was precisely what might have been anticipated; for, although Donaldson had endowments sufficient to raise him to distinction and opulence, his talents were in effect thrown away, and he died in indigence. While yet a child he was constantly occupied in drawing with chalk, on his father's cutting-board, those objects around him which attracted his attention. This natural propensity was encouraged by his father, and such was his success that the boy had hardly completed his twelfth year when he was enabled to contribute to his own support by drawing miniatures in India-ink. At that time, too, his imitations with the pen of the works by Albert Durer, Aldegrave, and other ancient engravers were so exquisite as to excite the astonishment and admiration of men of the most accomplished taste, and to deceive the eye of the most experienced connoisseurs. After prosecuting his profession for several years in Edinburgh, he removed to London and for some time painted likenesses in miniature with great success. But at length the mistaken notions of philanthropy just alluded to gained such an ascendancy over his mind as entirely to ruin his prospects. He conceived that in morals, religion, policy, and taste mankind were radically wrong; and, neglecting his profession, he employed himself in devising schemes for remedying this universal error. These schemes were the constant subject of his conversation, and latterly this infirmity gained so much upon him that he reckoned the time bestowed upon his professional avocations as lost to the world. He now held his former pursuits in utter contempt and maintained that Sir Joshua Reynolds must be a very dull fellow to devote his life to the study of lines and tints. Ultimately, from want of practice, he lost much of that facility of execution which had gained him celebrity in his early years.

To such a man the experience of the world teaches no lesson. He saw, with chagrin, the rise of greatly inferior talents, but failed to make that reformation in himself which would have enabled him to surpass most of his contemporaries. At the same time he was far from being idle, as the mass of manuscript scraps he left behind him abundantly testifies. These manuscripts, however, were found in a state too unfinished and confused to admit of their coming before the public. Before he became disgusted with his profession he had painted his well-known historical picture of "The Tent of Darius", which gained him the prize from the Society of Arts and was justly admired for its great beauty. About the same time he executed two paintings in enamel, "The Death of Dido" and "The Story of Hero and Leander", both of which obtained prizes from the same society. These two paintings were so much admired that he was urged by his friends to do others in the same style; but no persuasion could induce him to make the attempt. Among the various pursuits of this eccentric individual, chemistry was one, in the prosecution of which he discovered a method of preserving meat and vegetables uncorrupted during the longest voyages. For this discovery he obtained a patent, but his poverty and indolence and his ignorance of the world prevented his turning it to any account. The last twenty years of his life were spent in great misery; he was frequently destitute of the ordinary necessaries of life. Donaldson was a man of very rare endowments and of great talents; addicted to no vice, and remarkable for the most abstemious moderation. The great and single error of his life was his total neglect of his profession at a time when his talents and opportunities held out the certainty of his attaining the very highest rank as an artist.

The crowning touch—the most ludicrous incident—of Donaldson's extraordinary career was the fact that his last illness was occasioned by his having slept in a newly painted room, which brought on a total debility.

The general attitude to art in Scotland is well illustrated in what one of his biographers says of George Jameson, the first eminent painter produced by Britain, who was born at Aberdeen towards the end of the sixteenth century. "Previously to his appearance, no man had so far succeeded in attracting the national attention of Scotland to productions in painting as to render an artist a person whose appearance in the country was to be greatly marked. His father was a burgess of guild of Aberdeen and his mother the daughter of one of the magistrates of that city. What should have prompted the parents of the young painter to adopt the very unusual measure of sending their son from a quiet fireside in Aberdeen to study under Peter Paul Rubens in Antwerp must remain a mystery."

Donaldson's philanthropy perhaps had equalled the classic example of it practised by Dr. Andrew Duncan,

Professor of Medicine in Edinburgh (1744–1828), of whom we are told: "While his benevolence fell with the warmth of a sunbeam on all who came within the sphere of its influence, it was more especially experienced by those students of medicine who came from a distance, and had the good fortune to attract or be recommended to his notice. Over them he watched with a paternal solicitude. He invited them when in health to his house and his table. He attended them when in sickness with assiduity and tenderness, *and when they sunk the victims of premature disease the sepulchre of his family was thrown open for their remains*." Those who regard Scots as being of a mean and grudging disposition may safely be challenged to produce from any other country an instance of generosity that goes beyond that.

David Allan (1744–96) was another Scottish painter of great merit. He was prematurely born, his mother dying a few days afterwards. The young painter had so small a mouth that no nurse could be found in the place fitted to give him suck; at length, one being heard of, who lived at a distance of several miles, he was packed up in a basket amidst cotton, and sent off under the charge of a man who carried him on horseback, the journey being rendered additionally dangerous by a deep snow. The horse happened to stumble, the man fell off, and the tiny wretch was ejected from the basket into the snow, receiving as he fell a severe cut upon his head. "Such were the circumstances", says his memoirist, "under which Mr David Allan commenced the business of existence." His genius for designing was first developed by accident. Being confined at home with a burnt foot, his father one day said to him: "You idle little rogue, you are kept from school doing nothing. Come, here is a bit of chalk, draw something with it upon the floor." He took the chalk and began to delineate figures of houses, animals, and other familiar objects, in all of which he succeeded so well that the chalk was seldom afterwards out of his hand. When he was about ten years of age, his pedagogue happened to exercise his authority over some of the boys in a rather ludicrous manner; Allan immediately drew a caricature of the transaction upon a slate, and handed it about for the amusement of his companions. The master of the ferrule, an old, vain, conceited person, who used to strut about the school dressed in a tartan night-cap and long tartan gown, got hold of the picture and right soon detected that he himself was the most conspicuous and the most ridiculous figure. The satire was so keen, and the laugh which it excited sunk so deep, that the object of it was not satisfied till he had made a complaint to old Allan and had the boy taken from his school. When questioned by his father how he had the effrontery to insult his master by representing him so ridiculously on his slate, his answer was, "I only made it *like* him, and it was all for fun".

Too few Scottish artists have been concerned with what was *like* the life around them, or Scotland would have had—and have to-day—the greatest school of humorous artists the world has ever seen. Allan went on as he had begun. There is one of his caricatures well known to collectors; it represents the interior of a church or meeting-house at Dunfermline, at the moment when an imprudent couple are rebuked by the clergymen. There is a drollery about the whole of this performance which never fails to amuse. The alliance of his genius to that of our national poets led Allan to design illustrations to Burns' poems, the "Gentle Shepherd", and a collection of the most humorous of our old songs. As one of the historians of art says: "As a painter, at least in his own country, he neither excelled in drawing, composition, colouring, nor effect. Like Hogarth, too, beauty, grace, and grandeur of individual outline and form, or of style, constitute no part of his merit. He was no Correggio, Raphael, or Michael Angelo. He painted portraits as well as Hogarth, below the middle size; but they are void of all charms of elegance and of claro-obscuro and are recommended by nothing but a strong homely resemblance. As an artist and a man of genius, his characteristic talent lay in *expression*, in the imitation of Nature with truth and humour, especially in the representation of ludicrous scenes in low life. His eye was ever on the watch for every eccentric figure, every motley group, or ridiculous incident, out of which his pencil or his needle could draw innocent entertainment and mirth." Scotland could well dispense with all the beauties and elegances of nine-tenths of its artists for a few more social cartoonists of Allan's type.

In person, we are told, our Scottish Hogarth had nothing attractive. "The misfortunes attending his entrance into the world were such as nothing in after-life could repair. His figure was a bad resemblance of his humorous precursor of the English metropolis. He was under the middle size; of a slender, feeble make; with a long, sharp, lean, white, coarse face, much pitted by the smallpox, and fair hair. His large prominent eyes, of a light colour, were weak, near-sighted, and not very animated. His nose was long and high, his mouth wide, and both ill-shaped. His whole exterior to strangers appeared unengaging, trifling, and mean; and his deportment was timid and obsequious. The prejudices naturally excited by these disadvantages at introduction were, however, dispelled on acquaintance; and, as he became easy and pleased, gradually yielded to agreeable sensations, till they insensibly vanished, and at last were not only overlooked but, from the effect of contrast, even heightened the attractions by which they were so unexpectedly followed. When in company he esteemed, and which suited his taste, as restraint wore off his eye imperceptibly became bright, active, and penetrating; his manner and address quick, lively, and interesting; his conversation open and gay, humorous without satire, and playfully replete with benevolence, observation, and anecdote."

James Tassie, the famous modeller, having discovered the art of imitating precious stones in coloured paste and taking impressions from ancient gems—an art known to very few persons in Europe since the classic ages when it was practised, and by these few not brought to great perfection, while kept strictly secret—went to London to try his fortune in this profession.

"In 1766", says a memoir, in the Supplement of the *Encyclopædia Britannica,* "he arrived in the capital. But he was diffident and modest to excess; very unfit to introduce himself to the attention of persons of rank and affluence; besides, the number of engraved gems in Britain was small and those few were little noticed. He long struggled under difficulties which would have discouraged anyone who was not possessed of the greatest patience and the warmest attachment to the subject. He gradually emerged from obscurity, obtained competence, and, what to him was much more, he was able to increase his collection and add higher degrees of perfection to his art. His name soon became respected and the first cabinets of Europe were open for his use. He uniformly preserved the greatest attention to the exactness of the imitation and accuracy of the engraving, so that many of his pastes were sold on the Continent, by the fraudulent, for real gems. His fine taste led him to be peculiarly careful of the impression and he uniformly destroyed those with which he was in the least dissatisfied. The art has been practised of late by others, and many thousands of pastes have been sold as Tassie's which he would have considered injurious to his fame. Of the fame of others he was not envious; for he uniformly spake with frankness in praise of those who executed them well, though they were endeavouring to rival himself. . . . To the ancient engravings he added a numerous collection of the more eminent ones; many of which approach, in excellence of workmanship, if not in simplicity of design and chastity of expression, to the most celebrated of the ancients. Many years before he died he executed a commission for the late Empress of Russia, consisting of about fifteen thousand different engravings. At his death, in 1799, they amounted to near twenty thousand; a collection of engravings unequalled in the world."

Tassie practised for some time the art of modelling portraits in wax, transferring them to paste; and by this method preserved to the world the best likenesses of many of his most distinguished contemporaries. "A curious circumstance is told by his biographer of his feelings as to his facility in taking likenesses", says one writer, and quotes the following passage: "It is remarkable that he believed there was a certain kind of inspiration (like that mentioned by the poets) necessary to give him full success. The writer of this article in conversing with him always found him fully persuaded of it. He mentioned many instances in which he had been directed by it; and even some in which, after he had laboured in vain to realise his ideas on the wax, he had been able, by a sudden flash of imagination, to please himself in the likeness, several days after he had seen the original." But there is nothing in the least curious or remarkable about that, and the comments of these writers are not unlike the virtuous indignation with which a writer on Donaldson remarks that that wayward genius "had been known to deny himself even to Lord North, because he was not in the humour to paint. . . . With every due allowance for the whims and eccentricities of men of genius absurdities like these were not to be tolerated."

It is one of the favourite ideas of the bourgeoisie—who thereby get their culture and art-products cheap or whose mean souls are compensated by the indigence of their superiors—that artists are all the better for hardship, and that easy conditions and good living are apt to spoil them. If many artists are Bohemian enough to live in garrets and struggle against their Philistine environment, content to throw a few irradiations of their genius at random into the encompassing darkness, instead of the even distribution of which Sir James Mackintosh dreamed, it is no matter for surprise if now and again a man of very great gifts, secure in the knowledge of his own powers, does not care to struggle against unfavourable circumstance or think "the game worth the candle".

The *locus classicus* in this connection is the strange case of William Berry, and the phrases I italicise a few sentences further on supply, I think, the explanation of the matter, and it may be of a practice which is much commoner (though instances of it, and particularly instances of the Berry calibre, are naturally hard to come by) than "Pro Bono Publico" may care to believe. The Great Public likes to believe that, no matter what the handicaps are, Genius will out—and that it will get the benefits in due course without doing anything to deserve them; but, though the Great Public would not like to think so, Genius sometimes prefers to lie doggo and just keep itself to itself. Berry is a character I like to think of, and I often remember when I do the sentiments of that distinguished buccaneer, Leslie Charteris' hero, "The Saint", when he asked: "Why the hell should *I* bother? The country's got its salvation in its own hands. While a nation that's always boasting about its outstanding brilliance can put up with a collection of licensing laws, defence of the realm acts, seaside councillors, Lambeth conventions, sweepstake laws, Sunday observance acts, and one fatuity after another that's nailed on it by a bunch of blathering maiden aunts and pimply hypocrites, and can't make up its knock-kneed mind to get rid of them and let some fresh air and common sense into its life—when they can't do anything but dither over things that an infant in arms would know its own mind about—how the devil can they expect to solve bigger problems? And why should *I* take any trouble to save them from the necessity of thinking for themselves?"

Berry was born about the year 1730 and bred to the business of a seal-engraver. After serving an apprenticeship under a Mr Proctor at Edinburgh, he commenced business for himself in that city and soon became distinguished for the elegance of his designs, and the clearness and sharpness of his mode of cutting. At this time the business of a stone-engraver in the Scottish capital was confined to the cutting of ordinary seals, and the most elaborate work of this kind which they undertook was that of engraving the armorial bearings of the nobility.

Mr Berry's views were for several years confined to this ordinary drudgery of his art, but, by studying some ancient intaglios, he at length conceived the design of venturing into that higher walk, which might be said to bear the same relation to seal-engraving which historical painting does to portrait-painting.

The subject he chose for his first essay was a head of Sir Isaac Newton, which he executed with such precision and delicacy as astonished all who had an opportunity of observing it. "The modesty of Mr Berry permitted him to consign this gem to the hands of a friend in a retired situation of life who had few opportunities of showing it to others. He resumed his wonted drudgery, *satisfied*, we may suppose, *with that secret consciousness of triumphant exertion, which, to some abstracted minds, is not to be increased, but rather spoilt, by the applause of the uninitiated multitude. For many years this ingenious man 'narrowed his mind' to the cutting of heraldic seals, while in reality he must have known that his genius fitted him for a competition with the highest triumphs of Italian art*. When he was occasionally asked to undertake somewhat finer work, he generally found that, though he only demanded perhaps half the money which he could have earned in humbler work during the same space of time, yet even that was grudged by his employers; and he therefore found that mere considerations of worldly prudence demanded his almost exclusive attention to the ordinary walk of his profession. Nevertheless, in the course of a few years, the impulse of genius so far overcame his scruples that he executed various heads, any one of which would have been sufficient to ensure him fame among judges of excellence in this department of art. Among these were heads of Thomson, author of *The Seasons*, Mary Queen of Scots, Oliver Cromwell, Julius Caesar, a young Hercules, and Hamilton of Bangour, the poet. Of these only two were copies from the antique, and they were executed in the finest style of those celebrated intaglios. The young Hercules, in particular, possessed an unaffected plain simplicity, a union of youthful innocence with strength and dignity, which struck every beholder as most appropriate to that mythological personage, while it was, at the same time, the most difficult of all expressions, to be hit off by the faithful imitator of Nature. As an actor finds it much less difficult to imitate any extravagant violence of character than to represent, with truth and perspicacity, the elegant ease of the gentleman, so the painter can much more easily delineate the most violent contortions of countenance than that placid serenity to express which requires a nice discrimination of such infinitely small degrees of variation in certain lineaments as totally elude the observation of men, on whose minds Nature has not impressed, with her irresistible hand, that exquisite perceptive faculty which constitutes the essence of genius in the fine arts. Berry possessed this perceptive faculty to a degree which almost proved an obstruction, rather than a help, in his professional career. In his best performances he himself remarked defects which no one else perceived, and which he believed might have been overcome by greater exertion, if for that greater exertion he could have spared the necessary time. Thus, while others applauded his intaglios, he looked upon them with a morbid feeling of vexation, arising from that sense of the struggle which his immediate personal wants constantly maintained with the nobler impulses of art, and to which his situation in the world promised no speedy cessation. This gave him an aversion to the higher department of his art, which, though indulged to his own temporary comfort and the advantage of his family, was most unfortunate for the world. In spite of every disadvantage, the works of Mr Berry, few as they were in number, became gradually known in society at large; and some of his pieces were even brought into competition, by some distinguished cognoscenti, with those of Piccler at Rome, who had hitherto been the unapproached sovereign of this department of the arts. Although the experience of Piccler was that of a constant practitioner, while Mr Berry had only attempted a few pieces at long intervals in the course of a laborious life; although the former lived in a country where every artificial object was attuned to the principles of art, while Mr Berry was reared in a soil remarkable for the absence of all such advantages; the latter was by many good judges placed above his Italian contemporary. The respective works of the two artists were well known to each other; and each declared, with that manly ingenuousness which very high genius alone can confer on the human mind, that the other was greatly his superior. Mr Berry possessed not merely the art of imitating busts or figures set before him in which he could observe and copy the prominence or depression of the parts; but he possessed a faculty which presupposes a much nicer discrimination —that of being able to execute a figure in *relievo*, with perfect justice in all its parts, which was copied from a painting or drawing upon a flat surface. This was fairly put to the test in the head he executed of Hamilton of Bangour. That gentleman had been dead several years when his relations wished to have a head of him executed by Berry. The artist had himself never seen Mr Hamilton, and there remained no picture of him but an imperfect sketch, which was by no means a striking likeness. This was put into the hands of Mr Berry by a person who had known the deceased poet, and who pointed out the defects of the resemblance in the best way that words can be made to correct things of this nature; and from this picture, with the ideas that Mr Berry had imbibed from the corrections, he made a head which everyone who knew Mr Hamilton allowed to be one of the most perfect likenesses that could be wished for. In this, as in all his works, there was a correctness in the outline and a truth and delicacy in the expression of the features highly emulous of the best antiques; which were, indeed, the models on which he formed his taste. The whole number of heads executed by Mr Berry did not exceed a dozen, but, besides these, he executed some full-length figures of both men and animals, in his customary style of elegance. That attention, however, to the interests of a numerous family which a man of sound principles, as Mr Berry was, could never allow himself to lose sight of made him forgo these agreeable exertions for the more lucrative, though less pleasing, employment of cutting heraldic seals, which may be said to have been his constant employment from morning to night for forty years together, with an assiduity that almost surpasses belief. In this department he was, without dispute, the first artist of his time; but even here that modesty which was so peculiarly his own, and that invariable desire of giving perfection to everything he put out of his hand, prevented him from drawing such emoluments from his labours as they deserved. Of this the following anecdote will serve as an illustration, and as an additional testimony to his very great skill. Henry, Duke of Buccleuch, on succeeding to his title and estates, was desirous of having a seal cut with his arms properly blazoned upon it. But as there were no fewer than thirty-two compartments in the shield, which was of necessity confined to a very small space, so as to leave room for the supporters and other ornaments, within the compass of a seal of ordinary size he found it a matter of great difficulty to get it executed. Though a native of Scotland himself, the noble Duke had no idea that there was a man of first-rate eminence in this art in Edinburgh; and accordingly he had applied to the best seal-engravers in London and Paris, all of which declared it to be beyond their power. At this time Berry was mentioned to him with such powerful recommendations that he was induced to pay him a visit and found him, as usual, seated at his wheel. The gentleman who had mentioned Mr Berry's name to the Duke accompanied him on his visit. This person, without introducing the Duke, showed Mr Berry the impression of a seal which the Duchess-Dowager had got cut a good many years before by a Jew in London, now dead, and which had been shown to others as a pattern; asking him if he would cut a seal the same as that. After examining it a little, Mr Berry answered readily that he would. The Duke, at once pleased and astonished, exclaimed, 'Will you, indeed?' Mr Berry, who thought that this implied some doubt of his ability to perform what he undertook, was a little piqued, and turning round to the Duke, whom he had never before seen, he said, 'Yes, sir; if I do not make a better seal than this, I will charge no payment for it'. The Duke, highly pleased, left the pattern with Mr Berry and went away. The original contained, indeed, the various devices of the thirty-two compartments distinctly enough to be seen; but none of the colours were expressed. Mr Berry, in proper time, finished the seal, on which the figures were not only done with superior elegance, but the colours on every part so distinctly marked that a painter could delineate the whole or a herald blazon it, with perfect accuracy. For this extraordinary and most ingenious labour he charged no more than thirty-two guineas, though the pattern seal had cost seventy-five."

"Thus it was", concludes the chronicle of this astonishing case, "that, though possessed of talents unequalled in their kind, at least in Britain, and assiduity not to be surpassed,—observing at the same time the strictest economy in his domestic arrangements,—Mr Berry died at last in circumstances far from affluent. It had been the lot of this ingenious man to toil unceasingly for a whole life without obtaining any other reward than the common boon of mere subsistence, while his abilities, in another sphere, or in an age more qualified to appreciate and employ them, might have enabled him to attain at once to fame and fortune in a very few years. His art, it may be marked, has made no particular progress in Scotland, in consequence of his example. The genius of Berry was solitary, both in respect of place and time, and has never been rivalled by any other of his countrymen. It must be recorded to the honour of this unrequited genius that his character in private life was as amiable and unassuming as his talents were great; and that his conduct on all occasions was ruled by the strictest principles of honour and integrity."

THOMAS DAVIDSON

And the Fellowship of the New Life

THE persistence of the wayward, antinomian Scottish type—versatile, erudite, filled with wanderlust spiritual and physical, indifferent to or incapable of mere worldly prudence—from the earliest times to the present is easy of innumerable illustration. Of these characteristics, and their general radical tendency, recent times yield us a splendid example in Thomas Davidson, the incidental founder of the Fabian Society, a potent influence in the lives of Ramsay MacDonald, Havelock Ellis, and many other prominent men of to-day, whose description as "the Wandering Scholar" immediately calls up the memory of a host of Scotsmen equally entitled to it. William Knight has said of Davidson: "He educated others by a personality in which lay the slumbering fire of genius, a volcanic energy which was for long periods latent, and when active was sometimes slightly erratic in its mode of working. Continuity, or even consistency, was not possible to him in practical affairs. He chafed under constraint *ab extra*, while his whole being was alive and working out ideals *ab intra*. Testimony is borne from every quarter to the range of his learning, his marvellous memory, his knowledge of the ultimate problems of human thought, his mastery of many languages, his large humanity and affability, his loyalty as a friend, his unceasing toil in behalf of every pupil who came within the circle of his friendship, his hatred of superficiality and still more of all pretence, with his wonderful gift of appraising merit, or goodness of character, behind the ordinary shows of life. . . . Perhaps it was because he had no system to bequeath, no dogmas which he wished to see introduced into a school, and all-dominant there, that he was so altruistic in his endeavours. It is not as a doctrinaire philosopher that he will be remembered in Europe and America, but as the helpful comrade, who led many pupils out of the shallows of tradition and the back-water eddies of conventional belief, who made them think for themselves . . . helped them day by day to get quit of illusions . . . swept aside the sand of mere opinion. As to his own conclusions—so far as I can speak from personal knowledge—he was, as wise men are, both gnostic and agnostic; gnostic as to the root ideas of the true, the beautiful, and the good; agnostic as to the *terra incognita* which lies behind them, and the ultimate principle of things."

That is a portrait of a quintessential Scot; all Scotsmen of any consequence substantially correspond to it, and all who fail to embody and manifest these characteristics in considerable measure are unworthy of the name of Scotsmen. "He abjured finality, and rejected dogmas imposed on him, both *ab ante* and *ab extra*." He could have found no place for himself on the staffs of any of our modern Scottish Universities. "The raw material for tuition provided at our universities—young men and women who were preparing to enter the various professions, and were therefore to a large extent tied to ancient methods, some of them with already definitely formed opinions and who sought at college merely an outfit for professional success, —was not the material on which he could hope to work successfully." Defenders of our Universities to-day, who indignantly repel the charge that they are decadent and have ceased to be Universities in any true sense of the term, fail to realise that the gravamen of the charge to which they are replying is just this—that there is no place in them for great teachers like Davidson but that they are staffed by wholly inferior persons and catering almost entirely for very questionable requirements—a process which the tendencies towards the Leisure State and the increasing extent to which going through University courses and taking degrees has ceased to guarantee subsequent posts, while the numbers of would-be students have now to be more and more cut down, are to-day bringing to a perfect *reductio ad absurdum*; which must throw them back happily on to a purely cultural basis and conditions of free studentship uncontrolled by the contemptible rules and regulations of mere utilitarian considerations. "Like Socrates", Davidson "never cared about rewards for instruction; also, like Socrates, he had 'many scholars, but no school' with entrance examinations and well fenced traditional avenues to success. His was an educative rather than an academic ideal."

Writing his reminiscences of Davidson in 1903, Professor William James said: "I forget how Davidson was earning his subsistence at this time (*i.e.* in America, in the 1870's). He did some lecturing and private teaching, but I do not think they were great in amount. In the springs and summers he frequented the coast and indulged in long swimming bouts and salt-water immersions, which seemed to agree with him greatly. His sociability was boundless, and his time seemed to belong to anyone who asked for it. I soon conceived that such a man would be invaluable in Harvard University; a kind of Socrates, a devotee of truth and lover of youth, ready to sit up to any hour and talk with anyone, lavish of help and information and counsel, a contagious example of how lightly and humanly a burden of learning might be borne upon a pair of shoulders. In faculty business he might not run well in harness, but as an inspiration and ferment of character, and as an example of the ranges of combination of scholarship and manhood that are possible, his influence among the students would be priceless. I do not know whether this scheme of mine would under any circumstances have been feasible. At any rate it was nipped in the bud by the man himself. A natural Chair for him would have been Greek Philosophy. Unfortunately, just at the decisive hour, he offended our Greek department by a savage criticism of its methods which he had published in the *Atlantic Monthly*. This, with his other unconventionalisms, made advocating his cause more difficult, and the University authorities never, I believe, seriously thought of an appointment for him. I think that in this case Harvard University lost a great opportunity. Organisation and method mean something, but contagious human characters mean more in a university. A few undisciplinables like Davidson may be infinitely more precious than a faculty full of orderly routinists. As to what he might have become under the conventionalising influences of an official position, it would be idle to speculate. As things fell out, he became more and more unconventional, and even developed a sort of antipathy to academic life in general. It subdued individualism, he thought, and made for philistinism."

Davidson was vitally concerned with the solution of the educational problem of democracy, and in his paper on "The Higher Education of the Breadwinners" in 1899 he says (referring particularly to American conditions): "It cannot be said of our people that they are backward or niggardly in the matter of education. In no country is so much money expended upon schools and colleges as in the United States. And yet our people are very far from being educated as they ought to be. Ignorance is still widespread, and not only the ignorant but the whole nation suffers in consequence. In spite of our magnificent system of public schools and our numerous colleges and universities—over five hundred in all—the great body of our citizens lack the education necessary to give dignity and meaning to their individual lives, and to fit them for the worthy performance of their duties as members of the institutions under which they live. Our public schools stop too soon, while our colleges do not reach more than one in a thousand of our population. Moreover, neither school nor college imparts that education which our citizens, as such, require—domestic, social, and civic culture. What is imparted is defective both in kind and in extent. Even more regrettable is the fact that our schools and colleges for the most part confine their attention to persons who have nothing to do but study, who are not engaged in any kind of useful or productive labour. This results in two evils: (1) education for the great body of the people must stop at an early age since the children must go to work as soon as possible; (2) education is withheld just from those who are in the best position to profit by it; for every teacher with sufficient experience knows that people who have a knowledge of practical life and its duties are far better and more encouraging pupils than those who have not. . . . Thus it comes to pass that the lives of the great mass of our citizens are unintelligent, narrow, sordid, envious, and unhappy. Thus, too, it comes that our politics are base, and our politicians venal and selfish. The labouring classes are, through want of education, easily cozened or bribed to vote in opposition to their own best interests, and so to condemn themselves to continued slavish toil and poverty, which means exclusion from all share in the spiritual wealth of the race."

While admitting that the recent developments of training centres and "University extension" are steps in the right direction, he contends that neither go anything like far enough, and "worst of all, both exclude from their programmes some of the very subjects which it is most essential for the breadwinners to be acquainted with—economics, sociology, politics, etc." "I think," he says, in a letter to Wyndham Dunstan, "the time has come for formulating into a religion and rule of life the results of the intellectual and moral attainments of the last two thousand years. I cannot content myself with this miserable blind life that the majority of mankind is at present leading and I do not see any reason for it. Moreover, I do not see anything really worth doing but to show men the way to a better life. If our philosophy, our science, and our art do not contribute to that, what are they worth?"

"What shall we say of people who devote their time", he asks, "to reading novels written by miserable, ignorant scribblers—many of them young, uneducated, and inexperienced—and who have hardly read a line of Homer or Sophocles or Dante or Shakespeare or Goethe, or even of Wordsworth or Tennyson, who would laugh at the notion of reading and studying Plato or Aristotle or Thomas Aquinas or Bruno or Kant or Rosmini? Are they not worse than the merest idiots, feeding prodigally upon swinish garbage, when they might be in their father's house, enjoying their portion of humanity's spiritual birthright? I know of few things more utterly sickening and contemptible than the self-satisfied smile of Philistine superiority with which many persons tell me, 'I am not a philosopher'. It simply means this, 'I am a stupid, low, grovelling fool, and I am proud of it'."

Davidson was born in 1840 in the parish of Old Deer, at Drinies. Shortly afterwards the family moved to the village of Fetterangus, about a mile away. He had one brother, John Morrison Davidson, afterwards a well-known barrister-at-law and political and social journalist. A great reader from the beginning, Davidson received his early education in the local village school and later in the parish school of Old Deer, ultimately boarding with the headmaster of the latter, who taught him Latin, Greek, and mathematics in the evenings while his wife initiated him into French, which he was soon able to read with ease. At the age of sixteen (in 1856) he took sixth place in the Bursary Competition at King's College, Aberdeen, gaining a scholarship of fifteen pounds a year for four years. At the end of his first session he took the second prize in Greek and carried off the Simpson Greek prize of seventy pounds at the close of his curriculum. In his second year he took the first prize in senior Greek, and Principal Geddes, then Professor of Greek, spoke of him one day in his class as the best linguist he had ever taught. In his fourth year he was second in senior Humanity and fourth in Logic and in Moral Philosophy. Davidson graduated at Aberdeen University in 1860, and after teaching for three months at Oundle, Northamptonshire, became rector of the old-town Grammar School at Aberdeen and session clerk of Old Machar parish. These posts he held for about three years. The school did not flourish under him and he disliked the work of registering births, deaths, and marriages. He resigned in August 1863, taught a while at Tunbridge Wells, went to Canada, thence to St. Louis and afterwards to Boston, where he met Longfellow and through his influence got an examinership at Harvard University. He spent a year in Greece, chiefly at Athens, and later at Rome he was introduced to his Holiness the Pope, and had an hour's conversation with him in Latin in the Vatican garden, an honour rarely granted to any except intimate friends.

Davidson also spent a year in the north of Italy, while writing *The Philosophical System of Antonio Rosmini-Serbati*. As Wyndham Dunstan says: "Davidson's attachment to Rosmini's philosophical views had led some to suppose that he might eventually join the Church of Rome, which he respected and in a sense even venerated, and which had given every encouragement to his work on Rosmini. It was certainly an interesting spectacle in the early eighties to find Davidson in friendly communication with the Pope and the Cardinals in Rome and received literally with open arms by the priests and votaries of the Rosminian order throughout Italy. I spent the summer of 1882 with him at his villa above Domodossola, near the Rosminian monastery to which we constantly went to discuss philosophical questions with the learned fathers of the order, with whom Davidson was on the most friendly terms, though, so far as I am aware, he never attended any of their religious services. Between him and Pope Leo XIII there was much common intellectual ground. Both had consummate knowledge of Aristotle and the schoolmen, both were anxious to influence through philosophy the materialistic trend of current thought, and both had been influenced by the Rosminian philosophy. During my visits to Davidson in Rome and in Domodossola I saw much of those who represented the intellectual movement in the Roman Church, to whom Davidson was a *persona grata*. I have, however, no reason to believe that the idea of accepting the religious doctrines of Rome was ever present to Davidson's mind. Certainly no one who knew him could consider such an event even as a possible contingency."

Davidson's friendships soon spread all over Europe. "He had defects and excesses which he wore upon his sleeve, so that everyone could see them immediately. They made him many enemies, and if one liked quarrelling he was an easy man to quarrel with. But his heart and mind held treasures of the rarest. He had a genius for friendship; money, place, fame, fashion, and the vulgar idols of the tribe, had no hold on his imagination; he led his own life absolutely, in whatever company he might find himself; and the intense individualism which he stood for and taught is the lesson of which our generation stands perhaps most in need. . . . His broad brow, his big chest, his bright blue eyes, his volubility in talk and laughter told a tale of vitality far beyond the common; but his fine and nervous hands and the vivacity of his reaction upon every impression suggested a degree of sensibility which one rarely finds conjoined with so robustly animal a frame. . . . If you ask me what the *value* of Thomas Davidson was, what was the general significance of his life apart from his particular work and services, I shall have to say that it lay in the example he set to us all, of how—even in the midst of this intensely worldly social system of ours, in which every interest is organised collectively and commercially—a single man may still be a knight-errant of the intellectual life, and preserve freedom in the midst of sociability. Asking no man's permission, bowing the knee to no tribal idol, renouncing the conventional channels of recognition, he showed us how a life devoted to purely intellectual ends could be beautifully wholesome outwardly, and overflow with inner contentment. The memory of Davidson will always strengthen my faith in personal freedom and its spontaneities, and make me less unqualifiedly respectful than ever of 'civilisation', with its exaggerated belief in herding and branding, licensing, authorising, and appointing, and, in general, regulating and administrating the lives of human beings by system.

Surely the individual person is the more fundamental phenomenon, and the social institution, of whatever grade, is secondary and ministerial. The individual can call it to account in a deeper sense than that in which it calls him to account. Social systems satisfy many interests, but unsatisfied interests always remain over, *and among them interests which system as such violates*. The best commonwealth is the one which most cherishes the men who represent the residual interests, and leaves the largest scope to their activity. Davidson seemed to find the United States a more propitious commonwealth in this regard than his native land or other European countries." There was certainly little or no place for him in Scotland, which, nevertheless, strangely enough, has always produced—for export!—a far greater percentage of his type than any other country in Europe.

The need for an international brotherhood of great spirits has been frequently canvassed during the past century, and Davidson was one of the first to be seized with it. "A metaphysician who had read deep and widely, and an acute dialectician, Davidson's guiding motive in later life was, nevertheless, the practical one of founding a new society on an intellectual basis. In earlier life he had made himself acquainted with the best that had been said and done in religion, philosophy, art, and literature, and his rare intellectual ability, his remarkable power of memory and exposition, and his attractive personality, combined to make him feel that he might be able to bring into existence a new brotherhood which in time might grow and exercise a profound influence for good. Ultimately this lofty ambition actuated all that Davidson undertook." As he himself put it: "All great world movements begin with a little knot of people who, in their individual lives, and in their relations to each other, realise the ideal that is to be. To live truth is better than to utter it. Isaiah would have prophesied in vain had he not gathered round him a little band of disciples who lived according to his ideal. Again, what would the teachings of

Jesus have amounted to had he not collected a body of disciples, who made it their life-aim to put his teachings into practice?" So Davidson was bold enough to think that the new view of the world, the modern scientific view, makes it possible "to frame a new series of ethical precepts which should do for our time what the Deuteronomic Law did for the time of Isaiah, and the Sermon on the Mount for that of Jesus". And he was even more bold to state his conviction that "it is impossible to reach a better social and moral condition until we have rationally adopted an entirely new view of life and its meaning; a new philosophy truer and deeper than any that has gone before".

Davidson had consequently no sympathy with the efforts of those who, not knowing how to educate the masses of the people, offer them petty amusements to keep them off the streets and away from the public-houses. He did not believe in trifles. He stood for the highest culture for the breadwinners, for the people who have to "go to work" early. He was convinced that the way to lift the people above their degrading and vicious lives was to give them an intelligent view of the world, which will offer them an inspiring outlook on life. "One intelligent glimpse of the drama of life", he said, "will quench the desire for the pleasure of the dive and the prize-ring."

"The life of Thomas Davidson was essentially a heroic life", says Morris Cohen. "Though as I knew him one of the most sympathetic souls that ever trod this globe, he had no sympathy with anything unheroic. He had a generous faith in human nature, believing that there are heroes and heroines now, more than ever before, to be found in every street and on every corner, and that it is only our own blindness that prevents us from appealing to the heroic in them." He particularly loathed the tendency nowadays, especially among "practical people", to look down on all attempts to grapple with the deep problems of existence, and prophesy only easy things. The great defect in ordinary College and University education was, and is, as he said, "that it stops with knowing and does not go on to living and doing. It therefore never is really appropriated, for knowing that does not pass into act and habit is never ours, but remains an external thing, a mere useless accomplishment to be vain about."

In a paper on the foundation of the New York branch of the Fellowship of the New Life in 1884, Davidson ended: "The reason why people doubt the freedom of the will is because they never exercise it, but are always following some feeling or instinct, some private taste or affection. How *should* such persons know that the will is free? Our time is dying of sentimentality—some of it refined enough to be sure, but sentimentality—which destroys the will. We are on our way to all that heart ever wished or head conceived. But the greater gods have no sympathy with anything but heroism. When we will not be heroic they sternly fling us back to suffer, saying to us: Learn to will. The kiss of the Valkyre, which opens the gates of Valhalla, is sealed only upon lips made holy by heroism even unto death. The hosts of Ahura-Mazda are still fighting, and woe to us if we do not join them. It is the custom of the wise men of the world to laugh at all great heroism, all thirst for self-sacrifice; but we can afford to let them laugh. Somewhere in the shadow there are spectators who laugh at them, and will laugh when these have lost the will to laugh. The sons of Ahura-Mazda laugh for ever, and there is no uneasiness in their laughter. Their laugh is the beauty of the universe. But this will, perhaps, weary you and seem mere poetry to you. Poetry it is; but, as Aristotle said long ago, 'Poetry is more earnest and more philosophical than history'. The true poetry of the world is the history of its spiritual life, and is as much truer than what is *called* history as spirit is truer than outward seeming."

Writing to Havelock Ellis in 1883 he says: "Life is not mere emotion, nor is there in emotion anything moral or immoral, else the lower animals would be as moral or immoral as man. There is an intellectual life as well as an emotive one, and it is the former alone that is distinctively human. I know how strong the tendency is, in these sentimental dallying days of ours, to lay stress upon emotion, and all forms of passivity, to the detriment of intelligence, insight, and all forms of heroic activity. This is even the curse of our time. . . ."

The mottoes of his life were that line of the Greek tragedian, "Wisdom is by far the major part of well-being", and the other Greek text which was inscribed on the wall of his lecture-room at Glenmore, "Without friends no one could choose to live, even with all other good things". "The man of reflection", he wrote in 1899, "is not apt to be the man of action; and yet it is just he who ought to be so. It is the philosopher who ought to be the king. And yet just because philosophers have not been careful to cultivate their wills, they have always been bad kings; and kingship has been usually left to men deficient in insight and power of thought. But I do not believe that this need be always so. The difficulty arises from the fact that our philosophers, thus far, have been too abstract, ideal, and Platonic; concerning themselves with things and conditions too far remote from human experience, instead of with experience itself. This again has been largely due to the fact that all original thinkers have found the world in possession of certain ancient and traditional ideals, which it was regarded as impious to disturb, and that, therefore, they have had to betake themselves to unreal regions, philosophical and social Utopias. Even to this day there is no philosophy of actual experience, no working theory or norm of life, based upon the results of carefully digested science. Indeed, such philosophy is the great desideratum of our time, and the future will belong to the man who can furnish it. *Such* a philosophy will make men of strong wills, just because it will make them realise that thought, apart from action, is mere impotent flapping of wings in vacancy. The philosophers of the future will, like the early Greek philosophers, be men of action, the founders of societies, the chief agents in all social reform. They will be loyal not to the past but to the future—to the social order that is to be. . . . It is all in vain to imagine that we can have correct practice without correct thinking, and correct thinking implies correct metaphysics. . . . A life in which the deepest and highest thought is indifferent in relation to practice would be a life without intellectual endeavour and without poetry. Is not the deepest of all bonds, and the purest intellectual sympathy, community of insight?"

In his great paper on "Intellectual Piety" he says: "In the struggle, no doubt, many of our existing institutions must go down, indeed, in the end, they must all go down, in so far as they are in any way authoritative; for among men intellectually pious authority has no place or power. We ought always to remember that the amount of authority requiring to be exercised among a people is always in exact inverse ratio to its spiritual advancement, its intellectual piety." "Change is utterly impossible except on the supposition that there is an unchanging subject of change." "Get once into your mind the thought that being is an act (not an action) and all the talk about universal relativity becomes pure nonsense."

Dr. Felix Adler says: "To think wisely, to try to think so, was the greater part of his happiness. And this 'trying' is to be understood in a severe and thorough-going sense. His scholarship was admired by all who knew him. His vast command of languages and literatures, ancient and modern—Greek, Hebrew, Arabic, Italian, German, etc. —his minute acquaintance with the recondite learning of the Middle Ages, all this was astonishing. But still more astonishing was it how lightly he carried this heavy baggage, how entirely he forbore to intrude or make parade of his great erudition, how completely he converted into the tissue of his own thinking the elements he had absorbed from elsewhere. To be honest with himself, to be sure that he had a right to an opinion, was the stringent rule to which he subjected himself. He did not fail, I think, in due respect for beliefs held sacred by others, but he esteemed it a right and a duty to express his own with no uncertain sound, without any truckling show of conformity or timid apology. He believed that the progress of mankind depends on the acceptance of true ideas, and the rejection of false; and he rightly thought that the inherent strength and truth of ideas can be fairly tested only if all earnest thinkers shall freely and courageously state the results of their thinking, without fear of the social or material penalties that may follow such an avowal. In a world where inner convictions are so often veiled in timorous and guarded generalities, in a world in which the partial suppression rather than the full expression of the thoughts that relate to the highest interests of man is so often commended both by precept and example, his courage, his boldness, his perfect sincerity, his readiness to sacrifice interest to truth, appears to me to be one of his fairest titles to the respect of right-thinking men." "He refused", says Charlotte Daley, "to have disciples, insisting that everyone should 'think whole-thoughts' for himself. He was not a system-builder, and he purposely left no fully elaborated philosophy. 'There have been too many systems of philosophy already', he said to me. 'In the very nature of things there can be nothing final. It is not my duty to draw conclusions for anyone. What I want to do is to help people to think for themselves, and *to think round the circle, not in scraps and bits*.'"

It was his great desire to be influenced by as well as to influence current thought at all its centres which made him a wandering scholar. His life for years was divided between New York, London, Rome, Paris, Berlin, with excursions further afield to Cairo, Constantinople, and elsewhere. For money and worldly position he had no concern whatever. His permanent means were very slight indeed, and his simple tastes enabled him to depend upon the precarious and small pecuniary results of lecturing and writing.

It is interesting to find Professor James finding something in common between Davidson's personality and work and that of his countrymen, Carlyle and Ruskin. "Intellectually," as Percival Chubb said, "Davidson always bore the marks of his Scottish origin. He was modern in his equipment and in his outlook; but with this modernness was mingled a touch of the scholasticism and the sectarian fire, the *parti pris*, of a Knox." He was Scottish too in his appearance; there was always something rustic about him, something which suggested to the end his farm-boy origin. He had a sort of physical dignity, but neither in dress nor in manner did he ever grow quite "gentlemanly" or *Salonfähig*.

He was Scottish too in his endless sociability and volubility—the taciturn, non-committal, monosyllabic, canny Scot is the denationalised type, the product of Anglicisation. But he very seldom and very briefly ever returned to Scotland. Scotland was committed to a system the very antithesis of all that he had stood for—of all that appertained to its own true genius. Only within the past few years—in the Scottish Renaissance movement—has this appalling general servility and mindlessness been challenged, and the influence of Davidson made itself felt. The future of Scotland—and, above all, of a Scottish Scotland—depends upon it. For the present generation, however, these vital principles are less likely to be derived directly from the work of Davidson himself than from that of a more recent teacher of kindred truths, James Harvey Robinson: and it is important to note in the writings and speeches of the Renaissance group quotations such as these: "The astonishing and perturbing suspicion emerges that perhaps all that has passed for social science, political economy, politics, and ethics in the past may be brushed aside by future generations as mere rationalising", and "The fact that an idea is ancient and that it has been widely received is no argument in its favour, but should immediately suggest the necessity of carefully testing it as a probable instance of rationalisation", or, in relation to our educational system, "Political and social questions, and matters relating to prevailing business methods, race animosities, public elections, and governmental policy are, if they are vital, necessarily 'controversial'. School boards and those who control colleges and universities are sensitive to this fact. They eagerly deprecate in their public manifestoes any suspicion that pupils and students are being awakened in any way to the truth that our institutions can possibly be fundamentally defective, or that the present generation of citizens has not conducted our affairs with exemplary success, guided by the immutable principles of justice. How indeed can a teacher be expected to explain to the sons and daughters of business men, politicians, doctors, lawyers, and clergymen—all pledged to the maintenance of the sources of their livelihood—the actual nature of business enterprise as now practised, the prevailing methods of legislative bodies and courts, and the conduct of foreign affairs? Think of a teacher in the public schools recounting the more illuminating facts about the municipal government under which he lives, with due attention to grafts and jobs. So courses in government, political economy, sociology, and ethics confine themselves to inoffensive generalisations, harmless details of organisation, and the commonplaces of routine morality, for only in that way can they escape being controversial. Teachers are rarely able or inclined to explain our social life and its presuppositions with sufficient insight and honesty to produce any very important results. Even if they are tempted to tell the essential facts they dare not do so, for fear of losing their places, amid the applause of all the righteously minded."

So it comes about that almost the only men of any real value amongst the whole horde of Scottish teachers of the past fifty to a hundred years are John Maclean, who was thrown out of the profession and badgered to death by the authorities, and A. S. Neill, who struck out on a line of his own; while the general choice confronting Scotsmen is either to become, in some measure, a Thomas Davidson or a Ramsay MacDonald.

MacDonald was a disciple and associate of Davidson's in the early days. In 1883 Davidson came to London and held little meetings of young people to whom he introduced his ideas of a Vita Nuova, or a Fellowship of the New Life. Amongst those early attracted to this movement were Havelock Ellis, H. H. Champion, Frank Podmore, E. R. Pease, Mrs Hinton (widow of James Hinton), and Edith M. O. Lees, later the wife of Havelock Ellis. A minority soon tabled a plan for "the cultivation of a perfect character in each and all" as the essential aim of the Fellowship, and the principle of "the subordination of material things to spiritual". Out of the majority against this, on 4th January 1884, was born the famous Fabian Society. The Fellowship of the New Life continued for fifteen years, issuing from July 1889 to February 1898 a quarterly paper called *Seedtime*. Several attempts were made to run what Pease calls "associated colonies" (that is, the members living near each other), and a co-operative residence was established at 49 Doughty Street, Bloomsbury. According to Edward Carpenter, here some "eight or ten members of the Fellowship made their home, and were to illustrate the advantages of the community life". Ramsay MacDonald, not dreaming of Premierships, was among the chief inmates of the Fellowship House. Mr (later Lord) Olivier occasionally resided there. The Fellowship had for a time its own printing business at Thornton Heath, near Croydon, and also a Kindergarten in which it attempted to educate children aright. At Croydon, later on, there grew up an Ethical Church and a Boys' Guild. "Soon afterwards the Fellowship came to the conclusion that its work was done, the last number of *Seedtime* was published, and in 1898 the Society was dissolved." Edith Lees was the secretary, almost the factotum, of the idealistic Doughty Street establishment, where the individuals of the interesting experiment were pledged, after Goethe, to live resolutely "in the whole, the good, and the beautiful"; and MacDonald was her chief coadjutor. Alas, there was too little sociability, let alone socialism, in evidence there. As Mrs Ellis later shows in her novel, *Attainment*, the experiment, despite its Goethian aspirations, was headed from the first for much irresolute living in the partial, the bad, and the ugly. The best it has left are Havelock Ellis's reminiscences of Davidson, whom he declares to have been "one of the most remarkable men I have ever met. . . . He failed to make me his disciple, but he taught me a lesson I have never since unlearned. Before I met him I thought that philosophical beliefs could be imparted and shared; that men could, as it were, live under the same metaphysical dome. Davidson enabled me to see that a man's metaphysics, if genuinely his, is really a most intimate part of his own personal temperament, and that no one can really identify himself with another's philosophy, however greatly he may admire it or sympathise with it." But, as Isaac Goldberg says in his biographical and critical study of Ellis, Ellis came fully prepared to receive just such a lesson, for in his Australian *Notes*, set down years before his meeting with Davidson, he wrote: "For let us be very certain that the only right belief for every man is that which his own consciousness tells him is true, although our consciousness tells us something different".

"It was as a personal force", continues Ellis, "rather than as a profound intellect that Davidson made his mark on his time. It was this temperamental character that gave a curious, almost unique, imprint to his personality. He was well aware of his own emotional tendencies: I remember that he once referred to the attraction that mysticism had for him, as an attraction he had to guard against. Many of his characteristics were doubtless due to a certain struggle with his own exuberant emotionalism. His sense of the immense importance of education, training, and discipline was rooted there. Doubtless, also, a certain formality in his literary work showed that he wished to keep a curb on himself. But the result was that

Davidson never reached self-expression in literature. His personality—with that specially perfervid Scottish quality which he possessed in so high a degree—was much more potent than his works indicate. The enthusiasm and conviction, with which he advocated more or less impossible and unfamiliar ideals, could not fail to exert a stimulating influence on all who came near him. He helped to teach those who listened to him to think, even though it were to think that he was wrong, and to think why he was wrong. Few men, indeed, of his time were permitted to play a part so like to that of these early Greek philosophers whom he loved so greatly." One of Davidson's favourite quotations was always Carlyle's saying: "It does not so much matter what a man believes, as how he believes it".

Davidson went to America and established his Summer School of the Culture Sciences at Glenmore in 1889. Glenmore was a farm of 166 acres on East Hill in the north end of Keene valley in the Adirondacks, which Davidson had acquired. It lies in the wilderness, on the foothills of Mount Hurricane, about 2000 feet above sea-level. The attractions of the scenery were great; hill and dale, field and forest intermingled. It was made a home of simple living, assiduous and comprehensive study, and lively fellowship. "Twice I went up with Davidson to open the place in April", says William James. "I well remember leaving his fireside one night with three ladies who were also early comers, and finding the thermometer at 8° Fahrenheit, and a tremendous gale blowing the snow about. Davidson loved these blustering vicissitudes of climate. In the early years the brook was never too cold for him to bathe in and he spent hours in rambling over the hills and through the forest. His own cottage stood high on the hill in a grove of silver birches, and looked upon the western mountains; and it always seemed to me an ideal dwelling for such a bachelor scholar. . . . Individualist *à outrance*, Davidson felt that every hour was a unique entity to whose claim on one's spontaneity one should always lie open. Thus he was never abstracted or preoccupied, but always seemed when with you as if you were the one person whom it was then right to attend to. It was this individualistic religion that made Davidson so indifferent, all democrat as he nevertheless was, to socialisms and general administrative panaceas. Life must be flexible. You ask for a free man and these Utopias give you an 'interchangeable part', with a fixed number, in a rule-bound social organism. The thing to aim at is liberation of the inner interests. . . . Leveller upwards of men as Davidson was, in the moral and intellectual manner, he seemed wholly without that sort of religious sentiment which makes so many of our contemporary democrats think that they ought to dip, at least, into some manual occupation, in order to share the common burden of humanity. I never saw him work with his hands in any way. He accepted material services of all kinds without apology, as if he were a born patrician; evidently feeling that if he played his own more intellectual part rightly, society could demand nothing further. . . . When, in the last year of his life, he proposed his night-school to young East Side workmen in New York, he told them that he had no sympathy whatever with the griefs of 'labour', that outward circumstances meant nothing in his eyes, that through their individual wills and intellect they could share, just as they were, in the highest spiritual life of humanity, and that he was there to help them severally to that privilege. . . . His confidence that the life of intelligence is the absolutely highest made Davidson serene about his outward fortunes. Pecuniary worry would not tally with his programme. He had a very small provision against a rainy day, but he did little to increase it. He would write as many articles and give as many lectures, talks, or readings every winter as would suffice to pay the year's expenses, but would thereafter refuse additional invitations and repair to Glenmore as early in the spring as possible. I could not but admire the temper he showed when the principal building there was one night turned to ashes. There was no insurance on it, and it would cost a couple of thousand dollars to replace it. Excitable as Davidson was about small contrarieties, he watched this fire without a syllable of impatience. *Plaie d'argent n'est pas mortelle*, he seemed to say, and if he felt sharp regrets he disdained to express them. No more did care about his literary reputation trouble him. In the ordinary greedy sense he seemed quite free from ambition. During his last years he had prepared a large mass of material for that history of the interaction of Greek, Christian, Hebrew, and Arabic thought upon one another before the revival of learning, which was to be his *magnum opus*. It was a territory to which, in its totality, few living minds had access, and in which a certain proprietary feeling was natural. Knowing how short his life might be, I once asked him whether he felt no concern lest the work already done by him should be frustrate from the lack of its necessary complement, in case he was suddenly cut off. His answer surprised me by its indifference. He would work as long as he lived, he said, but would not allow himself to worry, and would look serenely at whatever might be the outcome."

He died in September 1900 and his great work never appeared. In 1894 he wrote that he had been working on it for fifteen years and intended that winter to consult original sources of information for it in the libraries of London, Paris, Berlin, and Rome. In 1896 he says: "My book progresses, but it grows terribly on my hands and the condensing is no easy matter. I must include in it a brief account of Arab thought, if I am to make the second period of scholasticism intelligible. I am not sure but you would do well to let me expatiate on Oriental thought, exclusive of the Hindu, even if I should need another volume. My book will practically be a History of the Rise and Fall of Authority in Thought. In mediaevalism authority or dogma takes the place of national spirit. . . . It is difficult to say when my book will be finished. It is a big subject; and the *Vorarbeiten* are not numerous, or good. The ordinary histories are mere congeries of facts, without internal connections. . . . The fact is there are no *Vorarbeiten*; indeed, there is no single book that really gives an intelligent, enlightening view of mediaeval thought. I could easily abridge Stockl's *Geschichte der Philosophie des Mittelalters* or expand Ueberweg-Heinze's *Grundriss der Geschichte der Philosophie*, but that would be useless hack-work. What I am trying to do is to give a living picture of dogma-limited mediaeval thought in all its relations and ramifications, showing its connection with Greek, Roman, Patristic, and Arabic thought, and its influence on modern thought. . . ."

As Professor Knight points out, though this book was never completed, there exist in manuscript a series of thirty-seven lectures on the "Philosophy of the Middle Ages", delivered at Glenmore, and taken down by a very competent student. They could not be printed as they now stand, but if other students took down similar ones (as many doubtless did), and if all were submitted to a competent editor (as the manuscript notes of the lectures on "Logic" and "Metaphysics" by Sir William Hamilton at Edinburgh were handed over to Professor Veitch and Dean Mansel), a work of real and lasting merit might be constructed. Although the printed output of Davidson's life is not large and probably does not do justice to his scholarly capacities, it is wrong to suggest that he frittered away his great powers and left an inadequate legacy. He published ten books. *The Parthenon Frieze*, published with other essays in London in 1882, was written to combat the prevailing opinions regarding the meaning of this monumental work. Modern archaeologists hold the subject to be the Parthenaic procession, or some ceremony connected with it. Davidson asserts that it may properly be called the Dream of Pericles—a vision of social union and harmony, never realised, but having in it a great, genial, human purpose, which, had it been fulfilled, might have changed the whole history of the world, and hastened the march of civilisation by two thousand years. He knew

Dante intimately and wrote a translation and commentary on Scartazzini's *Hand Book*, which was published in 1887. His knowledge of the history of education is not to be measured by his small though excellent book on that subject which appeared in 1900. His other books include *Aristotle and Ancient Educational Ideals; Education of the Greek People and its Influence on Civilisation; Rousseau and Education according to Nature;* and *Prolegomena to Tennyson's In Memoriam, with Index to the Poem.* Most important of all were his translations of *Rosmini's Anthropology* and *Rosmini's Psychology*, and his *Philosophical System of Antonio Rosmini-Serbati*, with a sketch of Rosmini's life, bibliography, introduction, and notes (London, 1882).

Rosmini was best known in this country as an Italian priest who was a reformer within the Church of Rome, and his *Seven Wounds of the Holy Church* was translated into English, with a preface, by Canon Liddon. Rosmini was also a metaphysician of a high order, however. His philosophy may be regarded as a restatement of the scholasticism of St. Thomas and the schoolmen in the light of Hegelianism and later German philosophy. Such a system had every attraction for Davidson. Deeply versed as he was in Greek philosophy, with a profound knowledge of Aristotle as well as of St. Thomas Aquinas and the schoolmen, and thoroughly imbued with the classical spirit, Davidson welcomed Rosmini's system as a means of reconciling the older philosophy and the later German metaphysics, which he had also mastered and whose subtlety he fully appreciated and admired; though he refused to accept them as a system of philosophy capable of being made the basis of ethical and practical action. "Leaving out the dogmatic part of them, I think they are the gospel of future thought", he writes, recommending Rosmini's works to Havelock Ellis. "With your freedom from prejudice, your desire to do the best you know, and your human sympathy, you would, I am certain, find great satisfaction in them, and be able to free yourself from the last remnant of that terrible monism from which hardly any English thinker escapes."

In view of the contemporary Thomist cult, it is interesting to find Davidson in another letter exclaiming: "Alas, that the philosophic value of the classical mediaeval philosophy stands in sad disproportion to its literary bulk. The achievements of Thomas Aquinas, for example, can be dismissed in a few pages; while Roscelinus and William of Ockham will require a good deal of attention."

But, if Davidson only published ten books, he wrote scores of articles or translations for the *Journal of Speculative Philosophy*, the *Western Educational Review*, the *Forum*, and other reviews, and left in manuscript nearly two hundred lectures, essays, translations, and diaries, amply testifying to his amazing range, his educative passion, his indubitable mastery, and his eager, devouring interest in all the manifestations of life.

ELSPETH BUCHAN

Friend Mother in the Lord

THE one Scottish woman (Note I) with whom I propose to deal in this volume may well be given pride of place, for Scottish women who can be classed as "eccentrics" are very few and far between, and in most of these the eccentricities displayed are of a very minor and moderate character, scarcely entitling them to more than a little local reputation as "queer customers"; while their careers as a whole had little or no general interest. Scottish women of any historical importance or interest are curiously rare, and although these may have played dramatic parts in great affairs and manifested no little courage and contriving power, their psychologies present next to nothing that is out of the ordinary. A long list of famous Englishwomen is easy to compile; it is impossible to draw up any corresponding list of Scotswomen. Only half a dozen or so of names come readily to mind, but even these compare poorly with the English "opposite numbers" whether in beauty, in social sway, or in mental or spiritual interest. For the most part our leading Scotswomen have been shrewd, forceful characters, with keen eyes to the main chance, but almost entirely destitute of exceptional endowments of any sort. Yet the women of Scotland have perhaps played a greater part, influenced the activities of the men to a greater extent, than the women of any other European nation. Can the absence in modern Scotland of all the rarer and higher qualities of the human spirit be attributed to this undue influence of the female sex? It may have something to do with it. It is, at all events, worth recalling that Galton in his study of genius maintains that it seldom comes where the mother's influence is strongest. Scotswomen are overwhelmingly not the sort to be "fashed with the nonsense" of any attention to the arts, or other precarious and comparatively unremunerative activities on the part of their offspring, as against due concentration on the business of getting on and doing well in a solid material sense.

Especially since the Reformation has this been the case, and the connection between industrial civilisation and Protestantism need not be stressed here. The Church has always been disproportionately—and in recent times to an ever greater extent—dependent upon women, and the subject of this essay deserves pride of place not only because she is the only representative of her sex in my contents-table but because she is a strange exception in the whole history of Scottish religiosity.

It is a curious fact that Scotland, despite the long obsession of its people with religious matters, has produced few religious characters of any great interest to those who are not particularly concerned with the truth (or considered tenability) or otherwise of their tenets, but only with the interest in and for themselves of the personalities in question. The intellectual and psychological processes involved seem incredibly poor and dull in relation to the course of affairs in which these people played such powerful parts. The fact that Scotland has produced practically no religious poetry or other religious literature of quality is probably a consequence of this defect. It is at least noteworthy that Scottish poets who have touched upon religious matters have only done so successfully when they have been in a flippant or sarcastic mood at variance with orthodoxy.

Literary issues apart, the national theological obsession seems to have had a general dehumanising effect, and it is certainly like looking for a needle in a haystack to look for interesting personalities in the interminable host of those bigoted people, any one of whom might well have been interchanged with any other one so far as personal attributes are concerned. Without a special interest in theological—rather than spiritual—matters the life-patterns of the vast majority of Scottish divines are of a singularly commonplace and uninteresting character, and the percentage of these which show significant, let alone sensational, characteristics and complications of temperament and raise curious psychological issues is as small as the occasional divergencies in question are themselves trivial. This great "cloud of witnesses", characterised by an appalling sameness, has little or no attraction for the connoisseur of human foibles. Whatever light and leading informed them seems to have been contained in the dark lanterns of natures almost as uniformly dingy as the covers of the Book with which they were so abnormally preoccupied. Many Scottish divines played very active and even astonishing parts in affairs, but the interest that attaches is to the affairs themselves—not to the individual personalities of the ministers in question. These historical dramas may be immensely important; the ecclesiastical actors filled their public rôles passionately and portentously enough—but, off the religio-political stage, are seen to have been as a rule very mediocre and insignificant men. To such an extent is this true—so negligible was their contribution to the Spirit of Man—that the hordes of dour and often fanatical Scots take on an extremely depressing aspect as they move through the pages of history, as if engaged in processes to which all that is colourful and vital and valuable in human nature had somehow, inexplicably, become irrelevant. It is with relief that we turn from the spectacle of that devastating steam-roller to the singular problem of Elspeth Buchan.

Elspeth was the daughter of John Simpson, who kept an inn at Fitney-Can, the half-way house between Banff and Portsoy. She was born in 1738 and educated in the Scottish Episcopal Communion. Having been sent when a girl to Glasgow, as a servant-girl, she married Robert Buchan, an employee in her master's pottery, with whom she lived for several years and had several children. "Having changed her original profession of faith for that of her husband, who was a burgher-seceder, her mind", we are told, "seems to have become perplexed with religious fancies, as is too often the case with those who alter their creed. She fell into a habit of interpreting the Scriptures literally, and began to promulgate certain strange doctrines, which she derived in this manner from Holy Writ. Having now moved to Irvine, she drew over to her own way of thinking Mr Hugh Whyte, a Relief clergyman, who consequently abdicated his charge and became her chief apostle. The sect was joined by persons of a rank of life in which no such susceptibility was to be expected. Mr Hunter, a lawyer, and several trading people in good circumstances, were among her converts. After having indulged their absurd fancies for several years at Irvine, the mass of the people at length rose in April 1784, and assembled in a threatening and tumultuous manner around Mr Whyte's house, which had become the tabernacle of the new religion, and of which they broke all the windows. The Buchanites felt this insult so keenly that they left the town to the number of forty-six persons, and proceeding through Mauchline, Cumnock, Sanquhar, and Thornhill, did not halt till they arrived at a farm-house, two miles south of the latter place, and thirteen from Dumfries, where they hired the outhouses for their habitation, in the hope of being permitted, in that lonely scene, to exercise their religion without further molestation. Mrs Buchan continued to be the great mistress of the ceremonies, and Mr Whyte to be the chief officiating priest. They possessed considerable property, which all enjoyed alike, and though several men were accompanied by their wives, all the responsibilities of the married state were given up. Some of them wrought gratuitously at their trades, for the benefit of those who employed them; but they professed only to consent to this in order that they might have opportunities of bringing over others to their own views. They scrupulously abjured all worldly considerations whatsoever, wishing only to lead a quiet and holy life, till the commencement of the Millennium, or the Day of Judgment, which they believed to be at hand."

The writer of the above account is, however, neither friendly disposed towards his subject nor too scrupulous, or perhaps sufficiently well informed, in matters of detail. What he says of the abandonment of marital relations, for example, carries unwarrantable implications. A fairer account occurs in a letter from the Rev. James Woodrow, minister of Stevenston, to Sir Adam Fergusson of Kilkerran, dated 19th October 1784. Sir Adam had been Member of Parliament for Ayrshire for ten years past; and had just surrendered that seat at the request of his party leaders in order to represent an Edinburgh constituency instead. Apparently he had written to Mr Woodrow asking for some account of the Buchanites, who, although Mrs Buchan had begun her "ministry" five years previously, had only recently become notorious owing to their flight from Irvine. Mr Woodrow copies out of a Glasgow newspaper a report of their movements, the authorship of which report he ascribes to Mr Millar, the minister of Cumnock. His letter then goes on to give the following picturesque and not unsympathetic account of Mrs Buchan and her followers: "Mrs Buchan was said to have come originally from Montrose or its neighbourhood, to have lived awhile in Glasgow, her character not good. There, and at Kilmarnock, she made some converts, but very few. She had been at Irvine occasionally for a year or two before, and had resided there constantly during the last winter and spring. She was a pretty old and ill-looking woman (her age at this time was only forty-six), but had something fascinating in her conversation and manners, particularly the appearance of much gentleness and kindness, joined with a cheerful piety and confidence in Heaven. The converts were all made by herself, the influence of her enthusiasm being confined to those who were within the reach of her conversation, and chiefly, though not entirely, to the Relief congregation. It did not spread in the smallest degree in the neighbouring parishes. Mr Whyte (the Relief minister who joined Mrs Buchan's followers) was a cheerful, lively young man of no learning or talents of any kind, except an easy flow of language. He was married and had a young family. Mrs Buchan lived in his house, and after she had in a few weeks infused her own spirit into him and perhaps a fourth part of his congregation, the rest were offended at him, deserted his ministry, and lodged a complaint against him with the Presbytery of Relief. They met at Irvine and without the formality of a trial gave Mr Whyte five or six queries relative to his obnoxious tenets, which he answered in writing immediately and unequivocally, and signed his answer at their desire. They then condemned him on his confession and suspended him from preaching *sine die*. Upon this he gave up the bond he had for his stipend and continued to preach to his little flock in his own house and garden. The people who became Mrs Buchan's disciples had been mostly serious and well-meaning people formerly; some of them of good sense and education. They conceived themselves as quite new creatures, and, indeed, they were strangely changed both in their principles and habits. They rejected and abhorred the doctrines of Election, Reprobation, and other high points for which they had been formerly zealous, and some of them disputed against these things with considerable acuteness, not from the Scriptures, but from other topics. Their turn of mind was cheerful, not gloomy. They entered easily into conversation on their favourite religious points and even attempted to turn every ordinary subject of discourse into that channel as if they had been wholly possessed by their enthusiasm; and in common with all other enthusiasts they had a great difference about the world and neglected business and the care of their families and children. There were more women among them than men, and they parted at last from their relations, their friends, and some of them from their lovers, without the least appearance of reluctance or regret. Besides the kind of inspiration which Mr Millar mentions, some of them, such as Mrs Buchan and Mr Whyte, laid claim to visions and revelations, and lay for many hours in a dark room covered with a sheet in confident expectation of them. One of these visions Mrs Buchan imprudently published, fixing the destruction of the town of Irvine to a particular short day. This exasperated the mob, who considered her a witch, and drove her and Mr Whyte from the town. The rest immediately followed their leaders. Patrick Hunter, a lawyer, was brought back by a warrant on account of some papers belonging to other people in his hands. He continued several days in Irvine, sold his house, a pretty good one, and the rest who had any property in furniture or clothes or shop goods took the opportunity of returning and selling off everything by roup. The money arising from this sale was not put into a common purse and given to Mrs Buchan as was expected, but retained by the individuals. It was still, however, a kind of common stock, for such is their mutual disinterested attachment that everyone was ready to part with whatever he had to any other of the fraternity who needed it. They had in truth a community of goods among them and were suspected by some and accused of having a community of a more criminal kind, yet I never heard anything amounting to a proof or presumption of such licentiousness. They lived together like brothers and sisters. They asked and took provision from other people on the road like those who were entitled to it, telling them that God would repay them, and never offering any payment themselves till it was insisted on." Mr Woodrow's letter concludes: "They are, indeed, an object of curiosity to an attentive and inquisitive mind. Several sets of enthusiasts resembling them made their appearance in Holland and Germany about the beginning of the Reformation, and some in America during this century, but the phenomenon is new and singular in Scotland."

Most of the accounts of the Buchanites were derived from hearsay and without first-hand knowledge, and were mostly prejudiced against them. It is good to find Mr Woodrow discrediting the allegation that they practised "free love" and insisting that at least there was no evidence to support that charge, which, nevertheless, along with other scandals, was widely retailed against them and all too readily believed in most quarters. Even Burns, in a letter from Mossgiel to his cousin, James Burness, showed a lamentable lack of Mr Woodrow's charitable scepticism in this connection, writing: "I am personally acquainted with most of them, and I can assure you the above-mentioned are facts". Burns's short account is, in fact, simply a credulous and unworthy rehash of the malicious countryside gossip. To be seen in its true light it only requires to be set against the account contributed to the *Scots Magazine* in November 1784, by a correspondent who signed himself "Glasguensis Mercator". This writer spent two days in their company during the month of August and studied them closely in "their daily walk and conversation". He denies all the popular and sensational reports of their conduct and beliefs, and ends as follows: "I found the Buchanites a very temperate, civil, discreet and sensible people, very free in declaring their principles, when they were attended to; but most of their visitants behaved in a rude, wicked, and abandoned way, which improper behaviour they met and bore with surprising patience and propriety".

Most of the reports do little or nothing to account for Mrs Buchan's strange hold over her followers—followers for the most part of intelligence and substance; and a hold that not only led them cheerfully to abandon all and follow her but did not loosen despite the falsifying of her successive predictions. It was the rowdy and vicious intolerance of the populace that dictated the flight from Irvine and harassed and finally broke up the community in Dumfriesshire—behaviour for which the conduct of the Buchanites, whether in sexual or other matters, seems to have afforded no justification whatever. The absence of the practices popularly imputed to them, however, only makes the problem of their motivation all the stranger and throws the greater stress on the peculiar powers of Mrs Buchan's little-studied personality.

Unfortunately there is altogether insufficient material for an adequate study. It is questionable whether the testimony of a recent writer, Mr A. S. Morton, author of *The Covenanters of Galloway* and other books, is more to be relied on than that of his predecessors when he writes that Elspeth, "on the death of her mother, was brought up by a distant relative, who taught her to read and write, to sew and cook. This lady married a West India planter, and Elspeth agreed to accompany her to Jamaica, but while waiting for a boat at Greenock she became enamoured of the gay life of the town and deserted her mistress. She entered domestic service, and afterwards married one of her master's workers, a potter named Robert Buchan. He found her wild and wayward, and hoping that she would settle down better in her native district he started a pottery in Banff, but this failed, and he went to Glasgow, leaving his wife and family to shift for themselves. She opened a dame's school, in which she expounded the Scriptures and the Shorter Catechism. Soon she became a religious fanatic, and even fasted for weeks. She neglected her school and her own children, till the neighbours were roused against her, and she found it necessary to return to her husband in Glasgow. Here she continued to neglect her house and family, ran everywhere to religious meetings, and took every opportunity to expound her views, which were far from orthodox." Mr Morton is wrong, however, when he goes on to say that the Rev. Hugh Whyte, having fallen completely under her sway and adopted her views, failed to appear when he was charged before the Presbytery at Glasgow with heresy, and was ejected from his charge. On the contrary, he appeared and answered the questions put to him in writing, defending the positions he had now taken up, and was temporarily inhibited from his pastoral duties. His final desertion of his ministry was his own action and due to the hostility of the Irvine populace to his continuance in their midst.

Following the heresy trial, as Mr Morton says, "a

Society was formed, and Mrs Buchan received the title, 'Friend Mother in the Lord', but to outsiders she was 'Luckie Buchan, the witch-wife who had cast her spell over the minister'. Violent opposition was raised, and the meeting had to be held after dark. Mrs Buchan proclaimed herself to be the woman described in Revelation xii. 1: 'There appeared a wonder in heaven; a woman clothed with the sun, and the moon under her feet, and upon her head a crown of twelve stars'. Whyte was the wonder 'man-child' of whom she was now spiritually delivered, who was to rule all nations with a rod of iron."

Mr Morton gives the best account of the subsequent developments. "The opposition", as he says, "became more intense, and the Society removed to the house of Patrick Hunter, the Burgh Fiscal, who had been an Elder in the Relief Church, but had joined the new Society. One night the mob smashed the doors and windows of his house, seized Mother Buchan, and started to drive her home to her husband. At Stewarton, eight miles on the way to Glasgow, she managed to escape, and made her way back to Irvine, to the house of James Gibson, one of her supporters. The mob attacked this house, and the magistrates, hastily convened, sent for Hunter and told him that the woman must be removed. She was taken to her husband's house in Glasgow. She and Whyte were invited to Muthill, the birthplace of the most ardent disciple, Andrew Innes. Here Whyte proclaimed his 'Friend Mother in the Lord' to be the new Incarnation of the Holy Ghost, and declared that Divine Vengeance would fall on all who did not accept her as such. The Lord, he said, was about to come and translate her and all her followers bodily to Heaven without tasting death, and all unbelievers would perish in the flames. This was too much for the simple folk of Muthill, and they refused to receive him into their houses, so he returned with Mother Buchan and the others to Irvine.

"The opposition was roused again, and the disturbances were renewed. The magistrates decided to banish Mother

Buchan, and allowed her two hours to clear out. Burns tells us that her followers 'voluntarily quitted the place likewise, and with such precipitation that some of them never shut the door behind them; one left a washing on the green, another a cow bellowing at the crib without food or anyone to mind her'. A cart was procured, in which rode Mother Buchan, Whyte, Gibson, and a few others not accustomed to tramping. Other carts were soon added to the procession, and afterwards a white pony, on which rode Mother Buchan, decked in a scarlet robe. The company numbered between forty and fifty, consisting for the most part of 'clever chiels and bonnie, spanking, rosy-cheeked lassies, many of them in their teens'. They found quarters in the barn at New Cample Farm, tenanted by Thomas Davidson, about a mile south of Thornhill. Here they had all things in common. Marriage was abolished and the children became the property of the Society. They occasionally wrought for neighbouring farmers, but never accepted remuneration. As harvest was approaching, the farmer needed his barn, but offered them ground on which to build a house for themselves. They gladly accepted, and had a place ready before harvest. This the neighbours christened 'Buchan Ha'', a name which still survives.

"At first crowds flocked to hear and see them, especially Mother Buchan, whom Whyte in his sermons declared to be 'the mysterious woman predicted in Revclation, in whom the Light of God was restored to the world, where it had not been since the ascension of Christ, but where it would now continue till the period of translation into the clouds to meet the Lord at his second coming'.

"Gradually curiosity gave place to hostility, and, on Christmas Eve 1784, about a hundred men attacked the house, smashed the windows and doors, and searched for Whyte and Mother Buchan, but did not find them. Mr Stewart, factor for Closeburn Estate, had heard of the plot and had persuaded these two to go to Closeburn Hall. Some of the rioters were tried at Dumfries and fined. About this time Whyte published '*The Divine Dictionary*, or a Treatise indicted [*sic*] by Holy Inspiration; containing the Faith and Practice of the people called (by the world) the Buchanites, who are actually waiting for the second coming of our Lord in the air, and so shall they ever be with the Lord. *There appeared a great wonder in Heaven —a woman. Rev. chap. xii. v. 1.* Written by that Society'. It extends to 124 pages octavo, and is a crude exposition of their beliefs under such heads as—'The propagation of the human race—a demonstration that the soul and person is the same—the person of Christ possessed of a divine nature only—God's method of calling men to true salvation—concerning the end of the world—a divine receipt instructing how all may live for ever—the meeting Christ in the clouds'. It is signed 'Hugh Whyte—revised and approved by Elspeth Simpson'. It showed them to be visionary and rhapsodical, and it is often quite beyond comprehension. Nobody took the slightest notice of it and it fell dead from the press. Mother Buchan was now doing everything to rouse the enthusiasm of her followers. One night when they were all employed as usual, a voice was heard as if from the clouds. The children shouted, clapped their hands, and started singing one of the hymns written by Whyte, beginning

> O hasten translation, and come resurrection,
> O hasten the coming of Christ in the air.

"Andrew Innes tells us that all the members downstairs instantly started to their feet, shouting and singing, while those in the garret hurried down to the kitchen, 'where Friend Mother sat with great composure, while her face shone so white with the glory of God as to dazzle the sight of those who beheld it, and her raiment was as white as snow'. The noise attracted the neighbours, and Davidson pressed into the house beseeching Mother Buchan 'to save him and the multitude by which the house was surrounded from the pending destruction of the world'. She told them, however, to be of good cheer, for no one would suffer that night, for she now saw her people were not sufficiently prepared for the mighty change she intended them to undergo. As the light passed from her countenance she called for a tobacco pipe and took a smoke."

Another writer says the little republic existed for some time, without anything occurring to mar its happiness, except the occasional rudeness of unbelieving neighbours. But at length, as hope sickened, worldly feelings appear to have returned upon some of the members; and notwithstanding all the efforts which Mrs Buchan could make to keep her flock together a few returned to Irvine. It would seem that as the faith of her followers declined she greatly increased the extravagance of her pretensions and the rigour of her discipline. It was said that "when any person was suspected of an intention to leave the Society, she ordered him to be locked up and ducked every day in cold water, so that it required some little address in any one to get out of her clutches". There is no direct or convincing evidence, however, that she was either able or inclined to take any such disciplinary measures or that her adherents were at any time otherwise than perfectly free agents.

Additional particulars, not to be found elsewhere, are set forth in a statement made in 1786 by some of the seceding members on their return to the West, but here again the evidence is to some extent suspect. According to this statement, "the distribution of provisions she kept in her own hand, and took special care that they should not pamper their bodies with too much food, and everyone behoved to be entirely directed by her. The society being once scarce of money, she told them she had a revelation, informing her they should have a supply of cash from Heaven; accordingly, she took one of the members out with her, and caused him to hold two corners of a sheet, while she held the other two. Having continued for a considerable time, without any shower of money falling upon it, the man at last tired and left Mrs Buchan to hold the sheet herself. Mrs Buchan, in a short time after, came in with £5 sterling, and upbraided the man for his unbelief, which, she said, was the only cause that prevented it coming sooner. Many of the members, however, easily accounted for this pretended miracle, and shrewdly suspected that the money came from her own hoard. That she had a considerable purse was not to be doubted, for she fell on many ways to rob the members of everything they had of value. Among other things, she informed them one evening that they were all to ascend to Heaven next morning; therefore, it was only necessary they should lay aside all their vanities and ornaments, ordering them, at the same time, to throw their rings, watches, etc., into the ash-hole, which many were foolish enough to do, while others more prudently hid every thing of the kind that belonged to them. Next morning she took out all the people to take their flight. After they had waited till they were tired, not one of them found themselves any lighter than they were the day before, but remained with as firm a footing on earth as ever. She again blamed their unbelief—said that want of faith alone prevented their ascension; and complained of the hardship she was under, in being obliged, on account of their unbelief, to continue with them in this world. She at last fell upon an expedient to make them light enough to ascend; nothing less was found requisite than to fast for forty days and forty nights. The experiment was immediately put into practice, and several found themselves at death's door in a very short time. She was then obliged to allow them some spirits and water; but many resolved no longer to submit to such regimen and went off altogether. We know not", thus concludes the statement, "if the forty days be ended; but a few expedients of this kind will leave her, in the end, sole proprietor of the Society's funds."

There are, however, no good grounds, so far as research can discover, for attributing any such fraudulent intentions to her, or for alleging that she took advantage of their credulity to enrich herself at their expense. That she did not need to undergo the penances the others had to suffer followed from the assumption of her divine character, and any privileges she had arose equally naturally from her special position amongst them. Nor could her opponents have it both ways; if they believed in the power of faith and in revelation, they were not in a position to deny the revelations she professed to receive nor to disprove that the only thing that prevented the miracles she anticipated taking place was the imperfect faith of her disciples. It is unfortunate that none of them kept a diary. The religious idiom they used, a mixture of Biblical English and Scots vernacular, is little heard to-day and it is therefore difficult to recreate the atmosphere in which they lived, nor are there any materials for a knowledge of the psychologies of even the leading members. Particularly interesting would have been an account book showing the initial capital, the incomings and outgoings, and final financial condition of the Society, but there is, alas, nothing of the sort.

If, however, "many of the members easily accounted", as we are told, for Mother Buchan's manœuvres, it is strange that the Society did not fall violently apart; but we hear little or nothing of internal differences and the "many of the members" in question seem to have been content to continue to be hoodwinked. The whole matter of the great fast and of the expected ascension are better described by Mr Morton in an account which significantly differs in many particulars from the foregoing statement:

"She declared that their failure to ascend to Heaven", says Mr Morton, "was because they had not been sufficiently purified from the corruptions of the flesh, and she ordered a forty days' fast—but not for her or Whyte. The authorities were induced to take action, as it was feared that some of the zealots would be starved to death, and there were vague rumours of infanticide. Constables made a thorough search, but discovered nothing incriminating. As the close of the fast drew near the excitement increased, and preparations were made for the triumphant translation to Heaven. Whyte dressed regularly in full clerical costume—gown, bands, and white gloves—and frequently surveyed the heavens for some sign of the coming event. The fateful night at length arrived, and the expectant company assembled on rising ground near the house, where they sang and prayed till midnight. They then proceeded to Templand Hill, the appointed scene of translation, half a mile away. Here they erected a frail wooden staging, which they mounted, with Mother Buchan on a higher platform in the middle. They had all cut their hair short (except Mother Buchan), leaving only a tuft on the top, by which they could be caught up from above, and on their feet they had light bauchels which they could easily kick off when the moment came to ascend. The air was filled with their singing and invocations as they stood stretching their hands towards the rising sun. Suddenly a gust of wind swept along; the flimsy platform collapsed, and instead of ascending to Heaven they crashed down to earth."

The "vague rumours of infanticide" were like the charges of "free love" and other scandals; but it is interesting to point out that, levelled against Roman Catholic convents, they have had a long currency in Scotland, every now and again rising to a fury of denunciation, popular agitation, and demands for thorough inspection of such premises—a vendetta of libel not dissimilar to that connected in other countries with the so-called Ritual Murder alleged to be practised by the Jews. With the general recession of interest in theological matters, scandals of this kind have nowadays found a new and fertile field in politics and the vast majority of intelligent people everywhere are the easy prey of atrocity mongers and find no more difficulty in swallowing the story of the German Corpse Factory or in crediting the Bolshevists with free love and unspeakable sadism than their ancestors had in discovering witches and crediting them with infernal cantrips or in attributing orgies of sexual licence and the practice of infanticide at one time to the Buchanites or at another to the Roman Catholic nuns. The interest attaching to the Buchanites is not that we have here any exceptional manifestation of human credulity and religious fanaticism; these are common enough at all times and the beliefs of the vast majority of people are of substantially the same character as those of the Buchanites. The latter only held opinions which showed a slight deviation from the no less absurd views generally entertained by their contemporaries, but they showed a disposition to insist on these literally and to practise what they preached, an inclination which certainly did not characterise the latter, although the failure of the Buchanites to square their doctrines with the practical requirements of existence was much less serious than it might have been. On the whole, the most that can be said of the attitude of their opponents is that the latter resembled Dr. Thomas Somerville, the historian, who, in his *Candid Thoughts on American Independence*, "maintained those opinions against the claims of the colonists, which were much opposed to the principles on which the Church of Scotland struggled into existence, however much they might accord with those of its pastors after it was firmly established", and displayed "an affection for the state of things existing at the time of writing, and such a respect for the persons who, by operating great changes, have brought about that existing state, as the writer would have been the last person to feel, when the change was about to be made". The orthodox mob were far more fanatical—and with no better foundations for their beliefs—than the little flock of the Buchanites, and again to the former may be well applied the phrases used to characterise Somerville's personality: "an alarmist on principle, he involved in one sweeping condemnation all who entertained views different from his own; and the wild impracticable theorist, and the temperate and philosophical advocate for reform, were with him equally objects of reprobation".

The fiasco of the Templand Hill ascension reminds me of the Icarian fate of that most interesting personality, James Tytler, a "poor devil, with a sky-light hat and hardly a shoe to his feet", who nevertheless, in the midst of the most multifarious literary labours, wrote several great songs, including "I canna come ilka day to woo". On the commencement of the balloon mania, after the experiments of Montgolfier, Tytler thought he would also try his hand at an aeronautic voyage. Accordingly, having constructed a huge dingy bag, and filled it with the best hydrogen he could procure, he collected the inhabitants of Edinburgh to the spot and prepared to make his ascent. The experiment took place in a garden within the Sanctuary, and the wonder is, we are told, "that he did not fear being carried beyond it, as in that event he would have been liable to the gripe of his creditors". There was no real danger, however; the balloon only moved so high and so far as to carry him over the garden wall, and deposit him softly on an adjoining dung-hill. The crowd departed, laughing at the disappointed aeronaut, who ever after went by the name, *appropriate on more accounts than one*, of "Balloon Tytler".

After the Templand Hill affair there were considerable defections from the Society and, since there had been very few accessions after public hostility first manifested itself, only a remnant of the faithful was left. The Kirk Session of Closeburn summoned Whyte to give security that none of the Society would become a burden on the parish. Whyte could give no such security, and as a consequence the fraternity were all ordered to leave Dumfriesshire on or before 10th March 1787. With the assistance of Davidson, the New Cample farmer, however, they took the farm of Auchengibbert, between Dumfries and Castle-Douglas, and after a temporary residence at Tarbreoch, near Kirkpatrick-Durham, removed there at Whitsunday. They put up fences and erected offices themselves, and all found outlet for their labour, but they no longer worked for nothing. A wheelwright made spinning-wheels, which several of the women used. A tinsmith made articles in his line, and these were bartered for wool to be spun and woven into cloth for both male and female wear. It was dyed light green—the distinctive colour of the dress of the Buchanites, who, in this respect, anticipated the Black Shirts, Brown Shirts, and other similar phenomena of to-day.

It would appear that dissensions were now developing between Mother Buchan and Mr Whyte. They no longer attempted to make proselytes," says Mr Morton, "but still clung to their own beliefs. Whyte, however, did his utmost to tone down the peculiarities of the Society, and on this he and Mother Buchan disagreed. When she attempted to assert her authority, he threatened to leave and break up the Society.

"Mother Buchan became really ill, but she would not lie down, and no one realised that the end was approaching—it was a cardinal point in their creed that she would never die. When she felt death near, she told them that though she might appear to die, she was only going to Paradise to arrange for their coming and if their faith remained firm she would return at the end of six months and they would all fly to heaven together. If they had not faith she would not return till the end of ten years, and if they were then still unprepared she would not return till the end of fifty years; when her appearance would be the sign of the end of the world and the final judgment of the wicked. Thus she kept up the delusion to the last, for immediately after this extraordinary pronouncement she died on 29th March 1791. Whyte wanted to have her buried, but the others wished to have her secreted about the house. Their dissensions showed that they would require to wait the ten years. The body was accordingly packed in dry feathers and deposited under the kitchen hearth. Sir Alexander Gordon, as Sheriff, had to inquire into the matter, but they hoodwinked him by a temporary burial in Kirkgunzeon Churchyard, and then brought the body back to the house. Ultimately Whyte became so overbearing that Andrew Innes and two others took a neighbouring farm, but informed Whyte they were willing to continue working at Auchengibbert if they got peace to do so, but would keep Larghill too. Whyte would not listen to this, and decided to go to America. The stock at Auchengibbert was accordingly sold and the proceeds divided among the members.

"On 11th June 1792, the seceders started for America. Two carts carried their goods, and thirty people walked beside them to Portpatrick, and eight weeks later they landed at Newcastle on the River Delaware. The remainder removed to Larghill, close to Crocketford, taking the body of Mother Buchan with them. They carried on successfully, and everyone had an allotted task. The women were noted for their spinning, and were the first to introduce into Galloway the two-handed spinning-wheel, in the use of which they were unrivalled. Time passed till the tenth anniversary of Mother Buchan's death arrived, but though they watched and prayed all day their expectations were doomed to disappointment, for nothing happened. As the lease of the farm was not to be renewed, they purchased about five acres of land at Crocketford and built houses, expending about £1000. For themselves they built Newhouse, which still stands, and the twelve remaining members removed to it, taking with them the body of Mother Buchan. Death gradually reduced their number, and a plot of ground behind the house became their burial ground. One by one they passed away, till only Andrew Innes and his wife remained. As the fiftieth anniversary of Mother Buchan's death approached, Andrew made great preparations for her return; but, alas, the fateful day came and went like any other, and Andrew was never the same again. His wife died in the end of November 1845, and so Andrew was left, the last of the Buchanites. A few weeks afterwards, finding his end drawing near, he sent for his friends and confessed to them for the first time that he had his revered Mother Buchan's body still in his possession, and desired them to bury it in the same grave as himself, but to place his coffin above hers, so that she could not rise without wakening him. Thus they were buried in the little enclosure behind the house."

I cannot agree that this is in any way an astounding story of religious imposture and childish credulity. The credulity and the element of imposture, or, as I prefer to believe, delusion, seem to me to be essentially the same as are to be found in any and every religion at all times. What I regard as interesting is the fact that the fraternity hung together so long. There was still a compact community of twelve eighteen years after the precipitate flight from Irvine, and Andrew Innes was faithful for an unbroken period of nearly seventy years. I have been unable to find out anything about the career of Whyte and his twenty-nine companions after their emigration to America. It is interesting to remark that after the establishment of the fraternity in Dumfriesshire Mrs Buchan's husband was still living in pursuit of his ordinary trade, and a faithful adherent of the burgher-seceders. One of her children, a boy of twelve or fourteen, lived with the father; two girls of more advanced age were among her own followers. Although the statement must be taken with reserve it is recorded that just before she died Mother Buchan told her disciples that she had one secret to communicate—that she was in reality the Virgin Mary, and mother of our Lord; that she was the same woman mentioned in the Revelations as being clothed with the sun, and who was driven into the wilderness; and that she had been wandering in the world ever since our Saviour's days and only for some time past had sojourned in Scotland. In regard to the Buchanites, however, and particularly their professions and rule of life and the personalities of the leaders, there is, as in so very many other directions in Scottish history, a sorry inadequacy of documentation, and it is impossible at this time of day to effectively check the statements made about them and in any way recapture the precise quality of their communal life. Andrew Innes's final precaution in the matter of the superimposition of his coffin over that of Mother Buchan's is of a type of burial safeguard and anticipation of the contingencies of the Resurrection Morn which informs many Scottish anecdotes from all parts of the country, and the whole conception of the flight to Heaven does not deviate essentially from the ideas of the Last Day, long and perhaps still generally held in our midst.

Certainly in these times of figures like Krishnamurtri, and Pastor Russell with his slogan that "millions now living will never die", and countless freak religionists of greater or less notoriety, the present day is in little condition to point the finger of scorn at Mrs Buchan and her followers. The preservation for over half a century of the unburied body is, of course, an unusual, and gruesome, feature, but the retention of unabated expectation despite disappointment after disappointment is no uncommon thing, and I might cite as a sort of parallel the story told of Sir James Stewart, of Coltness, the father of political economy in Britain—a science that perhaps more than most engenders, or, at least, calls for this quality of undaunted faith!

Among Sir James's intimate friends was Mr Alexander Trotter. Mr Trotter was cut off in early life; and, during his last illness, made a promise to Sir James that, if possible, he would come to him after his death, in an enclosure near the house of Coltness which, in summer, had been frequently their place of study. It was agreed in order to prevent mistake or misapprehension that the hour of meeting should be noon; that Mr Trotter should appear in the dress he usually wore, and that every other circumstance should be exactly conformable to what had commonly happened when they met together. Sir James laid great stress on this engagement. Both before and after his exile (which lasted from 1745 to 1763) he never failed, when it was in his power, to attend at the place of appointment, even when the debility arising from gout rendered him hardly able to walk. Every day at noon, while residing at Coltness, he went to challenge the promise of Mr Trotter, and always returned extremely disappointed that his expectation of his friend's appearance had not been justified. When rallied on the subject, he always observed seriously that we do not know enough of "the other world" to entitle him to assume that such an event as the reappearance of Mr Trotter was impossible. A very proper conclusion. A similar one may well cover the history of the Buchanites and it is by no means certain that, although their expectations were disappointed in the exact sense in which they were entertained, their faith was not abundantly justified in actual fact.

Unless I fell back upon a delightful character like "Jupiter" Carlyle, or his theological opponent, Dr. Webster, of whom the former declared that "he had no bowels and was always as ready for mischief as an ape", I should be hard put to it to find eccentrics, as opposed to mere fanatics, in the ranks of the Scottish ministry. "Divine irresponsibility" is not one of the attributes of the faithful; they are not given to what Gide calls *actes gratuits*; and they are lamentably lacking in the "humour of the saints". I should probably have to have recourse to George Sinclair (1618–87), the author of the famous *Satan's Invisible World Discovered* (1685), and the Rev. Robert Kirk of Aberfoyle (1641–92), author of the even more celebrated *Secret Commonwealth of Elves, Fauns and Fairies* (1691). The latter does not appear to have been printed before the issue of 1815 published by Messrs Longman, and it was edited and re-issued by Andrew Lang in 1893, while a new edition with an introduction by Mr R. B. Cunninghame Graham appeared in 1934.

The circumstances of Kirk's life are well enough authenticated. He was the seventh and youngest son of James Kirk, who had also held the charge of Aberfoyle, and he originally ministered at Balquhidder. A Celtic scholar, he translated the Bible and Psalter into Gaelic, publishing the latter in 1684. He was twice married and died in 1692, his tomb being inscribed "Robert Kirk, B.M., Linguae Hiberniae Lumen". "In Scott's time", says Lang, "the tomb was to be seen in the east end of the churchyard of Aberfoyle, but the ashes of Mr

Kirk *are not there*. His successor, the Rev. Dr. Cochrane, in his *Sketches of Picturesque Scenery*, informs us that as Mr Kirk was walking on a dunshi or fairy-hill, in his neighbourhood, he sank down in a swoon, which was taken for death." "After the ceremony of a seeming funeral," writes Scott, "the form of the Rev. Robert Kirk appeared to a relation and commanded him to go to Grahame of Duchray. 'Say to Duchray, who is my cousin as well as your own, that I am not dead but a captive in Fairyland; and only one chance remains for my liberation. When the posthumous child, of which my wife has been delivered since my disappearance, shall be brought to baptism I will appear in the room, when, if Duchray shall throw over my head the knife or dirk which he holds in his hand, I may be restored to society; but if this is neglected, I am lost for ever.' True to his tryst, Mr Kirk did appear at the christening and was 'visibly seen'; But Duchray was so astonished that he did not throw the dirk over the head of the appearance, and to society Mr Kirk has not yet been restored." As Lang points out, Kirk treated the world of Fairy as "a mere fact in Nature", his Presbyterianism notwithstanding. He did not believe the dwellers of fairyland to be the dead, but aery spirits, "an abstruse people", of a middle nature between men and angels, having intelligent spirits and "light, changeable bodies, best seen in twilight". As a recent writer, Mr Lewis Spence, says: "Kirk appears to have undergone much the same kind of adventures in Fairyland as did Thomas the Rymour, and to have shared a like fate with that ancient bard and with Merlin, who was also borne off to Fairyland. Like them, too, he had no convenient lady-love to free him from the Fairy bonds, as Tam Linn was redeemed. But it is strange to discover a Scottish minister spirited away in such a manner at so late a period as the close of the seventeenth century, when William and Mary occupied the throne, and who was caught up to Elfland only six years before the Darien Expedition sailed. Surely the whole circumstances of the Rev. Mr Kirk's disappearance merit thorough examination at the hands of someone who has the time and capability to lavish research upon them."

The best story about the fairies in Scotland is that told by James Hogg, the Ettrick Shepherd, about Will o' Phaup, his maternal grandfather, contained in his *Shepherd's Calendar of 1829*, and Will o' Phaup, who was "the last man of this wild region, who heard, saw, and conversed with the fairies, and that not once, or twice, but at sundry times and seasons" belonged to a later generation than Kirk, having been born in 1691.

We are not in this volume in search of strange happenings and queer stories—or even of the sort of credulity which could seriously relate as historical fact the episode of the Episcopalian cleric in whose chapel Satan administered the Communion, and that of the lady who rose in the air and flew up and down the garden, a tale that ends gravely with "the matter of fact is certain"—or we could find all we wanted without further ado in that treasure-house of oddities, Robert Woodrow's *Analecta or Materials for a History of Remarkable Providences* (which though the author died in 1734, was not published till 1842) and other volumes of a somewhat similar character.

Most of the material Scotland provides in regard to fairies, and brownies, and the Devil, and supernatural occurrences of all kinds, and mythical beasts, is of a puerile sort, and only very careful winnowing yields a few elements of perfect fantasy or horror. The horror pieces are by far the better of the two, and the very *crême de la crême* in this sort is to be found in the second category—the quiet subtle category—indicated by a recent writer who says: "That Calvinism, in a Scottish setting, should breed a devil worthy of its deity is hardly surprising, nor that the grimly fantastic age of witchcraft overlapping the opening of the Age of Reason should reach its height in the imagination born of the opposing qualities so strongly marked in the national character, hard logic, caution, and headlong recklessness. Combine with these the dry, unsparing humour whose perfect expression is in Lowland Scots, and you may well expect a masterpiece of the grotesque. There is the note of it as early as there is a surviving Scots literature; and it endures. Two of the very pinnacles of the kind come in the urbane age that built Charlotte Square in Edinburgh—*Tam o' Shanter* and the tale of *Wandering Willie*. Tam is a piece of flooding improvisation, a deil's spring on the fiddle; the narrator's laughing voice goes under the torrential sweep of the rhyme, with what Gothic gusto for the scolding wife, and the flash of the cutty sark in the riotous half-seen chaos of the dance to the pipes of that towsy tyke, Auld Nick. *Wandering Willie* comes gravely from under a long upper lip. France might have made *Tam o' Shanter*, but only Scotland, and only Lowland Scotland, could have produced that sobriety with the dancing fierceness behind it, the stark objective outline, and, at the climax, the sudden glint of an unearthly beauty, the vision of Claverhouse sitting a little apart, stately among the roistering of Hell." Keeping only to the best of such productions it is indeed an astonishing gallery that we have—Thrawn Janet; Tod Lapraik, "the commonplace weaver wi' the kind o' holy smile, a muckle fat white hash o' a man like creish, set in bright sunny daylight, among the sea-fowl"; Sawney Bean, the Galloway cannibal; Burke and Hare, the Edinburgh corpse-providers, to turn from literature to real life; and, one of the best of the lot, Hogg's Laird o' Ettrickshaw who used to dispose of his illegitimate children and their mothers with the help of "hurkle-backit Charley Johnston".

It is for the darker rather than the lighter humours that we can turn to religious Scotland, and all too seldom does bigotry and grim fanaticism develop into *diablerie* or the genuine *macabre*, though in fictional characters founded on the facts a fair amount has been carried to this desirable length and there is ample material for further developments along these lines. There is only one other Scottish minister—or near-minister—who appeals especially to me, and he is of a different type altogether. This is Flame, as he was nicknamed—Thomas Davidson (1838–70), the Scottish Probationer, whose life was compiled by the Rev. James Brown of Paisley, and published in 1877.

I agree with Mr George Burnett, who recently wrote commenting on the fact that copies of this can be picked up in second-hand bookstalls and street barrows for a few pence. "Now the life of Thomas Davidson at sixpence is better value for money than anyone has the right to expect even in these days of low prices. Davidson emerges from his letters—some of which, indeed, are masterpieces of the epistolary style—as one of the most lovable men one could meet in actual life or in the pages of literature." Licensed in 1864 as a probationer—that is to say, put on the "list" of supplies for vacant churches, and authorised to preach but not to dispense the sacraments—for two and a half years Davidson wandered over Scotland, England, and Ireland, gradually in these pre-railway days, and when he was perpetually hard up to make his expenses to go from point to point, undermining a constitution that was never robust. "It was a life that interested him because it afforded opportunities of seeing the world, and, better still, of studying human nature. The amusing side is fully related in his letters. "I've faced much this weary mortal round", he writes to the Rev. George Douglas, "since I saw your blessed face last, my darlint. I have been in England, Scotland, Ireland, France, this summer, and now in a fortnight I start polewards. This is great fun. I am going to Orkney this winter: I have a fancy that 'Orkney is nothing, if not stormy'. Still, this particular season cannot with confidence be called the very best for sailing purposes, and I confess I do feel inclined to exclaim with old Sir Patrick Spens:

> O who is this has dune this deed,
> And tauld the clerk o' me,
> To send me oot at this time o' the year
> To sail upon the sea.

However, what's the use of whining? I hate whining. Out upon whiners, moaners, groaners, lamentation-makers. Bah. Let us change the subject." The trip to Orkney results in a series of most interesting letters. "It was in 1866 that grave symptoms of consumption began to show themselves. 'Rather a necropolitan tone that, Bruce?' he asks his friend with reference to his cough. 'Aye, man, there's the ring o' the kirk-yard aboot it. It pits yin in mind o' the clap o' the shool [shovel].' His letters now contain frequent reference to successive colds—carrying a little of the old forward to the new—and pauses in the sermons owing to bouts of coughing. He fights against the disease, reporting improvements to his friends, but by the end of the year he has returned to his parents at Jedburgh. Here we find him learning German, writing poems, reading Marlowe, Ben Jonson, Boston, Homer, and imploring his friends to come and see him. Hopes of recovery alternate with relapses, but all the time he is growing weaker. 'I try to amuse and cheer myself by picturing what it will be like when spring is come round again. Then there will be blossom upon all the apple and pear trees; blackbirds and mavises will build their nests and sing songs; the ground will be covered with waving rye grass and leafy clover. The sun will shine and I will sit upon this big stone and rejoice and thank God that winter is past, and the summer come at last.' But the summer was not to come for him. He died on 29th April 1870, and they buried him 'on a gentle slope that lies to the sun and looks up Jed-water'."

To turn from ministers and think again of what I said at the beginning of the dearth of Scottish women to my purpose, there is, of course, that child prodigy, Pet Marjorie. There was that daughter of the Earl of Angus, Bessie Douglas, who ran away with Francy Faa, the gipsy, and is the heroine of the famous poem and not, as has until recently been generally supposed, one of the Countesses of Cassillis, and there is that redoubtable gipsy, Jean Gordon, born at Kirk Yetholm about 1670 and the reputed original of Meg Merrilees in Scott's *Guy Mannering*, although Scott may also have had in his mind's eye her granddaughter, Madge Gordon, whom he had met in the flesh.

Jean's death was a tragic one. She was a staunch Jacobite, and while on a visit to Carlisle one Fair day shortly after the '45 she gave the rabble great offence by taunting them regarding their behaviour during the Jacobite occupation of their town. In revenge they seized the gipsy and hurried her towards the Eden, where they ducked her to death. It is said that she struggled furiously with the mob, for she was a powerful and active woman, and while she had breath left she kept on shouting "Charlie yet, Charlie yet" whenever she managed to get her head above water.

But little is known about the great majority of the Scotswomen who may possibly have been worthy of a place in a gallery of eccentrics beyond what is sufficient to furnish an anecdote or two, and of the few exceptions to this rule, though enough is known of them to show that they were genuine characters worthy of a sizeable study, there is again a sad lack of detailed and trustworthy information. Little seems to be known, for example, of that unusual figure, Mrs Pierson, who led in the Debateable Land in the troubled days of Montrose's wars a private army carrying banners with stranger devices by far than ever floated in the snowy slopes of Switzerland—"Mrs Pierson, who passed as Carnwath's daughter, and whose commission was made out in the name of Captain Francis Dalziel; her cornet carried a black banner which displayed on a sable field a naked man hanging from a gibbet, under the motto 'I Dare'."

The subjects of the more than five hundred memoirs in Chambers's *Biographical Dictionary of Eminent Scots* include in addition to Mother Buchan only three women. One of these is the inevitable Mary Queen of Scots. But it would be extremely difficult for anyone who does not know the volumes in question to guess who the other two might be. One of them is Mrs Mary Brunton, described as "an eminent moral novelist of the present century", born in the Island of Burray, in Orkney, in 1778. Her novel *Self-Control* was published at Edinburgh in two volumes in 1811, and "the impression which it made upon the public was immediate and decisive. The modesty of Mrs Brunton, which was almost fantastic, induced her to give this composition to the world without her name. Four years afterwards she published a second novel in three volumes, entitled *Discipline*, which was only admired in a degree inferior to the first.—The whole mind and character of Mrs Brunton was 'one pure and perfect chrysolite of excellence.'"

The other is Lady Anne Halket (1622–99), "whose extensive learning and voluminous theological writings place her in the first rank of female authors. . . . Lady Anne was instructed by her parents in every polite and liberal science; and she became so proficient in the latter, and in the more unfeminine science of surgery, that the most eminent professional men, as well as invalids of the first rank, both in Britain and on the Continent, sought her advice." Her first publication was an "admirable tract" entitled *The Mother's Will to her Unborn Child*, written during her pregnancy with her eldest son, under the impression of her not surviving her delivery. She lived, however, to write no fewer than twenty-one volumes, chiefly on religious subjects.

I think I have made the best of an amazingly poor choice.

NOTES

I.—If one of the leading newspapers of Scotland set a competition for the best list of twenty most interesting, or beautiful, or important women Scotland has produced from the start of its history to the present day, the first few names would come readily enough to most of the entrants—though there would scarcely be agreement as to the order of their placing. Mary Queen of Scots would almost certainly be a universal first, and behind her would come (though most of these are not known to the great mass of the public) Flora MacDonald, the Margaret Douglas more than once proclaimed heir to the English throne, Black Agnes of Dunbar, Lady Grizel Baillie, Jenny Geddes, Margaret of Scotland (the Dauphine) "with the face like starlight", Deirdre perhaps, Jane Welch Carlyle, Susan Ferrier, Mary of the Songs, Clementina Walkinshaw, Mary Maitland or Lauder hailed as a third to Sappho and *Olimpia*, Mrs Oliphant, the Duchess of York, the Duchess of Atholl, Annie S. Swan, the Four Maries—but some of these are already absurd and a further choice of names would oblige competitors to fall back on Muckle-Mou'd Meg and Jean the Dumb and other such historical figures, or more modern women of little more consequence than what Dr. Agnes Mure Mackenzie calls John Knox's bourgeoise Egerias (the members of that spiritual harem who followed him about, rather reminding one of Shelley's soul-mates). One would have no similar difficulty in getting a list of twenty really celebrated and accomplished women in respect of any other country in Europe.

II.—If I had to add to the list of Scotswomen of some curious religious interest, "small beer" though they may be and not affording material for more than a few paragraphs, I would have recourse to some of those mentioned by the Rev. John Livingstone (1603–72) in the "Memorable Characteristics" appendices to his autobiography. One of these, Euphan McCullen, a woman of singularly quaint and pithy utterance, I have referred to elsewhere in this book. Then there is Dame Lilias Graham, Countess of Wigton. "Her chambermaid, that waited on her, told that so soon as she rose *and put on her night-gown*, before she went to her study for her devotion, she used to sit in a chair till that woman combed her head, and having her Bible open before her, and reading and praying among hands; 'and every day at that time', said the woman, 'she shed more tears than ever I did all my lifetime'." Lady Culross (Elizabeth Melville), the daughter of the Laird of Halhill, who professed he had got assurance from the Lord that himself, wife, and all his children should meet in Heaven, was famous for her piety, and for her dream anent her spiritual condition, which she put into verse. "Of all that ever I saw", said Mr Livingstone, "she was the most unwearied in religious exercises; and the more she attained access to God therein, she hungered the more. At the communion in the Shotts, June 1630, when the night after the Sabbath was spent in prayer by a great many Christians, in a large room where her bed was, and in the morning all going apart for their private devotion, she went into the bed, and drew the curtains, that she might set herself to prayer. William Ridge of Adderny coming into the room, and hearing her have great motion upon her, although she spake not out, he desired her to speak out, saying that there was none in the room but him and her woman, as at that time there was no other. She did so, and the door being opened the room filled full. She continued in prayer, with wonderful assistance, for large three hours' time." Lady Robertland was another "deeply exercised in her mind, and who often got as rare outgates". Dame Christian Hamilton, Lady Boyd, "used every night to write what had been the case of her soul all the day, and what she had observed of the Lord's dealing". Lady Binning, "before the time that the Service-Book was to be brought into Edinburgh, anno 1637," says Livingstone, "sent for me and told me that some friends had advised her that some days before it should be read she should change her seat out of the chief kirk, where it was to be first read; but, said she, 'that is some denying of my testimony to the truth; I have resolved to continue in my seat and when it is read to rise and go out'; and she desired me to advise with some honest ministers if they approved of her resolution. At that time, much of her neck and shoulders being bare, she said, 'It is a wonder that you or any honest man should look on me or stay in my company, for I am dressed rather like a strumpet than like a civil woman; but the truth is, I must either be thus dressed, or my lord will not suffer me in the house'; and while she thus said, the tears did not drop, but ran down, so as she was forced not to take notice of them."

III.—There are one or two other women with whom I might have dealt if I had wished to extend this essay, or of whom one regrets the absence of fuller information. There is the wife, for example, of the Rev. John Livingstone (1603–1672) who was courted in the following extraordinary way. She was the eldest daughter of Bartholomew Fleming, merchant in Edinburgh, "of most worthy memory", and had been recommended to Livingstone by the favourable accounts of many of his friends. Yet—and the fact is a curious trait of the age and of the man—he spent nine months "in seeking directions from God" before he could make up his mind to pay his addresses. "It is like", he says in his delightful autobiography, "I might have been longer in that darkness, except the Lord had presented me an occasion of our conferring together; for, in November 1634, when I was going to the Friday meeting at Antrim (the lady was then residing on a visit in Ireland), I foregathered with her and some others, going thither, and propounded to them, by the way, to confer upon a text, whereon I was to preach the day after at Antrim;

wherein I found her conference so just and spiritual, that I took that for some answer to my prayer to have my mind cleared, and blamed myself that I had not before taken occasion to confer with her. Four or five days after, I proposed the matter and desired her to think upon it; and after a week or two I went to her mother's house and, being alone with her, desiring her answer, I went to prayer, and desiring her to pray, which at last she did; and in that time I got abundant clearness that it was the Lord's mind that I should marry her, and then propounded the matter more fully to her mother; and, albeit I was then fully cleared, I may truly say it was about a month after before I got marriage affection to her, although she was, for personal endowments, beyond many of her equals, and I got it not till I obtained it by prayer; but, thereafter, I had greater difficulty to moderate it."

Then there is the wife of the Hon. Henry Erskine, one of the liveliest wits and most eloquent barristers Scotland has produced. "One of her peculiarities consisted in not retiring to rest at the usual hours. She would frequently employ half the night examining the wardrobe of the family to see that nothing was missing and that everything was in its proper place. I recollect being told this, among other proofs of her oddities, that one morning about two or three o'clock, having been unsuccessful in a search, she awoke Mr Erskine, by putting to him this important interrogatory: 'Harry, Lovie, where's your white waistcoat?' "

Lastly I should above all like, if she "came up to specification" (which I gravely doubt), a full account of the lady referred to in the following passage: "The domestic tranquillity of this excellent man [Sir John Lauder, Lord Fountainhall] was long harassed by the machinations of a stepmother—his father's third wife. This woman, Margaret Ramsay, to whom Sir John Lauder's father was united in 1670 at the ripe age of eighty-six, prevailed on her husband to procure a baronet's title, which he obtained in July 1688, and the lady, showing that she had more important designs than the gratification of female vanity, managed, by an artifice for which parental affection can scarcely form an excuse, to get the patent directed to her own son George, and the other heirs-male of her body, without any reference to the children of the previous marriage. A document among the papers of Sir John Lauder, being a draft of an indictment, or criminal libel, at the instance of the Lord Advocate, before the Privy Council against the lady and her relations, gives us his own account of the transaction. Neither the *Medea* of Euripides nor the old ballad of *Lord Randal my Son* gives a more *beau-ideal* picture of the proceedings of the 'cruel step-dame' than this formidable document: 'She tore the clothes off her body, and the hoods off her head, and sware fearful oaths, that she would drown herself and her children, and frequently cursed the complainers, and defamed and traduced them in all places, and threatened that she hoped to see them all rooted out, they and their posterity, off the face of the earth, and her children would succeed to all'."

JAMES BURNETT, LORD MONBODDO

WRITING to his friend Adam Smith, David Hume roundly expressed the opinion that, of all men of parts, "Ossian" Macpherson had "the most anti-historical head in the universe". Certainly the vast literature of the Ossian controversy shows what a mass of hocus-pocus can pass amongst intelligent and highly educated men as sound historical knowledge. But the description might rather have been applied to James Burnett (1714–99), better known by his judicial designation of Lord Monboddo. It certainly fitted the opinion entertained by most of his contemporaries concerning Monboddo's theories and beliefs; as one of his biographers says: "If he had the authority of Plato or Aristotle, he was quite satisfied, and, how paradoxical soever the sentiment might be, or contrary to what was popular or generally received, he did not in the least regard. Revolutions of various kinds were beginning to be introduced into the schools; but these he either neglected or despised. The Newtonian philosophy in particular had begun to attract attention, and public lecturers upon its leading doctrines had been established in almost all the British universities; but their very novelty was a sufficient reason for his neglecting them."

Monboddo is scarcely remembered to-day, except by some vague recollection that he upheld an extraordinary doctrine about men having tails; but he was a very able and interesting man and a singularly independent thinker whose conclusions on many matters will be as readily respected to-day as they were ridiculed by his contemporaries. He anticipated many modern findings in regard to all sorts of questions and instead of, as was commonly supposed, taking a fixed stand with the ancient Greeks and refusing in the most anti-historical fashion to admit any subsequent developments and discoveries, he was actually far in advance of his age. And his central principle was a splendid one (the adoption of which was, in itself, sufficient to render his views unintelligible to most people): "The laws by which the material world is regulated were considered by him as of vastly inferior importance to what regarded *mind*, and its diversified operations. To the contemplation of the latter, therefore, his chief study was directed."

We read in the *Tour to the Hebrides* that "Sir Adolphus Oughton laughed at Lord Monboddo's notion of men having tails and called him a Judge *a posteriori* which amused Dr. Johnson". Again: "I [*i.e.* Boswell] called on Mr Robertson, who has charge of Lord Findlater's affairs, and was formerly Lord Monboddo's clerk, was three times with him in France, and translated Condamine's *Account of the Savage Girl*, to which his lordship wrote a preface, containing several remarks of his own. Robertson said he did not believe as much as his lordship did; that it was plain to him the girl confounded what she imagined with what she remembered; that, besides, she perceived Condamine and Lord Monboddo forming theories and she adapted her story to them. Dr. Johnson said: 'It is a pity to see Lord Monboddo publish such notions as he has done: a man of sense, and of so much elegant learning. There would be little in a fool doing it; we should only laugh; but when a wise man does it we are sorry. Other people have strange notions; but they conceal them. If they have tails they hide them; but Monboddo is as jealous of his tail as a squirrel.'—I shall here put down some more remarks of Dr. Johnson's on Lord Monboddo, which were not made exactly at this time, but come in well from connection. He said he did not approve of a judge's calling himself *Farmer* Burnett, and going about with a little round hat. He laughed heartily at his lordship's saying he was an *enthusiastical* farmer, 'for (said he) what can he do in farming by his *enthusiasm*?' Here, however, I think Dr. Johnson is mistaken. He who wishes to be successful, or happy, ought to be enthusiastical, that is to say, very keen in all the occupations or diversions of life. An ordinary gentleman-farmer will be satisfied with looking at his fields once or twice a day; an enthusiastical farmer will be constantly employed on them, will have his mind earnestly engaged, will talk perpetually of them. But Dr. Johnson has much of the *nil admirari* in smaller concerns. That survey of life which gave birth to his *Vanity of Human Wishes* early sobered his mind. Besides, so great a mind as his cannot be moved by inferior objects; an elephant does not run and skip like lesser animals."

But we get a somewhat more flattering picture of Monboddo in Boswell's account of the visit Dr. Johnson and he paid to the eccentric judge at his place in Kincardineshire after which he took his title, and the conversation there. "Monboddo", he says, "is a wretched place, wild and naked, with a poor old house; though, if I recollect right, there are two turrets which mark an old baron's residence. Lord Monboddo received us at his gate courteously; pointed to the Douglas arms upon his house, and told us that his great-grandmother was of that family. 'In such houses (said he) our ancestors lived, who were better men than we.'—'No, no, my Lord (said Dr. Johnson), we are as strong as they, and a great deal wiser.'—This was an assault upon one of Lord Monboddo's capital dogmas, and I was afraid there would have been a violent altercation in the very close, before we got into the house. But his lordship is distinguished not only for ancient metaphysics but for ancient *politesse*, *la vieille coeur*, and he made no reply. His Lordship was dressed in a rustic suit, and wore a little round hat; he told us we now saw him as *Farmer Burnett*, and we should have his family dinner, a farmer's dinner. He said: 'I should not have forgiven Mr Boswell had he not brought you here, Dr. Johnson'. He produced a very long stalk of corn, as a specimen of his crop, and said: 'You see here the *laetas segetes*'. He added that Virgil seemed to be as enthusiastic a farmer as he, and was certainly a practical one.—Johnson: 'It does not always follow, my Lord, that a man who has written a good poem on an art has practised it. Phillip Miller told me that in Philips's *Cyder*, a poem, all the precepts were just, and indeed better than in books written for the purpose of instructing; yet Philips had never made cyder.' He and my lord spoke highly of Homer. Johnson: 'He had all the learning of his age. The shield of Achilles shows a nation in war, a nation in peace, harvest sport, nay, stealing.'—Monboddo: 'Ay, and what we (looking at me) would call a parliament-house scene; a cause pleaded'. —Johnson: 'That is part of the life of a nation at peace. And there are in Homer such characters of heroes, and combinations of qualities of heroes, that the united powers of mankind ever since have not produced any but what are to be found there.'—Monboddo: 'Yet no character is described'. Johnson: 'No; they all develop themselves. Agamemnon is always a gentleman-like character.' —Monboddo: 'The history of manners is the more valuable. I never set a high value on any other history.'—Johnson: 'Nor I; and therefore I esteem biography, as giving us what comes near to ourselves, what we can turn to use'.—Boswell: 'But in the course of general history we find manners. In wars we see the dispositions of people, their degrees of humanity, and other particulars.'—Johnson: 'Yes; but then you must take all the facts to get this, and it is but a little you get'.—Monboddo: 'And it is that little which makes history valuable'. Bravo, thought I, they agree like two brothers.—Monboddo: 'I am sorry, Dr. Johnson, you were not longer in Edinburgh to receive the homage of our men of learning'.—Johnson: 'My lord, I received great respect and great kindness'.—We talked of the decrease of learning in Scotland, and of the Muse's Welcome.—Johnson: 'Learning is much decreased in England, in my remembrance'.—Monboddo: 'You, sir, have lived to see its decrease in England, I its extinction in Scotland'."

Dr. Johnson was much pleased with Monboddo that day, remarking that "he would have pardoned him for a few paradoxes when he found he had so much that was good, but that, from his appearance in London he thought him all paradox, which would not do. He observed that his lordship had talked no paradoxes to-day." Johnson and Monboddo had disputed a little whether the Savage or the London Shopkeeper had the best existence, his Lordship as usual preferring the Savage. On their way to Aberdeen, Johnson reverted to this, and said, "I don't know but I might have taken the side of the savage equally, had anybody taken the side of the shopkeeper". There was one point of similarity between Johnson and Monboddo; they both had a black servant. Gory, Monboddo's negro, got on splendidly with Dr. Johnson's Joseph. Boswell observed how curious it was to see an African in the North of Scotland with little or no difference of manners from those of the natives of those parts themselves.

At the banquet of the Faculty of Advocates in commemoration of the centenary of the death of Sir Walter Scott, the then Lord Advocate (Mr Craigie Aitchison) conjured up the shades of those who had once frequented Parliament House—from John Ross of Montgrennan (in the fifteenth century), Sir Adam Otterburn, Gavin Dunbar, Alexander Myln, Johnston of Warriston, Sir George Mackenzie ("the bloody Mackenzie"), Viscount Stair ("the most commanding figure in the law of Scotland"), Forbes of Culloden, Lord Kames (who sat on the Bench till he was nearly ninety—a precedent beloved of Judges!—and who, in his farewell speech, called his brother Judges "auld bitches"—a precedent beloved of the Bar)—Cockburn, Jeffrey, Cranstoun, Horner, Inglis, Young, Balfour, Asher, Ardwall—what a tale! What a roll of ghosts! What a legend "emptied of all concern"!

Most of these great figures are not even names to the vast majority of Scots to-day. They are scarcely known to those who now hold the positions they once held. A society has only recently been formed to study Scottish legal history. Miss Elsie Swann, in her life of "Christopher North", gives us a picture of Edinburgh legal society at a date a little later than Monboddo's death. "Christopher North" was called to the Bar in 1815. "Many young men who were late distinguished in the profession passed about the same time as John Wilson. In the group of 1815–16 were Patrick Fraser Tytler, Thomas Maitland, a future Solicitor-General, Sir William Hamilton, the philosopher and metaphysician, Wilson's friend Patrick Robertson, and, most important for the future *Blackwood's Magazine*, young John Gibson Lockhart. It was as they paced the 'Hall of Lost Steps' that the two moving spirits of the *Magazine*—Wilson and Lockhart—became friendly enough to join forces later at the clarion call of William Blackwood. The young advocates were, upon the whole, 'a well-thriven looking race of juvenile jurisconsults', according to Lockhart. For the most part they were candid enough to wear their own hair, so allowing full scope to the devout craniologists who flourished ubiquitously. A few buried this source of information in the old bird's-nest of horsehair and pomatum, usually adhered to by seniors alone, for the costume of the Scottish Bar was much less regulated than that of Westminster Hall. The younger advocates were a care-free group, who either promenaded with an air of utter nonchalance, or collected into risible groups round the several iron stoves, there to gossip facetiously, retail anecdotes, and mimic the eccentricities of venerable judges and lawyers. The brilliant young men called to the Bar about 1815 formed thus what Lockhart called the 'Stovehood', since their journeyman days were spent in lounging around those centres of comfort on their particular side of the Hall. John Wilson, most exuberant of companions, was there among the 'Wits of the Stove School', and John Gibson Lockhart, the Glasgow scholar fresh from Oxford,—the 'hidalgo' with his lean face, grim blue jowl, and 'biting rude' wit. Then there was Patrick Robertson, styled 'a mighty incarnate joke', with round flabby face, gross lips that seemed ever smacking over an unseen repast, and a twinkle in his fat eye as if it saw eternally some funny scene—one of the wittiest and most warm-hearted of men, a Scottish Falstaff of infinite conviviality, a man 'cast in nature's amplest mould'."

But Monboddo's own colleagues, Lords Strichen, Kames, Auchinleck, Coalston, Barjarg, Alemoor, Elliock, Stonefield, Pitfour, Gardenstoun, Kennet, and Hailes, are a less-known but more remarkable group. Kames in particular is a great figure. Henry Cockburn described him as "an indefatigable and speculative, but coarse man". Kames, whenever he went on the Ayr Circuit, was in the habit of visiting Matthew Hay, a gentleman of good fortune in the neighbourhood, and staying at least one night, which, being both of them ardent chess players, they usually devoted to their favourite game. One spring Circuit the battle was not concluded at daybreak, so the Judge said: "Well, Matthew, I must e'en come back this gate in the harvest, and let the game lie owre for the present". Back he came in September but not to his old friend's hospitable house, for that gentleman had in the meantime been apprehended on a capital charge, and his name stood on the Porteous Roll, or list of those Kames had to try. Hay was found guilty and Kames pronounced sentence of death. Having concluded that awful formula, in his most sonorous cadence, Kames, dismounting his formidable beaver, gave a familiar nod to his unfortunate acquaintance and said to him in a sort of chuckling whisper: "And now, Matthew, my man, that's checkmate to you!"

Monboddo was educated at Marischal College, Aberdeen, then under the principalship of Principal Blackwell, previously for several years Professor of Greek, and "the great means of reviving the study of this noble language in the North of Scotland". Monboddo (Burnett as he was then) was infected by this enthusiasm and became a great Greek scholar and an enthusiast for all things pertaining to the ancient Greeks. "Having been early designed for the Scottish Bar, he wisely resolved to lay a good foundation and to suffer nothing to interfere with what was now to be the main business of his life. To obtain eminence in the profession of the law depends less upon contingencies than in any of the other learned professions. Wealth, splendid connections, and circumstances merely casual have brought forward many physicians and divines, who had nothing else to recommend them. But though these may be excellent subsidiaries they are not sufficient of themselves to constitute a distinguished lawyer. Besides good natural abilities, the most severe application and uncommon diligence in the acquisition of extensive legal knowledge are absolutely necessary. At every step the neophyte is obliged to make trial of his strength with his opponents, and as the public are seldom in a mistake for any length of time, where their interests are materially concerned, his station is very soon fixed. The intimate connection that exists between the civil or Roman law and the Law of Scotland is well known. The one is founded upon the other. According to the custom of Scotland at that time Burnett repaired to Holland, where the best masters in this study were then settled. At the University of Groningen he remained for three years, assiduously attending the lectures on the civil law. He then returned to his native country so perfectly accomplished as a civilian that during the course of a long life his opinions on difficult points of this Law were highly respected."

He happened to arrive back in Edinburgh from Holland on the night of the Porteous Riot. His lodgings were in the Lawnmarket in the vicinity of the Tolbooth, and hearing a great noise in the street, he sallied forth out of curiosity to witness the scene. Somebody recognised him, however, and as a consequence the rumour got about that he was one of the ringleaders in this affair. This might have got him into no little trouble, had he not been able to prove that he had just arrived from abroad and therefore could know nothing of what was in agitation. In later life "he was wont to relate with great spirit the circumstances that attended this singular transaction".

He became a member of the Faculty of Advocates in 1737 and in course of time developed a considerable practice. During the '45 rebellion, Burnett went to London, and prudently declining to take any part in the politics of that troublous period, spent the time chiefly in the company and conversation of his literary friends. Among them were Thomson the poet, Lord Littleton, and Dr. Armstrong. He returned to Scotland when peace was restored, and about 1760 married a beautiful and accomplished lady, Miss Farquharson (a relation of Marischal Keith, the great soldier), by whom he had a son and two daughters.

What first brought him into prominent notice was the share he had in conducting the celebrated Douglas cause —brought by the Duke of Hamilton and others against Archibald Douglas to reduce his claim to be, as he had for many years been accepted to be, the son of Lady Jane Douglas. "No question", it is asserted in one quarter, "ever came before a court of law, which interested the public to a greater degree. In Scotland it became a national question, for the whole country was divided, and ranged on one side or the other. Mr Burnett was counsel for Mr Douglas and went thrice to France to assist in leading the proof taken there. This he was well qualified to do, for, during his studies in Holland, he had acquired the practice of speaking the French language with great facility. Such interest did this cause excite that the pleadings before the Court of Session lasted thirty-one days, and the most eminent lawyers were engaged. It is a curious historical fact that almost all the lawyers on both sides were afterwards raised to the bench."

The case came up before the Court of Session in July 1767; Burnett, who had been made Sheriff of Kincardineshire the previous year, had been made a Lord of Session under the title of Lord Monboddo in February 1767, so he was now one of the Judges in the cause in which, during the earlier stages, he had been Mr Douglas's counsel. Lord Kames, another of the Judges sitting on this cause, described it as "the most intricate and singular that has at any time occurred, much more so than any set forth in the *Causes Célèbres*". Kames, like Monboddo and five others, voted to repel the reasons of reduction, while seven of the Judges voted to sustain them and the Lord President gave judgement according to his own opinion, which was on the latter side. Monboddo's speech shows what he thought of the extraordinary significance and importance of this case, for he said:

"Mr Douglas, though he has been so long in possession of his birthright, was acknowledged by father and mother, and was habit and repute their son, yet is obliged to prove his birth, like any other fact upon which he was to found a claim. This, my Lords, I hold to be a most dangerous doctrine, and it is *that* which makes this truly a *great* cause. For it is not great names of parties, it is not the value of the subject, nor is it the question of fact, of however great importance to the parties and particularly to one of them, that makes this cause great and important in the eye of law. But it is this question of such general importance which makes this cause not only the cause of Mr Douglas but of every person who hears me—I may say of mankind, and not only of the present race now living but of all future generations,

Et nati natorum, et qui nascentur ab illis

are concerned in this question. For, if this were law, who, of the age of this defender, can say that he is sure of his birthright, or that he has a state or belongs to a family? But such a doctrine I hold to be as erroneous as it is pernicious and subversive of the common rights of men. For the acknowledgment of parents, joined to the habit and repute, is the charter which every man has for his birthright, and which cannot be declared to be false, forged, or feigned, except upon evidence the clearest and most unexceptionable. As to the positive evidence of birth by the testimony of witnesses it must, of necessity, be confined to a very few, and those few in a few years will grow still fewer, till at last they must be quite gone. But, as was very well said by one of your Lordships, in proportion as the evidence by witnesses grows weak, the presumption of law grows strong, till at last it becomes so strong that nothing but evidence amounting to demonstration where there is not a *loop to hang a doubt on* can overcome it. But the case of Mr Douglas is much stronger than the common case; for his birthright is not only secured by the acknowledgment of parents, the habit and repute, and the lapse of so many years; but he has brought a direct proof of it by the only two witnesses now living, so far as appears, who were present at it. He has further brought a proof by many witnesses of what must have been necessarily precedent and subsequent to it, namely, the pregnancy and reconvalescence; and, over and above all that, he has brought a circumstantial proof, more pregnant perhaps than even the direct proof, and most wonderful at this distance of time. What, my Lords, can take away such an evidence as this? Nothing but proof, the strongest and most direct, of an imposture, by witnesses of greater number and more credible than those produced by the defender, or by an adamantine chain of circumstances which excludes even the possibility of a birth. In such a case, your Lordships are not to weigh and balance, and proceed upon conjectures and probabilities, as in ordinary cases, where the law allows you to find proved or not proved, according as the evidence appears, and is perfectly indifferent to either side. But, where there is such a weight of positive proof, as well as of legal presumption, in the one scale, there must be in the other such a preponderating weight of evidence as does not suffer the balance to remain a moment *in equilibrio*, but makes the opposite scale immediately to mount and kick the beam."

Few cases in law have created anything like equal interest throughout the country, but, along with it, may perhaps be bracketed the case of Kirkby's negro (to declare that having landed in Scotland automatically liberated a slave), Lord President Dundas's degradation for peculation, and the sedition trials of Muir and Palmer in 1793, others in the following year, and that of George Mealmaker, the leader of the Fife, Forfar, and Perth groups of the "United Scotsmen", allied to the United Irishmen who had been clamouring for independence since 1791. And along with this, as a curious sidelight on Scottish law, Duncan Forbes of Culloden's greatest feat of eloquence before he succeeded at the time of the '45 in persuading so many Highland gentlemen to play a coward's part, namely, in Compton Mackenzie's words, "to persuade a jury to acquit of a rape Colonel Charteris, the vilest blackguard of the century".

Language, and the question of the Savage, were two of the principal themes of study and speculation amongst learned Scots at this time—and, indeed, the former has always been. It was very natural, therefore, that Monboddo's first work should be on the *Origin and Progress of Language*. The first volume appeared in 1771, the second in 1773, and the third in 1776. "This treatise attracted a great deal of attention on account of the singularity of some of the doctrines it advanced. In the first part he gives a very learned, elaborate, and abstruse account of the origin of ideas according to the metaphysics of Plato and the commentators on Aristotle, philosophers to whose writings and theories he was devotedly attached. He then treats of the origin of human society and of language, which he considers as a human invention, without paying the least regard to the scriptural accounts. He represents men as having originally been, and continued for many ages to be, no better than beasts and indeed in many respects worse; as destitute of speech, of reason, of conscience, of social affection, and of everything that can confer dignity upon a creature, and possessed of nothing but external sense and memory and a capacity of improvement. The system is not a new one, being borrowed from Lucretius, of whose account of it, Horace gives us an exact abridgment in these lines: 'Cum prorepserunt primis animalia terris, mutum et turpe pecus', etc.—which Monboddo took for his motto, and which, he said, comprehended in miniature the whole history of man.

"In regard to facts that make for his system he is amazingly credulous, but blind and sceptical in regard to everything of an opposite tendency. He asserts with the utmost gravity and confidence that the oranoutangs are of the human species—that in the bay of Bengal there exists a nation of human creatures with tails, discovered one hundred and thirty years before by a Swedish skipper—that the beavers and sea-cats are social and political animals, though man, by nature, is neither social nor political nor even rational—reason, reflection, a sense of right and wrong, society, policy, and even thought, being, in the human species, as much the effects of art, contrivance, and long experience as writing, ship-building, or any other manufacture. Notwithstanding that the work contains these and many other strange and whimsical opinions, yet it discovers great acuteness of remark."

Most people to-day will, however, regard most of the positions taken up by Monboddo as thoroughly sound, and certainly the views of most of his opponents are far more likely to strike the modern mind as ill-founded, fantastic, and absurd.

Take, for example, the views of Dr. David Doig (1719–1800) "the most learned school-master Scotland ever produced". Lord Kames, Monboddo's fellow Judge, had, like Monboddo, stoutly maintained as the foundation of his system in his *Essay on Man* that man was originally in an entirely savage state, and that, by gradual improvement, he rose to his present condition of diversified civilisation. Doig, who in addition to a profound knowledge of the Greek and Latin languages, was a master of Hebrew, Arabic, and other Oriental tongues and deeply versed in the history and literature of the East, combated these subversive views and sought to prove that they were neither supported by sound reason nor by historical fact, while they were at the same time irreconcileable with the Mosaic account of the creation. "In the Bible the historical details of the earliest period present man in a comparatively advanced state of civilisation, and if we resort to profane history we find that the earliest historical records are confirmatory of the sacred books, and represent civilisation as flowing from those portions of the globe—from the banks of the Euphrates and the Nile—which the biblical history describes as the seat of the earliest civilisation. Modern history is equally favourable to Dr. Doig's system. In Eastern Asia, we find nations remaining for thousands of years in identically the same state of improvement, or, if they have moved at all it has been a retrograde movement. In Africa also we perceive man in precisely the same condition in which the Greek and Roman writers represent him to have been two thousand years ago. Europe alone affords an example of progress in civilisation, and that progress may be easily traced to intercourse with the Eastern nations. Man seems to possess no power to advance unassisted, beyond the first stage of barbarism. According to Dr. Robertson, 'in every stage of society, the faculties, the sentiments, and the desires of men are so accommodated to their own state that they become standards of excellence in themselves; they affix the idea of perfection and happiness to those attainments which resemble their own, and wherever the objects to which they have been accustomed are wanting, confidently pronounce a people to be barbarous and miserable.' The impediments which prejudice and national vanity thus oppose to improvement were mainly broken down in Europe by the crusades and their consequences, whereby the civilisation of the East was diffused through the several nations in Europe. America presents the only instance of a people having advanced considerably in civilisation unassisted, apparently, by external intercourse. The Mexicans and Peruvians, when first discovered, were greatly more civilised than the surrounding tribes; but, although this be admitted, yet, as it still remains a debateable question whence the people of America derived their origin, and as the most plausible theory represents them as having migrated from the nations of Eastern Asia, it may, after all be contended that the Mexicans and Peruvians had rather retrograded than advanced, and that, in truth, they only retained a portion of the civilisation which they originally derived from the same common source."

It was a friend of Doig's, John Callander, the antiquary, who affords perhaps the most diverting examples of the preoccupation with the problems of language of many erudite Scots of that period. In 1779 he published a curiosity in the shape of his "Essay towards a literal English version of the New Testament in the Epistle to the Ephesians", which proceeded on the principle of adhering rigidly to the order of the Greek words, and abandoning entirely the English idiom. The notes to this work are *in Greek*; "a proof certainly", as has been judicially remarked, "of Mr Callander's learning, but not of his wisdom" (Orme's *Bibliotheca Biblica*). His best-known work appeared in 1782, an edition of two ancient Scottish poems, *The Gaberlunzie Man* and *Christ's Kirk on the Green*. In this, he endeavours to make his readers acquainted with the true system of rational etymology, which, according to him, consists in deriving the words of every language from the radical sounds of the first or original tongue, as it was spoken by Noah and the builders of Babel. "Not attending", he remarks, "to this great truth, which we have recorded in the Scriptures, that the whole race of mankind formed at Babel one large family, which spoke one tongue, they have considered the different languages now in use all over our globe, as mere arbitrary sounds, names imposed at random by the several tribes of mankind, as chance dictated, and bearing no other than a relation of convention to the object meant to be expressed by a particular sound. They were ignorant that the primaeval language spoken by Noah and his family now subsists nowhere, and yet everywhere; that is to say, that at the dispersion of the builders of Babel, each horde or tribe carried the radical words of the original language into the several districts to which the providence of God conducted them; that these radical words are yet, in a great measure, to be traced in all the different dialects now spoken by men; and that these terms of primary formation are not mere arbitrary sounds but fixed and immutable, bearing the strictest analogy to the things they describe, and used, with very little material variation, by every nation whose tongue we are acquainted with. The proofs of this great etymological truth rise to view, in proportion to the number of languages the researches of the learned, and the diaries of the traveller, bring to our view; and we hope, by the small collection we have been able to form, and which, at some future period, we propose to lay before the public, to set the truth of our assertion beyond the reach of cavil." He afterwards states: "the large collection of those radical terms will one day be laid before the public under the title of a *Scoto-Gothic Glossary*, if Heaven shall bestow health and leisure to complete the work". He had previously announced a more magnificent project of a *Biblioteca Septentrionalis* (an universal dictionary, containing everything relative to the Northern Nations, from the sources of the Danube and Rhine to the Extremities of Iceland and Greenland); but he did not live to complete either of these undertakings, which, as Dr. David Irving suggests, he probably found more arduous than he had originally contemplated.

Monboddo's greatest work, which he called *Ancient Metaphysics*, consists of three volumes, the last of which was published only a few weeks before his death. "It may be considered as an exposition and defence of the Greek philosophy in opposition to the philosophical system of Sir Isaac Newton and the scepticism of modern metaphysicians, particularly Mr David Hume. His opinions upon many points coincide with those of Mr Harris, the author of *Hermes*, who was his intimate friend, and of whom he was a great admirer. He never seems to have understood nor to have entered into the spirit of the Newtonian philosophy; and, as to Mr Hume, he, without any disguise, accuses him of atheism, and reprobates in the most severe terms some of his opinions."

Monboddo was very unfortunate in his family life. His wife died in childbed. His son, a promising boy in whose education he took great delight, and whom Dr. Johnson examined in Latin on his visit to Monboddo, died young, as did his second daughter, in personal loveliness accounted one of the first women of the age, who fell a victim to consumption when only twenty-five. Burns, in an address to Edinburgh, thus celebrates the beauty and excellence of Miss Burnett:

Thy daughters bright thy walls adorn,
Gay as the gilded summer sky,
Sweet as the dewy milk-white thorn,
Dear as the raptured thrill of joy.

Fair Burnet strikes the adoring eye,
Heaven's beauties on my fancy shine;
I see the *Sire of Love* on high,
And own his work indeed divine.

About 1780 Monboddo first began to make an annual visit to London, which he continued for a good many years, indeed till he was upwards of eighty. As a carriage was not a vehicle in use among the ancients, he determined never to enter and be seated in what he termed a box. He esteemed it degrading to the dignity of human nature to be dragged at the tails of horses instead of being mounted on their backs. In his journeys between Edinburgh and London he therefore rode on horseback, attended by a single servant. On his last visit, he was taken ill on the road back, and it was with difficulty that Sir Hector Monroe prevailed upon him to enter his carriage. He set out, however, next day on horseback, and arrived safe in Edinburgh by slow journeys.

Being in London in 1785, Lord Monboddo visited the King's Bench, when, some part of the fixtures giving way, a great scatter took place among the lawyers, and the very Judges themselves rushed towards the door. Monboddo, somewhat near-sighted and rather dull of hearing, sat still, and was the only man who did so. Being asked why he had not bestirred himself to avoid the ruin, he coolly answered that he "thought it was an annual ceremony with which, being an alien, he had nothing to do".

Monboddo was an early nudist. When in the country, as Boswell mentions, he generally dressed in the style of a plain farmer; and lived among his tenants with the utmost familiarity, treating them with great kindness. He used much the exercises of walking in the open air, and of riding. He had accustomed himself to the use of the cold bath in all seasons, and amid every severity of the weather. It is said that he even made use of the air bath, or occasionally walking about for some minutes naked in a room filled with fresh and cool air. In imitation of the ancients the practice of *anointing* was not forgotten. The lotion he used was not the oil of the ancients but a saponaceous liquid composed of rose-water, olive oil, saline aromatic spirit, and Venice soap, which, when well mixed, resembles cream, and this he was in the habit of applying at bedtime before a large fire after coming from the warm bath.

"OSSIAN" MACPHERSON AND WILLIAM LAUDER

WILLIAM LAUDER

LEAVING out of account the ingenious gentleman of the name of Smith who flooded the market with bogus Burns holographs, Scotland's two main contributions to the curious records of literary imposture—though Ossian's imposture was completely outweighed by the real value of his work, and even Lauder did a considerable amount of good, except to himself, in doing wrong—were by two men whose lifetimes overlapped.

"Ossian" Macpherson, the principal subject of this essay, and by far the more important of the two, was one of these; the other was Milton's traducer, William Lauder, whose name and activities are little remembered to-day, for which reason I think it worth while to give some account of his astonishing and regrettable case before going on to pose and debate the problem of his famous contemporary. Their paths do not seem to have crossed, but they have, apart from an extraordinary obstinacy, at least this in common: that the portentous Dr. Samuel Johnson—that Scotophobe whose work and fame were ironically enough so bound up with Scotland and so dependent upon his wonderful Scottish biographer—had a finger in both their pies, but to very different effect, since he was one of the most determined denouncers of Macpherson's alleged frauds while there were grounds for supposing that he aided and abetted Lauder's.

Lauder's antecedents and early life are "wrapt in mystery", and though he claimed to be connected and that not distantly with the Lauders of Fountainhall, the connection is questionable. He was educated in Edinburgh, did well at the University, and turned to teaching for a living. But his career as a teacher was soon interrupted by a serious accident and it has been thought this may have been largely responsible for his subsequent developments, creating in him that kink which we now call an "inferiority complex". He was struck on the knee by a golf-ball while standing near a group engaged in that game (which has been responsible for surprisingly few serious accidents) on Bruntsfield Links. Through careless treatment the injury became septic and his leg had to be amputated. He deputised during Professor Watt's illness in 1734 in teaching the Humanity, or Latin, class, and on that gentleman's death applied with some confidence for the post, but, though he had, no doubt, all the necessary qualifications, lacked sufficient influence to secure the Chair. We are told in Nichol's *Anecdotes* that on this occasion the professors joined in presenting him with "a testimonial from the heads of the University, certifying that he was a fit person to teach Humanity in any school or college whatever", but it failed to prevent a rankling sense of injustice and frustration, which, in addition to the accident already mentioned, laid the foundations for what steadily grew into persecution mania.

According to Robert Chambers: "After this disappointment his ambition sank to an application for the subordinate situation of keeper to the University Library, but this also was denied him. He appears indeed to have been a person whose disposition and character produced a general dislike, which was only to a small extent balanced by his talent and high scholarship. 'He was', says Chalmers, with characteristic magniloquence, 'a person about five feet seven inches high, who had a sallow complexion, large, rolling, fiery eyes, a stentorian voice, and a sanguine temper', and Ruddiman has left, in a pamphlet connected with the subject of Lauder, a manuscript note, observing, 'I was so sensible of the weakness and folly of that man, that I shunned his company, as far as decently I could'. Ruddiman's opinion, however, if early entertained, did not prevent him from forming an intimate literary connection with its subject. In 1738 Lauder printed a proposal to publish by subscription 'A Collection of Sacred Poems', with the assistance of Professor Robert Stewart, Professor John Ker (Professor of Greek in Aberdeen, and afterwards of Latin in Edinburgh), and Mr Thomas Ruddiman." The promised work was published by Ruddiman in 1739, and forms the two well-known volumes called the *Poetarum Scotorum Musae Sacrae* (Note I). What assistance Stewart and Ker may have given to this work appears not to be known; Ruddiman provided several notes and three poems. It contains a beautiful edition of the translation of the Psalms and the Song of Solomon, by Arthur Johnston, and similar sacred poems of merit by Ker, Adamson, and Hog; it contains likewise a reprint of Eglisham's somewhat ludicrous attempt to excel Buchanan's best translated Psalm, the 104th, with the sarcastic "judicium" of Barclay on the respective merits of the competitors, and several minor sacred poems by Scottish authors are dispersed through the collection. The classical merit of these elegant poems has, we believe, never been disputed by those who showed the greatest indignation at the machinations of their editor; nor is their merit less, as furnishing us with much biographical and critical information on the Latin literature of Scotland, among which may be mentioned a well-written Life of Arthur Johnston, and the hyperbolical praises which proved so detrimental to the fame of that poet. To support the fame of the author he had delighted to honour, Lauder afterwards engaged in the literary controversy about the comparative merits of Buchanan and Johnston, known by the name "*Bellum Grammaticale*".

In 1740 the General Assembly recommended the Psalms of Johnston as an useful exercise in the lower classes of the grammar schools; but Lauder never realised from his publication the permanent annual income which he appears to have expected, "because", says Chalmers, "he had allowed expectation to outrun probability. In 1742 Lauder was recommended by Patrick Cumming,

Professor of Church History in Edinburgh University, and the celebrated Colin Maclaurin, as a person fitted to hold the rectorship of the grammar school of Dundee, which had been offered to his coadjutor Ruddiman in 1710; he was again, however, doomed to suffer disappointment, and in bitterness of spirit, and despair of reaching in his native place the status to which his talents entitled him, he appears to have fled to London, where he adopted the course which finally led to the ruin of his literary reputation."

It is likely that the Memoir of Arthur Johnston referred to, which reflects high classical acquirements, was Lauder's work. Although it is prefixed to Auditor Benson's edition of Johnston's Psalms, it had obviously appeared in the *Musae Sacrae*. Lauder may have pressed Arthur Johnston's (1587–1641) claims as against George Buchanan's with "a curious pertinacity" and greatly exaggerated the former's relative merit. It is difficult to recapture the atmosphere of these days when scholars canvassed their respective opinions on such matters with incredible industry and heat, and, indeed, made careers of such controversy, many of them. But even Robert Chambers admits that: "It cannot be said that the version of Buchanan is so eminently superior as to exclude all comparison; and, indeed, we believe the schools in Holland give Johnston the preference, with almost as much decision, as we grant it to Buchanan. The merit of the two is, indeed, of a different sort, and we can fortunately allow that each is excellent, without bringing them to a too minute comparison."

What led Lauder to fix upon Milton as his victim has never been determined. Probably, as Robert Chambers suggests, it was merely the accidental discovery of a few of the parallel passages and apparent echoes and similarities he afterwards adduced in support of his charge of universal plagiarism against Milton. What an obsession this hunting for precedent and correspondence in literary works can become is written large in the history of such controversies in all literatures and in every age (II), and that he was carried away by it, from very small and forfortuitous beginnings, is likely enough and argues no particularly venomous strain in Lauder. The criminal way in which he amplified his detective work suggests that more importance should be attached than many writers on the matter have been inclined to give to the possibility that what really set him off on his ruinous path was the angry feeling roused, and the real injury done to his interest, by a ludicrous contrast of his favourite author, Arthur Johnston, with Milton, in that passage of the *Dunciad* which is levelled at the literary predilections of Benson:

> On two unequal crutches propp'd he came;
> Milton's on this, on that one Johnston's name.

It is, indeed, from such very small causes that obsessions like that of Lauder's are most apt to develop. In my reading of the matter, I prefer to believe that the explanation lies here, and in the self-developing passion of the literary-detective game, rather than in any anti-English or party-political consideration. The consequences are out of all proportion to the cause. But that is the fashion in these affairs, and if my theory is right Lauder was again actuated by a disinterested passion for Arthur Johnston's reputation—disinterested except in so far of course as anything he did successfully to establish it would naturally redound to his own credit—rather than by meaner motives. The position would then be simply a transposition of that he took up in the previous controversy; a defence of Johnston in the one seemed to him to require a denigration of Buchanan—a defence of Johnston here, a denigration of Milton.

Lauder's initial allegations against Milton were contained in letters addressed to the *Gentleman's Magazine* in 1747. The *Gentleman's Magazine* had no hesitation in printing them: "The literary world, indeed, received the attacks on the honesty of the great poet with singular complacency, and the periodicals contained praises of the acuteness and industry of Lauder, some of which he afterwards ostentatiously published."

The Rev. Mr Richardson, author of *Zoilomastik*, was the first to subject Lauder's charges to critical examination, and early in 1749 he wrote to the *Gentleman's Magazine* declaring that some of the passages Lauder cited from books little known even to the learned world, accusing Milton of utilising them wholesale in his poems, did not, in fact, exist in the works in question at all. In particular Mr Richardson insisted that the passage "non me judice", which Lauder had "extracted" from Grotius, was not to be found in that author, and that passages said to be from Masenius and Staphorstius belonged to a partial translation of Milton's *Paradise Lost* by Hog, who had written twenty years subsequently to the death of Milton. It gives another amusing twist to this "comedy of errors" to learn that "although the editor of the *Gentleman's Magazine* arrogated to himself the praise of candour, for admitting the strictures of Lauder, yet this communication of Mr Richardson's was not published until the forgeries had been detected in another quarter, on the ground of unwillingness to give currency to so grave and unexpected a charge, without full examination". In the editorial opinion the living dog was of far greater consequence than the dead lion. Lauder's charges against Milton could be taken on trust and printed gladly as good "copy". But charges against the living Lauder were another matter.

Accordingly, nothing having occurred to give him pause—emboldened, probably, by the non-detection of his first series of fraudulent "extracts" and no doubt sufficiently confident that the range of writers upon whom he was ostensibly drawing were little enough known—Lauder continued to pursue his "studies" energetically and brought his plan to completion by the publication, in 1750, of his *Essay on Milton's Use and Imitation of the Moderns in his Paradise Lost*. He had a charming crooked sense of humour too, this Lauder, for he prefixed as a motto to his treatise "the very appropriate line" from Milton himself: "Things unattempted yet in prose or rhyme."

The book consists of a collection of passages from obscure authors, from which, Lauder maintains, Milton surreptitiously filched the materials of *Paradise Lost*. As Robert Chambers points out, two of these authors were fellow countrymen of Lauder's—Andrew Ramsay and Alexander Ross, both good scholars and Latin versifiers, "but neither likely to have been suspected of giving much aid to Milton". I find no good ground, however, for Chambers's suggestion—which savours a little too much of Lauder's own wire-drawn ingenuity—that Lauder may have gratified a little family pride by citing Ramsay, since Ramsay was Lord Fountainhall's father-in-law and consequently in some sort a connection or relative of Lauder's. That is a little too far-fetched. "Had the author confined his book to the tracing of such passages of Milton, as accident has paralleled in far inferior poems, he might have produced a curious though not very edifying book; and, indeed, he has given us a sufficient number of such genuine passages to make us wonder at his industry and admire the ingenuity with which he has adapted them to the words of Milton; but when he produces masses of matter, the literal translations of which exactly coincide with the poem unequalled in the eyes of all mankind, we express that astonishment at the audacity of the author which we would have felt regarding the conduct of Milton, had the attempt remained undetected. As he spreads a deeper train of forgery and fraud round the memory of his victim, Lauder's indignation and passion increase, and, from the simple accusation of copying a few ideas and sentences from others, passion and prejudice rouse him to accuse Milton of the most black and despicable designs, in such terms as these: 'I cannot omit observing here that Milton's contrivance of teaching his daughters to read, but to read only, several learned languages, plainly points the same way, as Mr Phillips' secreting and suppressing the books to which his uncle was most obliged. Milton well knew the loquacious and incontinent spirit of the sex, and the danger, on that account, of entrusting them with so important a secret as his unbounded plagiarism; he, therefore, wisely confined them to a knowledge of the words and pronunciation only, but kept the sense and meaning to himself'."

It is surprising perhaps how purely—that is to say, how merely—literary Lauder kept his whole arguments. Milton's treatment of his daughters in other respects—his political record—the religious bearings of *Paradise Lost*—and the origin (probably syphilitic) of his blindness, and a host of other such matters might well have suggested themselves to him as a means of attacking Milton on a variety of personal grounds, since an attack on Milton's character in other than literary connections would have had far greater effect and incidentally done more harm to his fame as a poet than any mere *exposé* of his borrowings, however extensive. Little or no value attaches even to the genuine portion of Lauder's treatise; a man of his erudition and energy might well have tracked down Milton's sources and explained his allusions in a most useful way. As a recent writer has said: "Out of his storehouse of memories from his years of Commonwealth service lines and phrases ride on the waves of Milton's verse, corks that indicate the widespread net below. . . . There is an imagination fed with knowledge of peoples distant and strange and many of them barbaric—yet more than mere names to this poet. Of this historical and political knowledge of his, so incomparably richer than that of all his poetical contemporaries put together, the evidence is hard to set out. It consists in an impressive accumulation of phrases and turns of thought and reference. It did not exist in the Milton who wrote *Comus* and *Lycidas*; it was put aside by the Milton who wrote *Samson Agonistes*, whose mind had withdrawn within to its memories and sense of an epoch closed in ruin. But it is everywhere in *Paradise Lost*, an unsuspected spaciousness of range and imagination and knowledge that range the globe. He is the only poet of his age who has not forgotten the sublime adventurers of the previous century, who sought for North-East and North-West Passages and as often as not left their bones in the icy solitudes. He who held that a great poem must be built out of familiarity with great affairs and great enterprises would have been astonished if he had been told that posterity would consider him 'pedantic', a sower and weaver of bookish riddles. It is not his verse that is obscure—it is our minds, which have let so much that is noble in the story of our race slide to oblivion." And the same writer points out that after his blindness Milton must have had to learn all this miscellaneous information largely from human life; there is far more—and other—in the rôle played by his daughters than Lauder imagined (Note III).

To return to Lauder himself, however, his motivation was, it seems, more mixed than Mr Chambers imagines. The motive for gain was there—to bring himself into public notice, to display his energy and erudition and his courage in attacking so great a reputation as Milton's, might be calculated to advance his worldly prospects. To acquire fame by such a bold act of dishonesty presumably appealed to his twisted humour and to his contempt for the unlettered upon whom he thought he could impose with impunity. He gambled on the chance of not being found out; but he probably reckoned with, and accepted, the risk of discovery, too—and in his disappointed and desperate circumstances he no doubt derived some masochistic satisfaction from the anticipation of that final evil. It is not unlikely that he even came to believe that the spurious passages he fabricated were genuine and that he was, indeed, performing a notable public service. The psychological process by which he could not forgive Milton for being the cause which had led him (Lauder) to fabricate these alleged plagiarisms, and his consequent intensification of denigratory zeal, is understandable enough.

He defends himself against possible aspersions with no little warmth. "As I am sensible," he says at the conclusion of his treatise, "this will be deemed most outrageous usage of the divine, the immortal Milton, the prince of English poets, and the incomparable author of *Paradise Lost*, I take this opportunity to declare, in the most solemn manner, that a strict regard to truth alone, and to do justice to those authors whom Milton has so liberally gleaned, without making the least distant acknowledgment to whom he stood indebted: I declare, I say, that these motives, and these only, have induced me to make this attack upon the reputation and memory of a person hitherto universally applauded and admired for his uncommon poetical genius; and not any difference of country, or of sentiments in political and religious matters, as some weak and ignorant minds may imagine, or some malicious persons may be disposed to suggest."

Lauder had not long to wait. In the same year (1750), another Scotsman, John Douglas, afterwards Bishop of Salisbury, published his first literary work, *Vindication of Milton from the Charge of Plagiarism, adduced by Lauder*, and, immediately, since "there is no crime so severely punished as injustice, which is always repaid by a repetition of itself, the learned world which applauded the courage and ingenuity of Lauder, on the appearance of this full and explicit detection of his crimes, were seized with a confirmed hatred against the person who had duped them, and would not admit to his degraded name the talents and information he undoubtedly possessed and displayed."

Lauder subscribed a confession, addressed to Dr. Douglas, explaining his whole conduct to have been caused by spleen and disappointment at the world's neglect of his previous labours sufficiently blackening his heart as to make him scruple at no means of gaining celebrity and triumphing over the world that had oppressed him.

Did this put an end to the matter, and Lauder forthwith relapse into obscurity? Not at all. "Notwithstanding his penitence, a desire to traduce the fame of Milton seems to have haunted this unhappy man like an evil spirit. In 1754 he published *The Grand Imposter detected, or Milton detected of Forgery against King Charles the First*. This too was promptly rebutted, and Lauder left England and for some time taught a school in Barbadoes. "His behaviour there", Nichols says in his *Anecdotes*, "was mean and despicable; and he passed the remainder of his life in universal contempt. He died some time about the year 1771." He did not pass out, however, without the perverse flame that consumed him giving a final flare-up, for some time after his retreat from London a pamphlet was published (no doubt written by himself or at his instigation) entitled *Furius: or a Modest Attempt towards a History of the Life and Surprising Exploits of the Famous W. L., Critic and Thief-catcher*.

Before passing from this curious case (unique, I think, in the annals of literary forgery and charges of plagiarism in that passages were taken from the poem of the author attacked, imitated nearly enough, and then ascribed to earlier books, not readily accessible), a brief paragraph must be devoted to the connection of Dr. Samuel Johnson with the matter. "The connection of Johnson with Lauder's work is, indeed, somewhat mysterious. On a manuscript note on the margin of Archdeacon Blackburne's remarks on the life of Milton, Johnson had written, 'In the business of Lauder, I was deceived, partly by thinking the man too frantic to be fraudulent'. But others have alleged that he did more than believe the statements of Lauder, and even gave assistance to the work. Dr. Lort had a volume of tracts on the controversy, in which he wrote: 'Dr. Samuel Johnson has been heard to confess that he encouraged Lauder to this attack upon Milton, and revised his pamphlet, to which he wrote a preface and postscript'. On the same subject, Dr. Douglas remarks: 'It is to be hoped, nay it is to be expected, that the elegant and nervous writer, whose judicious sentiments and inimitable style point out the author of Lauder's preface and postscript, will no longer allow one to plume himself with his feathers who appeareth so little to deserve assistance; an assistance which, I am persuaded, would never have been communicated, had there been the least suspicion of those facts which I have been the instrument of conveying to the world in these sheets.' Boswell repels the insinuation that Johnson assisted in the preparation of the body of the work, assuring us that Douglas did not wish to create such a suspicion, but he acknowledges the preface and postscript to have been the work of his hands."

It must be remembered, however, that Johnson always bore a grudge against Milton; and that Chambers is himself guilty of an inconsistency when he says that "the postscript contains matter much at variance with the other contents of the book, and had it been the work of Lauder, it might have gone far to redeem at least the soundness of his heart from the opprobrium which has been heaped upon him. It called for the admirers of Milton's works to join in a subscription to the granddaughter of Milton, who then lived in an obscure corner of London, in age, indigence, and sickness." But Lauder does, in fact, deserve that credit and to deny it to him is to act like those of whom Chambers himself had just declared that in their revulsion of feeling they would not admit to Lauder even the talents and information he really had, since, although Johnson wrote the postscript Lauder must have known what it contained and acquiesced in it. Lauder's confession is said to have been dictated by Johnson, and no doubt it was, but that does not clear Johnson of a greater or smaller measure of complicity.

"OSSIAN" MACPHERSON

Superficially Macpherson's case seems the antithesis of Lauder's. Lauder professed to discover passages which did not exist in little-known works, Macpherson—or so it was alleged—discovered poems by authors who had never existed. Lauder's object was to gain celebrity for himself on false grounds. Macpherson's procedure—if the allegations against him were true—could only result in his losing more or less of the celebrity to which he was genuinely entitled. Lauder caused only a storm in an ink-pot. Macpherson caused one of the greatest literary commotions in the history of the world. Macpherson's is a much more difficult and complicated—and an infinitely more important and interesting—case than Lauder's. But Lauder and Macpherson seem to have resembled each other a good deal in disposition. If Lauder was generally disliked, Hume calls Macpherson "so strange and heteroclite a mortal, than whom I have scarce ever known a man more perverse and unamiable". But he had undergone a profound psychological change by that time; earlier impressions of him were much more favourable—he was "a modest, sensible young man" in 1760 in the words of this same man who applied terms so extremely different to him only three years later.

The wrong posing of the Macpherson problem has been largely due to ignorance and to the unfortunate pre-eminence given to moral considerations over literary values. The great majority alike of those who attacked and defended Macpherson knew nothing of Gaelic, and even those who knew Gaelic had little or no knowledge of Scottish Gaelic literature and erroneous ideas regarding what little they did know owing to the lack of an adequate comparative-literary background. Dr. Johnson, who was always much taken up with what was against the authenticity of the Ossian poems *a priori*, voiced a general view when he said: "I look upon Macpherson's *Fingal* to be as gross an imposition as ever the world was troubled with. Had it been really an ancient work, a true specimen of how men thought at that time, it would have been a curiosity of the first rate. As a modern production, it is nothing." The contrary was the case, and if Macpherson had foreseen the effect *Ossian* was to have throughout

Europe he would have simultaneously realised the need to put it over in the way that he actually did, and would have been amply justified in the result. Had he published precisely the same works without ascribing them to ancient Gaeldom but frankly avowing them his own original compositions, they would have been still-born.

Boswell tells us too, in the *Journal of a Tour to the Hebrides*, that "One gentleman in company expressing his opinion 'that *Fingal* was certainly genuine, for that he had heard a great part of it repeated in the original', Dr. Johnson indignantly asked him whether he understood the original: to which an answer being given in the negative, 'why then' (said Dr. Johnson), 'we see to what *this* testimony comes—thus it is'".

"I mentioned this as a remarkable proof how liable the mind of man is to credulity, when not guarded by such strict examination as that which Dr. Johnson habitually practised. The talents and integrity of the gentleman who made the remark are unquestionable. Yet, had not Dr. Johnson made him advert to the consideration that he who does not know a language cannot know that something which is recited to him in that language, he might have believed and reported to this hour, that he had heard a great part of *Fingal* repeated in the original." Boswell goes on to say: "I do not think it incumbent on me to give any precise decided opinion upon this question, as to which I believe more than some and less than others. That *Fingal* is not from the beginning to end a translation from the Gaelic, but that *some* passages have been supplied by the editor to connect the whole, I have heard admitted by very warm advocates for its authenticity. If this be the case, why are not these distinctly ascertained? Antiquaries and admirers of the work may complain that they are in a situation similar to that of the unhappy gentleman whose wife informed him, on her death-bed, that one of their reputed children was not his; and, when he eagerly begged her to declare which of them it was, she answered, '*That* you shall never know', and expired, leaving him in irremediable doubt as to them all."

The story is told of George Buchanan that, when in France, having met with a woman who was said to be possessed with the Devil, and who professed to speak all languages, he accosted her in Gaelic. As neither she nor her familiar returned any answer, he entered a protest that the Devil was ignorant of that tongue. It is unfortunately an ignorance that is not confined to his Satanic Majesty, though it perhaps is to those who are possessed by the Devil. Certainly at the time of the *Ossian* controversy—and in Scotland to-day—most of those who pronounce most dogmatically on questions of Gaelic language and literature have devilish little knowledge of them.

M. Henri Hubert, the great French Celtic scholar, says, in his *The Greatness and Decline of the Celts*: "The literature of the Gauls was an oral literature, and so were those of the Welsh and Irish. Every oral literature is a paraphrase of known themes and centos. Since the most powerful memory has its limitations, their themes are few. Popular literature is poor, although there are so many collections of folklore: oral literature partakes of the nature of popular literature. It is not very varied. In Ireland the *ollamh*, or chief of the *fili*, had to know three hundred and fifty stories, two hundred and fifty long and a hundred short. We have catalogues of the resources of the *fili*. The prose parts of the Irish romances seem to have been a foundation on which all kinds of fancies could be built up. The metrical parts were those which acquired more permanence; they were usually *bravura* passages. The oral tradition went on long after the form of the story had been fixed by erudition. Some of the most famous and affecting passages in the heroic legends and even in the Mythological Cycle, to which the ancient parts merely allude, were only developed in late poems of the seventeenth or eighteenth century—for example, the story of the sons of Ler being turned into swans by their stepmother. From this point of view we may say that 'Ossian' Macpherson remained in the Celtic tradition;

only he took greater liberties than the ordinary arrangers of these themes."

The effect of *Ossian* in developing genuine Gaelic studies in a fashion that would probably never otherwise have been possible cannot be denied. When all is said and done it conveyed a Gaelic atmosphere like no previous work in the English language, which if, as Dr. Pryde says, "largely spurious", was nevertheless the most useful conductor to the genuine. And, since national literatures, like individual men, by "indirections find directions out", *Ossian* has been as incomparable a service to pure Scottish and Irish Gaelic literatures as it was a tremendous force in all the literatures of Europe. This is clearly brought out by Mr Aodh de Blácam in the following passage from his *Gaelic Literature Surveyed*:

"Through Gaelic Scotland the ancient Celtic genius exercised in modern times a remarkable influence on the course of European letters. The Scottish rising of 1745–6 is said to have struck such alarm into the ruling caste in Ireland as to arouse a new hostility to all things Gaelic. Carolan was dead, and none of his successors enjoyed the friendship of the Anglo-Irish. In Scotland, the rising brought about repressive measures—the banning of the kilt, for example, which thereupon became the theme of many a song, such as that satirical, *Hé an clo dubh, ho an clo dubh*, which vents the Gaelic contempt for the drab attire of the *bourgeoisie*. In Lowland Scotland and in England, however, the rising had an unpredictable effect. Did that picturesque, exotic, Northern race, which lately had swept southward with targe and claymore, possess a literature of its own? This was the question debated in literary circles, and an answer came from James Macpherson of Kingussie. In 1760, this strange and somewhat furtive genius published a volume entitled, *Fragments of Ancient Poetry*, collected in the Highlands of Scotland and translated from the Gaelic or Erse langue.

"In rapid succession followed the so-called epics *Fingal* and *Temora*. These works purported to be translations from Ossian (*i.e.* Oisin). He was represented as a Gaelic Homer, whose verses had come down traditionally even as Homer's; Macpherson's translations consisted of confused and cloudy versions of tales from the Fenian and Red Branch sagas, set forth in a rhythmical prose. An Irish setting remained—Temora is Tara—but many episodes were represented as taking place in 'Morven' and other Scottish regions. These volumes became the centre of violent controversy. Enemies of the Scots argued that such an extensive literature could not be transmitted orally; and, alternatively, that it had no merit. Any man could write such stuff, said Dr. Johnson, if he would stoop to it. Highlanders subscribed large funds for the publication of the originals, but, to this day, owing to Macpherson's shifty tactics, the credentials of the Gaelic texts that were printed remain obscure.

"Whatever the truth regarding the originals, Macpherson's *Ossian* became one of the most influential books of the age, and one of the main sources of the Romantic movement. Not in the English-speaking world alone, but throughout the Continent, where *Ossian* was translated into many tongues, this wind from the Highlands blew the powder from polite perukes. Imaginative minds, ready to revolt against the stiff artificiality of the eighteenth century, found in *Ossian* a summons to the open air, and learnt from these curious pages a new and passionate delight in the ocean and the moor, and in the splendour of the tempest on the mountains. We, who are familiar with Gaelic originals or authentic translations, too easily scorn Macpherson. We note the jumbling together of different cycles, the vagueness of narrative, the sentimentality, and the absence of the true Gaelic firmness and maturity. We observe in the diction phrases that never came from Gaelic, phrases which Macpherson got from the Bible and his Classical reading. The wrong things are so numerous as to exasperate us, so that we fail to recognise how largely the Gaelic spirit *did* inform this work. When, however, we read MacNeill's literal translations of

Ossianic lays in *Duanaire Finn* we are struck by many similarities, and are brought to realise that Macpherson certainly had heard lays of the same sort."

Probably Macpherson composed his prose poems in the form of original work, seeking to recapture vague memories floating in his mind of lays heard long since, in Gaelic or in translation. It may be, however, that he had before him Gaelic originals which were themselves corrupt—lays that had grown confused in oral transmission.

In either case, two truths must be borne in mind. First, that Macpherson's *Ossian* is far removed from the Gaelic classics. And second, that it nevertheless conveyed a Gaelic atmosphere like no previous work in the English language. Even to-day it is an insensible reader who cannot find freshness in many a passage: "Our youth is like the dream of the hunter on the hill of Neath"; "Colamon of troubled waters, dark wanderer of distant vales, I behold thy course between trees, near Car-ul's echoing halls"; "I have seen the walls of Balclutha, but they were desolate. The fire had resounded in the halls, and the voice of the people is heard no more." Macpherson's *Ossian* is important to us for other reasons than the fact that it was the first manifestation of the Gaelic genius in the English tongue. It exerted a curious reaction on subsequent Gaelic letters. Scottish writers of Gaelic began to compose in the Macpherson tradition. A good deal of falsity thus entered Scots Gaelic literature. Many Scottish writers derived their conception of the Gaelic past principally from Macpherson's distorted version thereof. Directly and indirectly, Macpherson exerted a tardy influence on Ireland. An Irish "Ossianic Society" was founded, which did fine work, and it was as a result of the European romantic movement, to which he contributed so much, that Anglo-Ireland discovered in the nineteenth century an interest in Gaelic literature.

The absence of the true Gaelic firmness and maturity, and other faults from a strictly Gaelic standpoint, in

Macpherson's work are due to a variety of causes—the vague and adulterated conception of the Gaelic spirit at the time, the contemporary standards of English composition, the intrusion of Biblical and other overtones, and a lack of that technical experimentalism alike in the choice of words and the rhythms and uses of alliteration, assonance, and other devices employed, which might have enabled more authentic Gaelic effects to be secured if these had been properly understood to begin with.

It is not true, as many Gaelic enthusiasts aver, just as other Gaels disavow or conceal their knowledge of the ancient language, that English is an impossible medium for the effective translation of Gaelic texts, but the task certainly calls for a very unusual adroitness in the choice of the right English words and in the employment of technical devices. To some of these English is to-day returning in the work of some of the younger poets, but it has been more or less a stranger to them since it became more and more inspissated with alien modes and alienated from its own native basis and rhythms. Macpherson's alleged faults in this connection, as listed by Mr De Blácam, are by no means peculiar to Macpherson but characterise the great bulk of translations from Irish and Scottish Gaelic into English; it is only necessary to compare the renderings of Irish Gaelic poetry by Sir Samuel Fergusson and other early translators with the recent re-renderings by Professor Bergin, Mr Robin Flower, and others which are much harder and far nearer to the spirit of the originals than the quite misleading products of the Celtic Twilight school. But it is true, obviously, that a highly inflected language will only correspond with another highly inflected one. Greek, for instance, cannot be livingly translated except into a highly inflected language. Some languages, however, which possess inflections corresponding more exactly with those of Greek than the Latin ones do—having a dual, for example—are also unsuitable because their vocabulary has taken its meaning from a set of circumstances so different that there must always be a tremendous gap between the meaning of a Greek sentence and the meaning of its however literal rendering. Greek poetry will not bear translation into our poetry. If the attempt is made the result may be poetry, but it is English poetry (or would be Scots or Gaelic poetry were these media used), and poetry that could be written by no one else than that particular translator.

> Where has he of race divine
> Wandered in the winding rocks?

Surely no one imagines he is reading anything but a lyric by Shelley when he sees this translation of a Euripidean chorus, or that it is Homer rather than Pope he hears in:

> Thus having spoke, th' illustrious chief of Troy
> Stretch'd his fond arms to clasp the lovely boy.

Actually the only excuse for printing these translations is to cease regarding them as translations, and give them attention as pieces of imitative verse. Pound is right, however, when he declares Gavin Douglas's *Eneados* better than the original, Douglas "having heard the sea", but wrong when he speaks of "the starters of crazes, the Ossianic Macphersons, the Gongoras whose wave of fashion flows over writing for a few centuries or a few decades, and then subsides, leaving things as they are". He is wrong in this alike to the Scottish and to the Spanish writer; but less to Gongora, because while there are Gongoras—Euphuists, Marinists, and such like—who, however, serve a very necessary and valuable purpose, there are no Macphersons—Macpherson's achievement was absolutely unique.

It is a pity there is not a great deal more thinking and writing about the problems of language and translation in Scotland. The "common sense" attitude to language—the "man in the street" attitude—has meant a complete and grotesque misprisal of the efforts that have been made in Scotland to revive the Scots Vernacular as a literary language; and little study seems to have been devoted to the thorny problems of translation since Alexander Fraser Tytler, afterwards Lord Woodhouselee, published his admirable *Essay on the Principles of Translation*, anonymously, in 1790.

The problems of language are far more profound and intricate and important to-day than ever. The mediaeval Scottish scholars were great linguists, but not in a useful sense so far as creative literature was concerned; what they knew of the numerous languages almost all of them boasted was pretty much the same in each of these tongues. The vast majority of those who take modern languages in our schools and Universities to-day learn far less than that, however, but even so it is highly regrettable that the special Scottish aptitude for languages is not exercised far more than it is; every educated Scot should be multilinguistic. Only so can he put himself in possession of the diverse heritage of his own race even. A significant feature of the current new Scottish Movement—apart from the interest in Scots and in Gaelic—is the increase of translations, into Scots in particular, by Scottish writers. German, French, Russian, the Auvergnat dialect, Dutch, and others have been drawn upon. It is to be hoped that this may develop much further and embrace prose as well as verse. For in many instances Scots is a much superior medium to English; and Gaelic would be immensely the better for a constant and ample stream into it of renderings of contemporary work from various European languages—it has been far too long cut off from European influences.

It must not be supposed that I am anxious that the protagonists of the Scottish Renaissance should receive more ample, direct, and speedy "news of civilisation" in order to be affected by it otherwise than Gerard Manley Hopkins was affected by great poems—namely, not with a desire to imitate them but to do something entirely different. My wish to see Scottish writers equipped with a far more extensive knowledge of European languages and literatures is so that they may be enabled to keep themselves free from influences inappropriate or confusing to the fullest possible realisation of their own distinctive genius, and especially that they may be disabused of the misconceptions even in matters closely relating to their own languages and literatures and the potentialities of these and reduced as the *Ossian* controversy reduced so many of them, and as the current new departures in Scottish letters have reduced almost all of them, to a state of literally not knowing what they are talking about, a condition principally induced so far as Scotsmen are concerned by the state of affairs best summarised in these two sentences: "But I am afraid it is rather partisan"; "Anything un-English is bound to be".

"In Scotland, particularly since the time of the Covenant and the Montrose wars," says Mr J. L. Campbell in the introduction to his *Highland Songs of the 'Forty-Five*, "partisan writers have always been wont to describe the Highlanders as barbarous in manners and uncouth in speech. This propaganda, which is of a type now familiar to many of us, crystallised into an accepted opinion, adopted by most Scottish (and practically all English) historians, who have been almost without exception ignorant of the language of the people whom they condemned. ('To the southern inhabitants of Scotland,' says Dr. Johnson, *A Tour of the Hebrides*, 'the state of the mountains and the islands is equally unknown with that of Borneo or Sumatra. Of both they have heard only a little and guess the rest. They are strangers to the language and the manners, to the advantages and wants of the people, whose life they would remodel and whose evils they would remedy.') 'The dominating thought in the mind of the average Highlander in the '45 rising', says Hume Brown in his *History of Scotland*, 'was that he was engaged in a Highland raid on a large scale which ought to result in a proportionate profit.' 'The common people north of the Grampians', says D. N. Mackay in his introduction to the *Trial of Simon, Lord Lovat*, 'had little idea of the great political movements of their day.

They could be swayed, deceived, or goaded into war by any alleged insult to their immediate community. The larger issues were unrealised. Few could read or write, which mattered little, for there was little to read and no occasion to write.' So two highly respected Scottish scholars, one of whom bears a Highland name. It matters not to Professor Hume Brown that not even the then enormous sum of £30,000 could procure a traitor from among the Highlanders to betray the Prince *even from among the clans who had regarded his enterprise with indifference* (as if the uncorruptibility of the Highlanders were too much to be believed, it has even been suggested that the idea of money had no meaning for them, and the offer no temptation!) or to Mr Mackay that the people whose illiteracy he derides had by 1745 been deprived of all education through the medium of their mother-tongue for more than a hundred years, and yet maintained an oral literature of no small extent and beauty, and, in the remote island of Uist, the traditions of the old Gaelic culture which centuries earlier had made Ireland the illumination of the western world. But '*omne ignotam pro barbaro*' seems to have been the proverb of the Highlanders' critics, maintained more recently as a reaction against the literary exploits of James Macpherson and the effusions of the Jacobite and Highland romanticists. And here indeed there is to be found some measure of excuse, though from the critical point of view there is no condonation, for the historians' bias against the Gael. For if the Highlanders have been undeservedly criticised, they have also been undeservedly praised, and in fact the controversy over their merits and faults has often been waged in an atmosphere of complete unreality, the imaginations of the contestants frequently relieving them of the arduous task of historical research. And it is also necessary to point out in fairness that Scottish Gaelic literature has never been until recently well edited or easily available. The text of the principal poet (Alexander MacDonald) whose poems are included in this anthology was not translated until 1924 and has never been properly annotated yet; and about a third of the poems printed here have never been previously annotated at all. Though such a state of affairs may be considered an extenuation for the pronouncement of such opinions as are quoted above, it still remains in itself a gross reflection upon Scottish scholarship and the methods of Scottish historians. It is very little to their credit that so much interesting and important material has for so long been permitted to go unworked and neglected. To refer again to the remarks of Professor Hume Brown, 'The dominating idea in the mind of the *average* Highlander . . .' It would be interesting to know where Professor Hume Brown obtained the insight into the mind of the *average* middle-eighteenth-century Highlander that would qualify him to make this sweeping assertion. It cannot have been from a first or even a second-hand source; and it would not be going far wrong to say that this statement, like others of the same kind, owes its conscious or unconscious genesis to what would now be described as the influence of anti-Gaelic propaganda. In its unenlightened aspect it was represented by the dread of English mothers that the Prince's followers would devour their children alive."

It was against that background of ignorance and prejudice that the *Ossian* controversy ran its furious course; and it is against a very similar background of ignorance and prejudice to-day that the questions of a Scottish Renaissance, the re-writing of Scottish History, and the literary potentialities of Scots and Scottish Gaelic are being posed—alike by those who are opposed to them and by almost all of those who are advocating them. I have used the word barbarism, and my attitude, and the tissue of misconceptions in which these issues are involved to-day on all sides are ably described in a recent editorial in *The Modern Scot*. "The modern world, the world of the modern history of the text-books, is a post-Renaissance world, and it is a matter of profound and far-reaching significance that every thriving national culture in Europe to-day has been made or remade in post-Renaissance times. There are important respects in which the Celtic culture of Scotland has not been reborn in the modern world, whereas the culture of Lowland Scotland has: Celtic art and thought in their various branches clearly demonstrate this. The reason lies to a large extent in the imperviousness of Celtic art to the classical influences, emanating chiefly from Graeco-Roman sources, that made, say, a Shakespeare possible in England and an Adams possible in eighteenth-century Edinburgh. Much has been made by a certain type of writer of the classical influences on Celtic culture, of the Gael's knowledge of ancient Greece, and so on, but although one can recall at random the use Irish writers have made of, say, the *Odyssey*, the *Aeneid*, Lucan, Heliodorus, etc., the fact remains that there are stronger affinities between Celtic art and the art of the East than between Celtic art and modern European art (we are not here concerned with qualitative differences, but with differences of kind). For the commonly drawn comparisons between Celtic art and eastern art boil down to an insistence on the non-participation of these arts in the major developments of modern European art. Mr T. D. Kendrick emphasised this when he wrote: 'The art of the Celtic lands and of Scandinavia . . . were . . . both of them *barbarian*, although this may well sound a rather irreverent description of the lovely works produced by early monastic Ireland; but the meaning is clear—they were both on the edge of the world wherein classical art progressed through Carolingian, Ottonian, Italian, and Byzantine phases, and neither of them was strong enough to stand aside from this main stream of European art. They aped it and whenever they did they fell from grace, as is the way with barbarian art.' By comparison with this 'barbarian' art, European art is a humanist art. The organisation, ordering, centripetal quality in European art and thought, first exploited by the Greeks, is opposed to the spirit of the Celt and the Oriental. The art of classical Europe was an art of selection, an ordering and organising of experience, it has an aerated quality deriving from its humanism; it is not so much organic as architectural in form. It is easy in the light of Mr Kendrick's and similar remarks to see how the cultural inbreeding of the Celt came about, to appreciate its rich fruits and yet recognise, whilst bemoaning, the virtual death of Celtic culture in the modern world. Of all the people talking so glibly about a Celtic revival, we can think of only one who sees the consequences of what a Celtic revival would be (supposing it possible). He would welcome it, not because he is ignorant of the European tradition, but because he has no use for it." And as this one the writer mentions the present author. I do think a Celtic Revival possible, but the question does not arise here. What I am concerned with is the bearing of these arguments on my initial thesis—that the Scots are, as Shaw says, "incompatible with British civilisation".

An understanding of what *The Modern Scot* writer says is not all that is necessary, however, if this problem is to be effectively grappled with. There must also be what the late Mr A. R. Orage deplored as being so lacking in literary circles to-day—a thorough understanding of the achievements of all other literatures, as indispensable before one can value works in any and not be in the position of mere reviewers who have no such background and whose judgement accordingly lives in a mere hand-to-mouth fashion. There must also be a clear appreciation of the fact that "the 'poetry' of the Gael of popular fiction is a chaotic and perverse notion. The Gael of the great past was a poet if he wrote poetry. For him, as for all the people of his age, the term 'poetic' as used by the romantics of our day would be meaningless. Fighting was fighting, and building was building, and love-making was love-making, and so on—poetry might be written about these and all the other myriad aspects of his life, but his life itself was not 'poetic'." What those who prate about "the 'poetry' of the Gael" need in regard to the matter is an experience similar to that of the little boy who exclaimed:

"Mummy, there's a man in the dining-room". When he learnt that it was his father in dress-clothes he knew his father more surely and saw him more clearly than when "Daddy" was merely "Daddy". Gaelic literature is a literature and it needs to be seen as such and not as some special unshared soulfulness having little or nothing in common with the mere literatures produced by other peoples who lack this divine endowment. The discovery that individual objects have fundamental resemblances does not, as a matter of fact, tend to minimise their individuality, but rather to accentuate it. To get rid of Gaelic glamour and see Gaelic literature just as literature instead would be a far more stupendous change than the transformation of "Daddy" into the "man in the dining-room", and is the only way to get to know it surely and clearly.

Unfortunately almost all Scots have only seen their country or any aspect of any Scottish national issue in such diverse terms simultaneously as did the stranger of whom S. T. Coleridge wrote: "Some folks apply epithets as boys do in making Latin verses. When I first looked upon the falls of the Clyde, I was unable to find a word to express my feelings. At last, a man, a stranger to me, who arrived about the same time, said: 'How majestic'. It was the precise term, and I turned round and was saying—'Thank you, sir. That *is* the exact word for it'—when he added *eodem flatu*, 'Yes. How very *pretty.*' " This is typical of what has always happened to all Scots in matters of art. At the very point where the impulse should undergo that objectification necessary to art, it is deflected into the banal. True, few Scots seem to have had any artistic tendency—the elements that in other peoples would have become the materials of art have always been abundant enough amongst them, but instead of being applied to artistic purpose they flare up to great heights and then are suddenly thwarted and beaten down by contrary forces generally of a moral (which, of course, includes immoral) sort. As a rule, too, these stultifying forces come from without—they are the European influences the barbarians are unable to withstand, which prevent them being fully themselves. It is this selecting, organising, and ordering of experience which is alien to the Scottish genius, which lacks the necessary architectonic faculty and purpose—it is the acceptance of a code of any sort. The Scots should sample all philosophies and religions and enjoy their various savours, but switch about freely from one to the other, accepting none—which is, of course, moral anarchy. "In the field of metaphysics", as Shestov says, "rules the daemon of whom we are not even entitled to assume that he is interested in any 'norm' at all. Norms arose among the cooks and were created for cooks. What need is there then to transfer all this *empiria* thither whither we flee to escape *empiria*? . . . The whole art of philosophy should be directed towards freeing us from the 'good and evil' of cooks and carpenters, to finding that frontier beyond which the might of general ideas ceases." It is certainly there that Scottish genius has most abundantly manifested itself—in the play of personality, the indulgence of impulses, not in stated terms of dialectic or art. The true Scot is known by his continual propensity for a genuine "transition into another field".

This leads us to the real nature of *Ossian*. Macpherson entirely misconceived the nature of his achievement; if he had not done so—if it had been a true expression of the Gaelic genius—*Ossian* would have been a meaningless feat to Europe and quite incapable of meeting the widespread need and exercising the stupendous influence it did. It was, as a matter of fact, necessary to Europe but only of very slight, indirect, ultimate benefit to Gaeldom. Dr. Laurie Magnus, in his *History of European Literature*, puts the matter perfectly when he says of *Ossian* that, despite the exposure of the fraud, "its 'merits' remain. It served the needs of its own time, and, paraphrasing a famous saying of Voltaire, we may add that, since Ossian was not extant, it was necessary to invent him. His immense vogue is the measure of the need."

Macpherson would not have met that need, or achieved any European fame, if he had been a true Scottish poet, a true translator of true Gaelic poetry into English, or, in his own right, the greatest Gaelic poet to date. In any of these rôles he would scarcely have been heard of. The fact that the English and European interest insists upon a fraudulent conception of the Gaelic genius—that it is incapable of assimilating other than the most erroneous ideas of that genius and, having done so, has the power to carry these back and pollute the very springs of Gaelic genius—it only justifies a fraud such as Macpherson's is generally assumed to be in this strictly literary sense. It would also have rendered anything other than he actually did in translating Gaelic originals into English no less of a fraud, and a species of fraud that belongs to all translating and which is not generally regarded as fraudulent at all. The motive in such cases is not fraudulent; the result inevitably is. Dr. Magnus found gentler terms for the process when he said that, in literature generally at this time, the appeal of the writers "was couched in language which found a ready way to men's hearts. That human feeling and natural phenomena were fused or forced into harmonious relationship—

All, all conspire
To raise, to soothe, to harmonise the mind,

this was an implement of its success, and it is arguable that the success was quickened by the fact *that many of the writers were not in the first rank*. The mood was communicated more readily to the middle classes. Burke perceived this imminent danger in the new thought, and there is a sense in which the note of the eighteenth century was sublimated after the ordeal of the French Revolution. Fused, or forced, we said just now, and amid all this transfusion of feeling and translation of books, there was bound to be some forcing of sentiment. The conspiracy between Nature and man would sometimes have to be assisted. James Macpherson and Thomas

Chatterton both forced the sentiment at which they aimed. By hook or by crook—and their extreme cases illustrate the crooked means—writers between 1700 and 1778 satisfied with increasing zeal the demand for surprise and difference. The worn sameness of experience was proving intolerable. So earth had to be remapped for the survey of the sons of man." A false Scotland was accordingly added to it—and it is amusing to hear its falsity condemned by writers like Dr. Pryde whose own conceptions of Scotland are still more false—just as, later, a false Russia was added to it (*vide* the comments of Mrs Virginia Woolf and D. S. Mirsky on the entirely erroneous conceptions propagated by the principal enormously influential translations of Dostoevski and others).

"The work of the young Speyside schoolmaster [Macpherson] formed, in fact, one of the most important headwaters of the world-phenomenon described as the Renascence of Wonder. Of that fact, a Scots delegate to an international literary congress in Poland in 1932 was thrillingly reminded", says William Power, "when an announcement of his regarding the Gaelic movement in Scotland was received with a burst of applause. When he recovered from his astonishment, he had the presence of mind to refer to Macpherson's *Ossian*. The Ossianic rage was something quite unparalleled in the history of European literature, before or since. What was the real secret of it?

"A key to the mystery was suggested by a remark made to me by 'A. E.', to the effect that a congenial mythology is needed for poetry. The way had been paved for *Ossian* by the Vernacular revival (Gay, Ramsay, Lady Grizel Baillie), the growing love of natural beauty (James Thomson), and the emotional ferment and idealistic revolt initiated by Rousseau. What was still lacking was the embodiment of the vague feelings thus aroused—the congenial projection, shadowy but simple, of awakened subjectivity. The classic mythology was hackneyed and shop-soiled, and literary people had grown tired of it. The

Norse mythology was familiar only to a few scholars in Scandinavia and England. Both mythologies were too local and remote, too definite in scheme and characterisation, too closely associated with certain archaic ways of life and thought. They had too much solidity and 'body colour'. The unexpressed demand was for cloudland figures that would take on the colours of the atmosphere and shape themselves to the mood of the age; Harz mountains giants, so to speak, in which any dreamily poetic young European could at any moment behold the grandiose image of himself or herself. And the age found what it wanted in the vaguely beautiful, vaguely grand, vaguely plangent figures of Macpherson's *Ossian*. . . . The world went on, licked its war-wounds, increased the number of its red corpuscles, conquered Nature, grew wealthy and strong; but still fought and loved, lost or won, laughed and feasted and wept and died; and the elemental hankerings after a topical mythology—a generalised poetic bodying-forth of the spirit of the age—revived.

"This time it was supplied, in soul-conquering, polyphonic music, by a far greater artist than Macpherson—Richard Wagner, exploiting the old mythology of the Teutonic races. 'Except for *Die Meistersinger*', remarks W. J. Turner, 'not one of his operas contains human beings. They are all monsters—called, euphemistically, gods—or they are legendary figures of an equal monstrousness. All Wagner requires of them is that they shall rave, fight, love, and declaim—as though they were ten feet high with the chests of bulls and the legs and arms of Cyclops. From the beginning to the end of the *Ring* there is nothing but sheer vitality personified into the figures of myth: Wotan is the power of knowledge, Loge is cunning, Fricka is woman, Freya is joy, Brunnhilde is maidenhood, Siegfried is boyhood, and so on.' That is true, but unfairly put: for within the simple framework of each personification, there are vast and subtle differentiations of passion raised to the height of spiritual beauty. Through this extraordinary spell, the hearers identify themselves, they cannot tell how, with those magnificent 'monsters', who, like the Ossianic figures, are both less and more than human."

It is difficult either to convey any idea of the passionate controversy Macpherson's work created in Scotland—estranging friends, dividing households, leading, in some cases, almost to bloodshed—or of the Continental vogue it enjoyed. From the first the genuineness of the poems became a matter of dispute. Among those who believed in their authenticity were Dr. Blair, Dr. Gregory, Lord Kames, the Rev. Dr. Graham of Aberfoyle, and Sir John Sinclair; and among the most distinguished of those who denied their genuineness were David Hume, Dr. Samuel Johnson, Dr. Smith of Campbeltown, and Malcolm Laing, the historian. Sir James Mackintosh, too, in his *History of England*, expresses himself very strongly against their authenticity. There was no effort, however, to make a systematic study of Scottish Gaelic literature, to collect and publish the old tales and legends, or to translate into English such texts as were available. The curiosity aroused failed to produce what would seem to have been its natural result.

How differently Germany would have tackled such a matter. "It was in 1757 that attention was called for the first time to the wealth of Northern Mythology locked up in mediaeval manuscripts, and the pioneer work was Bodmer's publication, *Chriemhilden Rache und die Klage* (Chriemhilde's Revenge and the Lament). But the Teutonic cast of mind could not leave to one man so much credit of discovery, hence it was that commentator tumbled over commentator with translations and editions, accumulating 'a whole system of antique Teutonic Fiction and Mythology'." According to Carlyle "the *Nibelungen* is welcomed as a precious national possession, recovered after six centuries of neglect, and takes undisputed place among the sacred books of German literature".

But nothing at all has eventuated from a parallel case

in our own country, though a vast mass of material concerning it has been set out by a Scottish writer, Professor L. A. Waddell, with his book *The British Edda*, the great epic poem of the Ancient Britons on the exploits of King Thor, Arthur, or Adam, and his knights in establishing civilisation, reforming Eden, and capturing the Holy Grail about 3380–3350 B.C., reconstructed for the first time from the mediaeval MSS. by Babylonian, Hittite, Egyptian, Trojan, and Gothic keys, and done literally into English.

"The collection of very ancient epic poems known as the *Edda* and hitherto called 'Icelandic'—from one circumstance that its parchment manuscripts were found preserved over eight centuries ago in the far-off fastnesses of Iceland—has been little known and unappreciated by the educated British public. This neglect has arisen not only from the supposed foreign character of its poems and heroes, but in a more especial degree from the unattractiveness of its theme and literary form as presented in the hitherto current confused and misleading English 'translations'," says Dr. Waddell. "The translators have totally failed to recognise that the *Edda* is *not* at all a medley of disjointed Scandinavian mythological tales of gods as has been imagined; but that it forms one great coherent epic of historical human heroes and their exploits, based upon genuine hoary tradition; that it is an ancient British epic poem written with lucid realism in the ancient British language; and that it is one of the great literary epics of the world, and deals circumstantially with the greatest of all heroic epochs in the ancient world, namely, the struggle for the establishment of civilisation, with its blessings to humanity, over five thousand years ago." This great book, published in 1930, was still-born. English literature is not open to fundamental revaluations of its bases.

Profoundly influential in every other European country, *Ossian* was practically without effect on English literature, and it was the English and Anglo-Scottish elements who were most concerned to destroy its influence by proving the non-existence of the alleged originals, and, even if these had been forthcoming, would still have been most concerned by every possible means to minimise the value of the work and restrict it to the least possible measure of influence. It is no accident that three Scottish writers have had a far greater European vogue than any English writer—Ossian, Scott, and Byron; that Ossian and Byron are relegated in English literature to a far smaller degree of importance than Europe concedes them; and that there is the same discrepancy between the English and the European estimate in the case of another Scottish writer, Carlyle.

While the *Ossian* controversy prompted no genuine Scottish nationalist effort, ill-founded prejudices and false sentiment were greatly in evidence. And when Malcolm Laing denied the authenticity of the *Ossian* poems, producing similes and trains of ideas derived or plagiarised from the writings of other authors, particularly from Virgil, Milton, Thomson, and the Psalms, and entering into a curious comparison between the method of arranging the terms and ideas in the poems of Ossian and that exhibited in a forgotten poem called *The Highlanders*, published by Macpherson in early life, "the author of such an attack on one of the fortresses of the national pride of Scotland did not perpetrate his work without suitable reprobation; the Highlanders were 'loud in their wail', and the public prints swarmed with ebullitions of their wrath. Mr Laing was looked upon as a man who had set all feelings of patriotism at defiance; to many it seemed an anomaly in human nature that a Scotsman should thus voluntarily undermine the great boast of his country; and, unable otherwise to account for such an act, they sought to discover in the author motives similar to those which made the subject sacred to themselves. (Laing was a native of Strynzia on the Mainland of Orkney.) 'As I have not seen Mr Laing's History,' says one gentleman, 'I can form no opinion as to the arguments wherewith he has attempted to discredit Ossian's poems: the attempt could not come more naturally than from Orcadians. Perhaps the severe check given by the ancient Caledonians to their predatory Scandinavian predecessors raised prejudices not yet extinct. I conceive how an author can write under the influence of prejudice, and not sensible of being acted upon by it.' " This is typical enough of the arguments used in nine-tenths of the controversial writing evoked, and the hopelessly unscientific grounds on which the discussion proceeded may be illustrated by the fact that the Rev. Dr. Graham, in a long and elaborate work designed as a confutation of Laing, "made a somewhat unlucky development of his qualifications for this task, by quoting the *De Moribus Germanorum* of Tacitus, referring entirely to the Teutonic nations, as authority concerning the Celts".

Meanwhile, *Ossian* had taken Europe by storm. "Turgot translated it into French and Melchiore Cesaroti into Italian. The Italian version accompanied Napoleon all the way from Egypt to St. Helena and may have helped to make European history. Certainly it helped to make Goethe's poetry and to create a new literature in far-off Russia. Joined with the genuine *Reliques of Ancient English Poetry* by Bishop Percy, it gave a most powerful impetus to the revival of mediaeval studies in folklore and ballad and is one of the pillars on which the Romantic Movement was established." "Ossian, that poet of the genius of ruins and battles," wrote Lamartine, "reigned paramount in the imagination of France. . . . Women sang him in plaintive romances, or in triumphal strains, at the departure, above the tombs, or on the return of their lovers. . . . I plunged into the ocean of shadow, of blood, of tears, of phantoms, of foam, of snow, of mists, of hoar frosts and of images the immensity, the dimness, and the melancholy of which harmonise so well with the lofty sadness of a heart of sixteen which expands to the first rays of the infinite. . . . I had become one of the sons of the bard, one of the heroic, amorous, or plaintive shades who fought, who loved, who wept, or who swept the fingers across the harp in the gloomy dominions of Fingal."

"Ossian has long ago retired to his misty hill-tops," says Professor Gregory Smith, "and James Macpherson, who conjured him forth to vex the world of letters as no ghost has done, before or since, has 'tholed his assize'. It is hard for us to understand what a pother the son of Fingal caused in the critical coteries, or to measure the effects, in some ways for good, of this fiction, so impudently conceived, upon the literature of Europe. Ossian *is* the modern Homer, said Madame de Staël. To Klopstock he is the rival of Homer; to Voss 'Ossian of Scotland is greater than Homer of Ionia'; and Herden, having at last found his soul's desire, had thoughts of going to Scotland that he might be touched more closely by this inspired writing.

"All this and more, especially of the enthusiasm of Germany, is familiar. It would appear that in our own day *Ossian* (in translation) is, or was, accepted in Italian schools as the standard 'English' classic—a pedagogical enormity very distressing to a correspondent in the *Spectator* of 26th October 1918. But one or two reflections suggest themselves not impertinently. In the first place, the Scotticism, as found by Herden in Macpherson's pages, was illusory. If, as their author claimed, the Ossianic poems are far removed from the fantastic work of the Irish bards, they are not any nearer, in trait and sentiment, to what must pass for Scottish, even if by that we mean only Gaelic. No literary critic nowadays could, even were all clues of provenance and language to fail, mistake this Ossian and his brethren as representative. The Dean of Lismore would have had no doubts; and there would have been fewer in the classical Edinburgh of Blair's day willing to be convinced of the ancient and abiding Scottish *timbre* of the epics, had not the contempt shown by Johnson and other Englishmen made defence of Macpherson and his work a plain matter of national honour. Had these good people been as wise as posterity, they would have seen that Scotland's credit in the matter was based not on the local or representative character of Macpherson's work, but on the larger issue, that it voiced the new mood of Romanticism, and in terms which immediately won the attention of every literature ready to break with the ennui of Rule. If, as Percy said of the *Fragments*, there is 'not one local or appropriate image in the whole', there is at least genius, and genius which promised a new dispensation.

"This suggests a second observation, that Macpherson, even more than Thomson, was unconscious of the trend of his effort towards Romanticism. Like the Lowlander he was attracted by the homiletic and rhetorical fashions, which not a few in England were already of opinion 'had been carried too far'. Isaac Taylor's dainty vignette on the title-page of *Temora*, with its Greekish hero, helmeted, and reclining as the gods do on Olympus, tells us how the author and artist interpreted their mission. The quaint protest in the 'Dissertation' which Macpherson prefixed to the piece shows, notwithstanding its hint of his sensitiveness to the situation, how thoroughly he failed to understand the true direction of his work. In answering, with a complacency so astounding that Johnson must have smiled, the 'absurd opinion' which 'appropriated' the 'compositions of Ossian' to 'the Irish nation', he describes the Irish poems as 'entirely writ in that romantic taste, which prevailed two ages ago'. . . . In every way, in the interests of his peculiar patriotism, and the originality of his work, he resisted Irish pretensions,—even to the renaming of Finn MacCoul (so known to Dunbar and every Scottish writer) as Fingal. Irish scholarship showed temper, and a triangular duel ensued between Scot, Englishman, and Irishman, to the increasing of Macpherson's credit not a little. Clearly, he had convinced himself that the *poems*—the 'original' documents of his affection—were immune from all romantic disease. Ten years later he actually threatened to impose the 'classical' couplet on his spasmodic prose. Europe, indifferent alike to his deceit and his wrong-headed criticism, thanked him, past the dreams of more ambitious bards, for his gift of Romance. If the mystery of his popularity becomes a little less mysterious when we knew how well prepared the public was, even in England, and as far back as the time of Temple's *Essay of Heroic Virtue*, how greedy that public had grown, and that the things which it coveted were not those which he offered with most ceremony, we may still be allowed to wonder, when we think of what Romanticism has meant since his day, how this impudent antiquarian fraud fared so well, and how men, by no means fools, came to believe that thus (as Gray said) 'Imagination dwelt many hundred years ago in all her pomp on the cold and barren mountains of Scotland'. So, in the third place, we may ask ourselves, are these poems Scottish in any other way than may be assumed by us from our knowledge of the nationality of their author and of their setting? Could we dispute their Hibernian origin had Macpherson called himself O'Flaherty and hailed from Dublin? We are almost tempted to ask, Could we have tracked him back to Caledonia had he disguised the names of his heroes and hills in Choctaw and had his poems published posthumously at the charges of the Smithsonian Institute? . . .

"It is easy to see why Europe found this unreality so real. The infinite melancholy of the Ossianic books, their sentiment and lyrical appeal, their Biblical sublimity of expression, were welcomed by writers, not so much as a revelation, as the first adequate satisfaction of a general yearning. The stranger Macpherson, bent on a Chattertonian frolic, had stumbled in their way. He seemed to give them what their passion for mystery and gloom and their eighteenth-century ennui demanded, an excuse, a place, a setting, for the freer exercise of imagination. Macpherson gave them, as Goethe has pointed out, 'ein vollkommen passendes Local' for this exercise, by taking them to far-away Thule with its *mise en scène* of heath, moss-grown grave-stones, wind-tossed grass, and lowering sky. Young France and Germany had been dreaming of adventure in the cloud-scapes of a spiritual twilight. In *Fingal* and *Temora* came the answer to the longing. Amid the imaginary mists of an imaginary Caledonia Macpherson's heroes fought and loved and lamented as a Chateaubriand, a Goethe, or a Lamartine craved. To each, as to the last,

> La harpe de Morven de mon âme est l'emblème;
> Elle entend de Cromla les pas de morts venir;
> Sa corde à mon chevet résonne d'elle-même
> Quand passe sur ses nerfs l'ombre de l'avenir.

"Here was Macpherson's triumph, and with it the beginning of Scotland's literary reputation throughout Europe. It mattered not that the general impression was confused, or the gratitude extravagant, or the universality of appeal overstated, when a French poet could identify his own mountains by the details of a Northern picture, and his own passion on the lips of Ossianic lovers. This welcome made the way easier to others whose task was to show the realities. Indeed, it may be doubted whether the true Scottish temper of the *Border Minstrelsy* and *Waverley* would have been so readily accepted had not Macpherson's pretty fiction put the world in such good humour with its 'Caledonians'." The present writer, however, boggles at the adjective "true" in the foregoing sentence, and the noun "realities" in the preceding one. While he does not doubt that *Ossian* paved the way for a readier acceptance of *Waverley* and the *Border Minstrelsy*, he doubts whether these do not also appertain to an imaginary Scotland, which has little or no relation to the actual fact. He objects, too, to the phrase "impudently conceived". Was Macpherson's indeed a deliberate antiquarian imposture? It is better simply to say that "the investigations that were set on foot by Sir John Sinclair and others sufficiently establish the fact that, long before the name of Macpherson was known to the literary world, a collection of poems in Gaelic did exist which passed as the poems of Ossian, and the publication of the Gaelic manuscripts at length settled the question of their authenticity in the minds of all unprejudiced persons. . . . That Macpherson, with the poetical fragments which he translated, took the liberty of adding to, transposing, or completing where he deemed it necessary, there can be no reason to doubt. On this point the Committee of the Highland Society reported that they were inclined to believe that he 'was in use to supply chasms, and to give connection, by inserting passages which he did not find, and to add what he conceived to be dignity and delicacy to the original composition, by striking out passages, by softening incidents, by refining the language, in short, by changing what he considered as too simple or too rude for a modern ear, and elevating what in his opinion was below the standard of good poetry. To what degree, however, he exercised these liberties it is impossible for the committee to determine.' And this is all that can now be said on the subject." It is certainly going far too far to say: "It was an unkind fate which compelled Macpherson to produce the goods. But the scholars demanded the 'originals', and late in life, as Professor W. P. Ker writes (in the *Cambridge History of English Literature*, vol. x, p. 230), 'he had to sit down in cold blood and make his ancient Gaelic poetry. He had begun with a piece of literary artifice, a practical joke; he ended with deliberate forgery, which, the more it succeeded, would leave him the less of what was really his due for the merits of the English Ossian.' "

These originals were not published posthumously at the charge of the Smithsonian Institute, but at Macpherson's own charge. At his death in 1796, he left to John Mackenzie of Figtree Court, London, £1000 to defray the expense of the publication of the originals of the whole of his translations, with directions to his executors for carrying that purpose into effect. Various causes contributed to delay their appearance till 1807, when they were published under the sanction of the Highland Society of London. It is, of course, the case that these "originals" were all in Macpherson's own handwriting or that of his amanuensis, and, if not simply translations into Gaelic of the poems originally written in English, at most records of what Macpherson obtained by oral communication.

The "originals" are well debated by Robert Chambers. "Macpherson", he writes, "has said that they are the originals, but this is all we have for it. He had a control over these documents which greatly lessens, if it does not wholly destroy all faith in them as evidences; while his interest in producing them must lay them open, under all circumstances, to the strongest suspicions. But it is said that it is not likely that he would be at the trouble of going through so laborious a process as this, merely to support an imposture—that, though willing, he was, from his want of skill in the Gaelic language, unfit for the task, and could not have produced poems in that language of such merit as those which he gave as originals—that the Gaelic poems are superior to the English—and lastly, that from impartial and critical examination, the former must have been anterior to the latter. With regard to the first of the assertions, it seems to be merely gratuitous, as it rests upon a question which Macpherson himself alone could determine, and can, therefore, be of no weight as an argument. That Macpherson was greatly deficient in critical knowledge of the Gaelic language, and that he could not consequently produce poems in that language of such merit as those which he represents as the originals of Ossian is certain, because it is established by the clearest evidence and by the concurring testimony of several eminent Gaelic scholars; but although he could not do this himself he could employ others to do it, and it is well known that he was intimate, and in close correspondence with several persons critically skilled in the Gaelic language, of whose services he availed himself frequently and largely when preparing his 'Translations'. Might he not have had recourse to the same aid in translating from the English to the Gaelic. . . . It is said that the Gaelic is superior to the English and that on an impartial and critical examination it appears that the former must have been anterior to the latter. Now, the first of these is again matter of opinion, and, as such, entitled to no more consideration than opinions generally deserve. To many their merits will appear on the whole pretty equal; to others, the Gaelic will, in some instances, seem the more beautiful; and in some, again, the English. The second assertion, however, is not of this description. It is not founded on opinion but on an alleged positive internal evidence. It is to be regretted, however, that that evidence had not been pointed out in more specific terms than those employed—that it had not been distinctly said what are those peculiar circumstances which, on a perusal, establish the relative ages of the Gaelic and English versions, for on an impartial and critical examination lately made by a person eminently skilled in the Gaelic language, it does not appear, at least from anything he could discover, that the Gaelic poems must, of necessity, have preceded the English. They certainly contain nothing that shows the contrary—nothing that discovers them to be of modern composition; but neither do Macpherson's English poems of Ossian. Neither of them betray themselves by any slip or inadvertency, and this, negative as it is, is yet all that can be said of both as to internal evidence. . . . The 'Originals' correspond exactly with the 'Translations', in language and indeed in every point. How can this be reconciled to the fact admitted by Macpherson himself, that he took certain liberties with the original Gaelic? The 'Originals', when published, might be expected to exhibit such differences with the 'Translations' as would arise from Mr Macpherson's labours as an emendator and purifier of the native ideas. But they do not exhibit any traces of such difference."

Certainly Macpherson knew how to keep his own counsel. If he obtained such assistance as is suggested above from persons skilled in the Gaelic, none of them ever admitted having assisted or been approached to assist, in such a task. Macpherson was a busy public man, but none of his intimates were, apparently, in a position to throw any light on the matter. And the "several eminent Gaelic scholars" referred to were at least in the extraordinary position of not knowing whether or not the Ossian originals existed in Scottish Gaelic literature. Macpherson refused to settle the matter, and, though Dr. Johnson might declare that "to revenge reasonable incredulity, by refusing evidence, is a degree of insolence, with which the world is not yet acquainted; and stubborn audacity is the last refuge of guilt", the fact remains that the British practice is to assume a man's innocence until he has been proven guilty, but here the whole attempt was to attach the onus of proof to Macpherson himself. He simply insisted that his translations were from authentic originals and left it to those who might suspect him of fraud to establish his guilt if they could. It was a natural and creditable attitude for him to take up—I had almost written "the right attitude"—and he adhered to it for thirty years, declaring that the charges against him gave him no concern, "since I have it always in my power to remove them", but promising to publish the originals in due time. This, to Chambers, was "pursuing exactly the course which an impostor would have done". It has not that significance to me, and I read with amusement the indignant sentences: "He was accused of being guilty of an imposition. He took no steps to rebut the charge. He was solicited to give proofs of the authenticity of the poems. He refused, and for upwards of thirty years submitted to wear the dress of a bankrupt in integrity, without making any attempt to get rid of it. He affected, indeed, a virtuous indignation, on all occasions, when the slightest insinuation was made that an imposition had been practised; and, instead of calmly exhibiting the proofs of his innocence, he got into a passion and thus silenced, in place of satisfying, inquiry."

But surely there is nothing very extraordinary in such an attitude when a man is confronted with accusations for which his accusers have no proof. Why should he satisfy persons who lacked the knowledge to entitle them to advance any such suspicions? Their floundering in the morass of impotent surmise may have amused him, and the vast European success of his work more than offset their malevolent gibing. I have referred earlier to the amount of falsification necessary in any case to get over anything Gaelic via English to the consciousness of Europe, and it is curious that, in a passage the significance of which I am inclined to think has been generally missed, Macpherson shows himself very much, and very bitterly, alive to that. It is at variance too with what Professor Gregory Smith says of his passionate concern to identify his work with Scotland and to resent Irish claims. In his preface to *Temora* he says: "If the poetry is good, and the characters natural and striking, it is matter of indifference whether the heroes were born in the little village of Angles, in Jutland, or natives of the barren heaths of Caledonia. That honour which nations derive from ancestors worthy or renowned is merely ideal. It may buoy up the minds of individuals, but it contributes very little to their importance in the eyes of others. But of all those prejudices which are incident to narrow minds, that which measures the merit of performances by the vulgar opinion concerning the country which produced them is certainly the most ridiculous. Ridiculous, however, as it is, few have the courage to reject it; and I am thoroughly convinced that a few quaint lines of a Roman or Greek epigrammatist, if dug out of the ruins of Herculaneum, will meet with more cordial and universal applause than all the most beautiful national rhapsodies of all the Celtic bards and Scandinavian skalds that ever existed."

If he wore for thirty years the disgraceful garb of a bankrupt in integrity he contrived to do so with no little equanimity and aplomb. There is a delightful incongruity in the thought of the greatest literary influence of his age acting as agent to Mohammed Ali Chan, Nabob of Arcot, and issuing several effective appeals to the public on behalf of that dusky potentate; and becoming M.P. for

Camelford in 1780, and being re-elected in 1784 and 1790. He was a silent member, but it is as odd to think of him as a worthy member of our legislative assembly as it would be to conceive of Shakespeare as M.P. for Stratford or of Burns as Secretary of State for Scotland. "Man in his time plays many parts", and it tickles my fancy to think of the pen that wrote *Fingal* inditing *The History and Management of The East India Company*, and writing on behalf of the Government pamphlets against the claims of the American colonists. "He also wrote a *Short History of the Opposition during the Last Session of Parliament* (1779). The merit of this production was so remarkable that it was, at the time, generally ascribed to the pen of Gibbon, a compliment which, however, it is very questionable if its real author appreciated." "In an evil hour for his literary reputation, Macpherson, with more confidence than wisdom, began a translation of the *Iliad* of Homer. This work he completed and gave to the world in 1773. Its reception was mortifying in the extreme. Men of learning laughed at it, critics abused it; and, notwithstanding some strenuous efforts on the part of his friends, particularly Sir John Elliot, it finally sank under one universal shout of execration and contempt.

"There is nothing", says Dr. Graham, "which serves to set Macpherson's character and powers in a stranger light than his egregious attempt to render the great father of poetry into prose, however natural it might have been for him to make this attempt, after his success in doing the same office to Ossian. The temerity of this attempt will not be deemed a little enhanced by the consideration that Pope's elegant translation was already before the world, nor will the awkwardness of its failure be thought lessened by a recollection of the sentiment its author himself expressed on another occasion, viz. that he 'would not deign to translate what he could not imitate, or even equal'."

Macpherson went his strange and industrious way, materially at least unaffected by his enemies, and died in opulent circumstances in Inverness-shire on 17th February 1796, at the age of fifty-eight. He directed by his will that his body should be taken to London and interred in Westminster Abbey. This was complied with, and he was buried in the Poets' Corner. Whatever the final verdict may be on the question of forgery, it is well to remember that no great Scottish writer has failed to display questionable, if not criminal, characteristics in regard to his personal character or in connection with his work, and that, even if the charges against Macpherson were fully proved, it would be entirely fitting that Scotland should impress itself most powerfully on the consciousness of Europe through the agency of an imposture, just as it is in perfect keeping that the genius responsible for such a phenomenon as *Ossian* should also pen *The Rights of Great Britain asserted against the Claims of the Colonies* and the *Letters from Mohammed Ali Chan, Nabob of Arcot, to the Court of Directors*.

NOTES

I.—It is a ridiculous state of affairs that the representation of Scottish poetry in anthologies and the discussion of it in literary histories and critical essays is invariably confined to poems written in Scots or English but leaves out of account work written in Gaelic and in Latin. Many of the best poets Scotland has produced have written in one or both of these two last-mentioned languages, and if it be inevitable that few readers nowadays can read them in the originals it is highly discreditable to Scottish Letters that excellent translations of their principal poems should not have been made long since and given their proper place in our anthologies, failing which no all-round view of Scotland's contribution to poetry can be had. Alas, it is only in keeping with the modern Scottish attitude to all the phases of our country's past inconvenient to Anglophily that much should be made of those who are relatively the veriest poetasters —Tannahill, Stevenson, Lang, and others—while, if it is remembered at all that in George Buchanan Scotland yielded the first Latin poet since Imperial Rome, and in Arthur Johnston one scarcely if at all his inferior, literary Scotland is content enough to take the matter on trust and make no attempt to explore their writings. Of Buchanan and Johnston it has been said: "It may be enough to prove the elegance and accuracy of Arthur Johnston's Latinity to say that his version of the 104th Psalm has frequently been compared with that of Buchanan, and that scholars are not unanimous in adjudging it to be inferior. As an original poet, he does not aspire to the same high companionship, though his compositions are pleasing and not without spirit. One curious particular concerning these two authors has been remarked by Dr. Johnson, from which it would appear that modern literature owed to the more distinguished of them a device very convenient for those whose powers of description were limited. When a rhymer protested his mistress resembled Venus, he, in fact, acknowledged his own incapacity to celebrate her charms, and gave instead a sort of catchword by means of which, referring back to the ancients, a general idea of female perfections might be obtained. This conventional language was introduced by Buchanan, 'who', says the critic just named, 'was the first who complimented a lady by ascribing to her the different perfections of the heathen goddesses; but Johnston', he adds, 'improved on this, by making his mistress at the same time free from their defects'." "Johnston", says another writer, "has been universally allowed to have been the more accurate translator, and few exceptions can be found to the purity of his language, while he certainly has not displayed either the richness or the majesty of Buchanan. Johnston is considered as having been unfortunate in his method: while Buchanan has luxuriated in an amazing variety of measure, Johnston has adhered to the elegiac couplet of hexameter and pentameter, except in the 119th Psalm, in which he has indulged in all the varieties of lyrical arrangement which the Latin language admits—an inapt choice, as Hebrew scholars pronounce that Psalm to be the most prosaic of the sacred poems." Tennant says: "Johnston is not tempted like Buchanan by his luxuriance of phraseology, and by the necessity of filling up, by some means or other, metrical stanzas of prescribed and inexorable length, to expatiate from the psalmist's simplicity, and weaken, by circumlocution, what he must needs beat out and expand. His diction is, therefore, more firm and nervous, and, though not absolutely Hebraean, makes a nearer approach to the unadorned energy of Jewry. Accordingly, all the sublime passages are read with more touching effect in his than in Buchanan's translation: he has many beautiful and even powerful lines, such as can scarce be matched by his more popular competitor, the style of Johnston possessing somewhat of Ovidian ease, accompanied with strength and simplicity, while the tragic pomp and worldly parade of Seneca and Prudentius are more affected by Buchanan."

II.—The lengths to which the academic habit of tracing literary influences can go—a habit that grows till its victims seem to do it almost unconsciously—is illustrated in Miss Janet Spens' recent book on Spenser's *Faerie Queen.* In a comparison between *Prince Arthur* and Marlowe's *Tamburlaine*, for example, in which she quotes Spenser's line

His glitter and armour shined far away,

she interrupts herself to say, for no reason but its own sake, "a line which may have suggested Milton's 'farre off his coming shone'", as though Milton had no mental capacities but assimilation. Lauder was by no means outstandingly bad in this respect; and as to his inventions of non-existent passages alleged to be in obscure books, there is surely little enough to draw between that crime and Victor Hugo's "Shakesperian defiance of historic fact" in writing *Marie Tudor*, since an analysis of the bibliography he gave for this play shows "that of the thirty-seven learned works he quotes he cannot have seen more than four or five at the most. And among the ones quoted are some laughable confusions, such as the *Panégyrique de Marie, reine de l'Angleterre*, which is a panegyric upon Mary, wife of William III. To swell his list he quotes as two separate works the English or French and Latin versions of one document. The erudition vanishes before a close scrutiny." In the case of *L'Homme qui rit*, "the sources chiefly used by Hugo were Chamberlayne's *Angliae Notitae* and *L'État présent de l'Angleterre*, and Beeverell's *Délices de la Grande Bretagne.* Anyone who will read the parallel passages of these two authors and what Hugo has made of them will be amazed at the trickery and ingenious adaptation of the sources."

III.—Several books (advancing different conclusions) on the causes of Milton's blindness have appeared recently. More to our point is to set alongside Lauder's the very different methods presently being employed by Professor Mutschmann of the University of Tartu (Dorpat), who has published two books on the subject. "For those who do not know the methods of Miltonic research employed by Professor Mutschmann, an imaginary analogy may perhaps serve as a suitable form of introduction. Suppose that Tennyson's ballad of *The Revenge* had never been written, or, if written, destroyed and never published, while plenty of evidence remained to show that

Tennyson contemplated writing such a historical poem and in the interests of historical accuracy studied closely the original accounts of the fight; suppose also that a critic having familiarised himself with those original accounts were, on reading Tennyson's *Relief of Lucknow* (which for the purpose of this analogy must be taken as later than any '*Revenge*' study of Tennyson's), to find such parallelisms in language in it and in *The Revenge* originals that he could declare that here was Tennyson writing of Lucknow with many of the very words which he must have thought of using when he was meditating on writing about the *Revenge*, it would be, as Dr. Mutschmann claims, a discovery of a most extraordinary kind. In this particular investigation Dr. Mutschmann is concerned mainly with the war in Heaven (*Paradise Lost*, VI), and with the documents open to Milton for a study of the story of the Armada, which, as he shows, was intended by Milton to form part of a projected but afterwards abandoned national epic. With this intention of Milton's in mind, he turns to the three or four pre-Miltonic writers who describe the great sea-fight, and by his method of watching for word-groups arrives at the conclusion that when writing long afterwards of the war in Heaven Milton used and adapted materials which he had collected in the first place for a treatment of the Armada. It is true that the celestial encounter is no longer a sea-fight and that the combatants are no longer Englishmen and Spaniards but spiritual beings: but enough can be detected, Dr. Mutschmann argues, to show how old materials stored in Milton's memory for one purpose were brought out from the treasury of his mind when the time came and repolished for another purpose. It is indeed a curious discovery: 'it may be safely maintained that there exists nothing in the whole range of English literature . . . that will furnish anything like the word-constellations brought forward'. Of course, as Dr. Mutschmann sees, it does not in the least detract from Milton's credit as a poet; but it throws an illuminating beam upon his mental processes and brings out the power which words and their connotations in association with one another had upon him. . . . It is hard to pass over one of the heroes of the Armada who—the name, not the meaning—survives *totidem literis* in *Paradise Lost*, VI, 215. In that line the word 'cope' is traced by Dr. Mutschmann to one Cope, who, according to a contemporary document in the British Museum, lost his life in the fighting; unless the reasoning is too far-fetched, it seems that he was to have figured in Milton's Armada as a proper man, and that he survives in *Paradise Lost*, the same in form, but utterly different in function, after the strangest of sea-changes."

EPILOGUE: THE STRANGE PROCESSION

IT was an element in him common to the vast majority of his brilliant countrymen that led David Hume, more than any other, to give its impetus to that movement in psychology and in philosophy of which, as McDougall has said, "no man can yet see the final issue" but of which at least one issue has been the scientific psychology of the present day. Here is Baldwin's estimate of Hume: "His psychology is one of those systems whose very radicalness and freedom from ambiguity make them typical and influential, not only positively, but as targets for the practice of riflemen generally". The concise and belligerent Scot! And, again, "In method he was an experimentalist, a positivist, admitting no intrusion from metaphysics, no dogmatic assumptions. His results were in a measure personal to him . . . but in his principles of association and habit, no less than in his sensational theory of knowledge, Hume worked out views which have been and still are of enormous importance." Hume must, indeed, be reckoned as one of the first and greatest of the prophets of modern psychology and in this respect too he is typical of his people, for, with the exception of literature and the arts, there is hardly a department of human knowledge and affairs in which Scotsmen have not played foremost rôles to a degree out of all proportion to the number of the Scottish people compared to that of many other nations.

But Hume was even more characteristic of his people in his experimentalism, his freedom from dogmatic assumptions. They have no use for any *a priori*; they are ready, it is the first law of their nature, to go from nowhere to anywhere at a moment's notice and their more or less accidental discoveries *en route* have been of incomparable moment to mankind. Restless, impelled by a universal curiosity, going off continually at all sorts of tangents, they turn up continually in the most unlikely quarters. It is this—and the wanderlust which is one of the outward expressions of their temperamental instability—which led to the old saying that when the Poles were reached Scotsmen would be found sitting at the tops of them. It is this in them which continually presents us in Scottish biography with achievements or evidences of interests so out of all keeping with the general run of their work as to be almost incredible as pertaining to the same individual. It is this that has led them in innumerable cases to the most surprising applications of knowledge obtained in one pursuit to other and apparently quite unconnected fields. An admirable example of this is the way in which Professor P. G. Tait, busy with the theory of brachistochrones, the phenomena of mirage, the theory of knots, and the foundations of the kinetic theory of gases, hit upon that discovery of the fundamental importance of "underspin" in determining the length of drive of a golf-ball and the accuracy of approach with well-played iron shots which threw a wonderful new light on the whole process of play, and taught the intelligent player how to improve his game.

All this may seem singularly out of keeping with that seriousness and Presbyterian rigour which is generally understood to have been the principal if not almost the only moulding force on modern Scottish mentality. But the facts show that this force has been enormously overrated—at least so far as the intelligent section of our people is concerned.

It must not be forgotten that the grim religiosity of our people found amongst us too its most irreconcilable and contemptuous enemies. It was a Scotsman, Thomas Gordon, who was mainly responsible for that weekly organ, *The Independent Whig*, of which Mr Murray says in his *Literary History of Galloway*: "It is a fortunate circumstance that this work is known only by name, for it is disfigured by sentiments which are deserving of great reprehension. It was more immediately directed against the hierarchy of the Church of England, but it was also meant, or at least has a direct tendency, to undermine the very foundation of a national religion, under any circumstances, and to bring the sacred profession, if not religion itself, into contempt. The sacerdotal office, according to this book, is not only not recommended in Scripture, but is unnecessary and dangerous; ministers of the gospel have ever been the promoters of corruption and ignorance, and distinguished by a degree of arrogance, immorality, and a thirst after secular power that have rendered them destructive of the public and private welfare of a nation. 'One drop of priestcraft', say the authors, 'is enough to contaminate the ocean'."

Despite Mr Murray's opinion, few students of history to-day would side against the view taken by these authors, and at least a third of the population of Scotland has now (on the admission of the General Assembly itself) no Church connection of any kind. Ludicrous examples of the restraints and prejudices against which knowledge in Scotland has had to labour abound on every hand. Typical is the Wernerian-Huttonian conflict in geology. One of the two chief protagonists was the great Scottish geologist, James Hutton (1726–97). Two impressive thoughts rise from Hutton's theory; the one is the immensity of time required to develop a landscape when progress is so slow that Roman roads are still traceable across British hills; the other is the inevitable end to which erosion seems to be tending, namely, the obliteration of all dry land. "From the top of the decaying Pyramids to the sea," says Hutton himself, in summarising his argument, "throughout the whole of this long course, we may see some part of the mountain moving some part of the way. What more can we wish? Nothing but time!" But there had to be a long-drawn-out battle before his conclusions could be established. "How bitter party feeling had been in the matter", we are told, "can now scarcely be credited—unless, as Lyell points out, allowance is made for the political circumstances of the time.

The French Revolution was an ever-present source of terror. Hutton's mechanical interpretation of the earth, and the glimpse that it gave into an immeasurable depth of time, seemed calculated to loosen the restraints of authority—and this was a danger that could not be tolerated!"

Happily Scotland has always been more than most countries productive of men on the other side—of completely radical spirits. One of these was the distinguished judge, Lord Gardenstone (1721–93), whose "political principles", we are told, "were always on the side of the people, and so far as may be gathered from his remarks, he would have practically wished that every man should enjoy every freedom and privilege which it might be consonant with the order of society to allow or which might with any safety be conceded to those who had been long accustomed to the restraints and opinions of an unequal government". These Safety First suggestions were not Lord Gardenstone's own; his attitude has in these phrases been very carefully qualified in a way upon which it would have been amusing to have heard this redoubtable lawyer's own view, since he had satirical gifts of a singular pungence and acuteness. An anonymous biographer, who seems to have been intimate with him, describes him as having expressed great contempt for the affectation of those who expressed disgust at the indelicacies of Horace or Swift, and it must certainly be allowed that, in his humorous fragments, he has not departed from the spirit of his precepts, or shown any respect for the feelings of these weaker brethren. Garden is a typical Scot in another respect; his failure to husband his gifts and order them to the best practical effect. "His *Travelling Memorandums*", we are told, "display the powers of a strongly thinking mind, carelessly strewed about on unworthy objects; the ideas and information are given with taste and true feeling, but they are so destitute of organisation or settled purpose that they can give little pleasure to a thinking mind searching for digested and useful information, and are only fit for those desultory readers who cannot, or like the author himself will not, devote their minds to any particular end.''

It is unfortunate that those who have so greatly revolutionised modern life or are still more greatly changing it should be of little or no interest to the vast majority of people as compared with royalties, politicians, stage and cinema stars, sports champions, and the like. It is not that their personalities are less interesting, but the attentions of the people are carefully kept in certain directions. A nation of football spectators and picture-house fans is far more easily controlled than would be one with a like passion for being *au fait* with science and speculative ideas. Any development of the general level of intelligence encounters foes far more formidable than those who feared the danger to established authority of the promulgation of Hutton's conceptions. The consequence is that the twentieth century is still populated (save for an infinitesimal minority) by Neolithic Man. "Only incidentally'', says Professor Knott, "do our scientific men of the past receive a passing notice from those who have earned our gratitude by rescuing from oblivion the national services, the heroic deeds, the quaint humour, and the kindly foibles of our predecessors. The developments of Science do not appeal to the multitude with the force and fascination of social and political changes, which are oft-times the outcome of an upheaval of human passions. History of an attractive kind still busies itself with the outstanding personalities of the age that is being depicted. Men and women who fill a large space in the shifting scenes of their time will always receive special homage from those who follow, and round their memories haloes of romance will gather and grow in the dimness of the receding past. The brilliant episodes and the pathetic tragedies which spring to mind with the mere mention of Queen Mary and of Prince Charlie never fail to command attention, especially when they can be linked with existing palace or castle, or even with the remains of an ancient keep. For these and other thrilling tales of long ago, and for lively pictures of life and manners changing with the centuries, we turn with absorbing interest to the pages of Robert Chambers's *Traditions*, Robert Louis Stevenson's *Picturesque Notes*, John Geddie's *Romantic Edinburgh*, Rosaline Masson's *Edinburgh*, and the like. Or we delight in those rich records of the past which are poured forth in inexhaustible profusion by the great Sir Walter in such of his tales as touch on Edinburgh life. Yet Sir Walter Scott, President though he was for twelve years of the Royal Society of Edinburgh, found no occasion to refer to the scientific aspects of the life of his native city, except when, as 'Malachi Malagrowther', he wrote on questions of currency. In his *Journal* he speaks of a meeting of the Council of the Royal Society convened to consider the question of allowing Robert Knox to read an anatomical paper at the very time when public feeling ran high over the Burke and Hare revelations. In his novels Scott is content to introduce those picturesque purveyors of pseudo-science, the astrologer and the alchemist; and even the honest-minded Antiquary is made the butt of genial persiflage. If Sir Walter Scott so neglected the scientific side of Edinburgh society, what can we expect in the works of other writers?"

Many other Scottish writers had, like Scott himself, their own scientific interests, however. R. L. Stevenson's paper on *The Thermal Influence of Forests* is, unfortunately, not nearly so well known as his *Treasure Island*; and few of his admirers associate with the author of the *Confessions of an English Opium-Eater* his *Logic of Political Economy* (also described as *Prolegomena to all Future Systems of Political Economy*), which De Quincey wrote during his residence in Edinburgh. The propensities of the mob are perhaps to any interest in science and scientists as the cheap jokes, the broad obvious humour, of the English to our subtle Scottish wit. At all events it requires something other than the vulgar taste to appreciate, say, John Bell's account (the first account given) of the effects produced by paralysis of the seventh nerve (Bell's palsy): "It appears that whenever the action of any of the muscles of the face is associated with the act of breathing, it is performed through the operation of this respiratory nerve, or *portio dura.* I cut a tumour from before the ear of a coachman. A branch of the nerve which goes to the angle of the mouth was divided. Some time after he returned to thank me for ridding him of a formidable disease, but complained that he could not whistle to his horses."

It demands an old Scottish delight in words (a characteristic that is one of the most marked in our history and has produced among us an exceedingly curious and extensive literature of its own) to delight in coming upon facts such as the following: "It will convince any one of the continuity of geological thought from the seventeenth century onwards to find George Sinclair (Professor of Mathematics and Philosophy at Glasgow University for twenty years and author of a short *History of Coal* as part of a work entitled *The Hydrostaticks*, 1672) using the words 'cropp', 'dipp', 'rise', and 'streek', with the same meaning, though not the same spelling, as holds good to-day. Moreover, he employs the terms 'gae', 'dyke', or 'trouble', just as Scots miners still do, to cover both the 'dykes' *and* the 'faults' of modern text-books. He also speaks familiarly of the 'Great Seam' of Midlothian. And, finally, when he refers to clays and shales, it is by their Scots name, 'tilles', which, with restricted application, had found its way into the glacial literature of the world. Sinclair understood thoroughly the geometry of an ordinary faulted coal-basin. As regards 'gaes', he cites the experience of the coal-hewers that the direction of inclination of the 'vise' or 'weyse' shows the side on which the coal will be found to be 'down'. As regards dip, he agrees with those who contend that dip, unless interrupted by a gae, continues to a centre, where the coal, or whatever it may be, 'takes a contrary course' which brings it up once again to the 'grass'. This proposition he applies to the Midlothian basin, boldly accepting a hypothesis that carried him in imagination 3000 feet below the limit of his experience. What appealed to him was the fact that he could follow the outcrop of the Great Seam fairly satisfactorily round the landward margin of the basin."

It may seem a matter in which, like Lord Balmuto with the point of most of Erskine's witticisms, we may not "see the joke" that (to refer to a few subsequent Scottish geologists) "Peach observed minute organisms in certain Arenig-Llandeilor cherts, and these were shown to be radiolaria by Professor Nicholson and Dr. Hinde; Macconochie and Tait found fish remains in Downtonian shales, and these placed in Traquair's system 'opened out to us a new vista in the field of palaeozoic ichthyology'." But when we think of the hosts of Scots making like discoveries in all the sciences, of all the Scottish scientists of the very first importance in their various departments, and of the extent to which Scottish science and invention is responsible for the amazing changes in the organisation, methods, and ideas of the world to-day, it is impossible to deny that without taking into view the scientific aspect we omit one of the major elements of Scottish genius and necessarily relapse upon a hopelessly false view of the nature, functions, and values of our national psychology. Even the broadest human appeal is not lacking—as in the fact that that tremendous genius, the discoverer of the electro-magnetic field, Clerk-Maxwell, was known at Edinburgh University as "Dafty Maxwell"; that John Law of Lauriston, once the most famous man in the world, the Napoleon of Finance, was sentenced to death at twenty-one for killing another man in a duel; or that Adam Smith, the author of the *Wealth of Nations*, began life by being stolen by gipsies.

It is, however, when we think of the great groups of Scottish scientists at various times that, in this pre-eminently scientific age, we are forced to consider the present state of affairs. Let us take psychology, say.

"What a galaxy of psychological talent is represented in the Edinburgh of Hume's and the following generations. David Hume himself, Adam Smith, Lord Kames, Adam Ferguson, Dugald Stewart, Thomas Brown, John Abercrombie, Sir William Hamilton, George Combe—all these were Edinburgh men by birth, or by adoption, and all were notable in the history of modern psychology. James Mill was a student at the University of Edinburgh, as were also both the Darwins, Erasmus and Charles, James Braid, W. B. Carpenter, and Thomas Laycock. Many of these names stand high among the representatives of other thought developments; but their position is also secure in the records of British psychology. . . . The exact position of the Scottish School in the development of modern psychology is worthy of special notice. Perhaps the leading characteristic of the Scottish School was that all its representatives, carrying on the tradition of Locke, attempt to base a metaphysical and ethical philosophy on a psychological foundation, in contradistinction to the German school of thought—Leibniz, Kant, Hegel, and their followers and successors—the representatives of which deduced a psychology from their metaphysical principles. As a result of this fundamental characteristic the Scottish School developed introspective psychology to the highest pitch, and this introspective psychology may be said to have become the orthodox psychology, not merely in Britain, but also abroad, and more especially in France."

Glance at another sequence of Great Scotsmen in a different department of science altogether. "Most distinctive of the product of Edinburgh University is the series of naturalist travellers who have left her walls to gather knowledge in the ends of the earth. Some gathered nature knowledge by the way, their minds set on other pursuits—Mungo Park, James Bruce, William Baikie, William Scoresby in the Arctic regions, Alexander Dalrymple in the Southern Seas. But to others natural history was a chief end, and they added many pages to the book of zoological knowledge. The Franklin expeditions were staffed by Edinburgh naturalists; John Macgillivray sailed for Torres Straits and the East Archipelago in 1842 as naturalist on the 'Fly', and his life was made up of a succession of exploring expeditions; William Spiers Bruce laboured in both Arctic and Antarctic regions and by his 'Scotia' Expedition (1902–4) added perhaps more than any other to our knowledge of the animal life of the far southern Atlantic and western Antarctic seas. Then there have been J. Graham Kerr's South American explorations and Nelson Annandale's surveys of the peninsula of Siam and of typical Asiatic lakes . . ." The list could be extended indefinitely.

A glance at Agriculture is particularly useful at the moment when the relations of Scotland to England are again in debate. "Macintosh's well-known *Essay on the Ways and Means for Inclosing, Fallowing, Planting, etc. Scotland* (1729) consists, for the most part, in an attempt to persuade Scottish landowners and farmers to adopt English methods; and he recommends, among other things, the bringing north of a battalion of 640 skilled English labourers who were to instruct his countrymen in the arts of husbandry. Nearly all the early improvers were men of the landlord class who had travelled in England, and their improvements consisted mainly in attempts, sometimes rather slavish and undiscerning, to imitate the practices of the South. Progress in Scottish agriculture was concurrent with the general economic and intellectual development of the country, and was astonishingly rapid. No widespread or general improvement took place till after the '45, yet by 1800 a complete revolution had been effected in the Lothians, and in the remoter districts rapid progress was being made. It is a sufficient commentary on the relative progress of Scottish and English agriculture during this period to mention that, less than a century after Macintosh wrote, Cobbett was complaining of the multitude of Scotch bailiffs who had overrun England." To-day Scotland is much under-populated; it looks as though (indeed experiments are already taking place to that end) a determined attempt will be made to settle colonies of the English unemployed on Scottish land.

What an amazing, if gruesome, story the history of the provision of human bodies for the purposes of science in Scotland would make! "The body of a single malefactor in the year failed to meet the needs of the growing School of Anatomy in Edinburgh, and the Town Council made a further grant of 'these bodies that dye in the correction house' and 'the bodies of foundlings that dye upon the breast . . . for the encouragement of so necessary a work as the improving of Anatomy'. Later, yet another demand was made, for 'the bodies of foundlings who die betwixt the time that they are weaned and their being put to schools or trades; also the dead bodies of such as are stifled in the birth, which are exposed and have none to own them; also the dead bodies of such as are *felo de se*, and likewise such as are put to death by sentence of the magistrate, and have none to own them'. In granting this last request the Town Council made it conditional on the Corporation building an anatomical theatre and publicly holding in it once a year 'ane anatomical dissection as much as can be shown upon one body'." The first public dissection took place in 1703.

The roving eye looking hither and thither over this vast expanse of our crowded and too little surveyed national life hits upon many an eccentric figure, ludicrous incident, strange fact, heroic effort. There is Edward Sang who devoted the greater part of a long and active life to logarithmic calculations. He calculated to as many as twenty-eight figures the logarithms of all prime numbers up to 10,037, and a few beyond, and from these, with the help of his daughters, he constructed a great table of logarithms to fifteen figures, with first and second differences for all integers from 100,000 to 370,000. The natural limitations of life prevented him carrying on to the million, as originally intended. The forty manuscript books containing these logarithms were presented to the British nation and are now in the custody of the Royal

Society of Edinburgh for use and reference. Professor John Leslie's famous experiment in which water is made to boil at a low pressure and temperature, and by its rapid evaporation becomes cooled and frozen—in other words, freezes in the very act of boiling—which requires that the partial vacuum in which the evaporation is being promoted must be kept dry, for which purpose roasted oatmeal was first used, led Christopher North in the *Chaldee Manuscript* to describe Leslie as a "cunning spirit, which hath his dwelling in the secret places of the earth, and hath command over the snow and the hail, and is as a pestilence to the poor man; for when he is hungry he lifteth up the lid of his meal-girnel to take out meal, and lo! it is full of strong ice!"

Among eccentric figures there is Charles Piazzi Smyth (1819–1900), the Astronomer-Royal, "with red fez on his head, and an extraordinary rhetorical manner. His micrometrical measurements of gaseous spectra and his visual solar spectrum (1884) are illustrated by magnificent coloured plates of spectra of high dispersion arranged according to a scale expressing the number of wavelengths to the inch. This unusual mode of representation has seriously diminished their usefulness for other investigators. It was also Piazzi Smyth who drew special attention to the predictive value of the rain-band in the yellow region of the solar spectrum. The rock thermometers on the Calton Hill installed by J. D. Forbes engaged Piazzi Smyth's close attention. He found indication of a cycle of change corresponding to the eleven-year cycle of sunspots. On the meaning of the Great Pyramid and the sacredness of the English inch, Smyth was a sublime 'paradoxer' in De Morgan's meaning of the term. His extraordinary style of composition is displayed in all his papers, but in none so appositely as in his picturesque obituary of Leverrier, the brilliant but intensely autocratic French Astronomer." The essay of Sir James Young Simpson—the discoverer of chloroform and its introducer into obstetric practice—on Hermaphroditism in Scotland is perhaps the only article yet written on this curious subject. He also wrote on leprosy in Scotland. It was a Scottish medico too who in London disposed of the pretensions of Mrs Maria Tofts, who had for some time imposed even upon educated people by pretending every now and again to have an accouchement at which she brought forth no human progeny but litters of rabbits! And sight should certainly not be lost (see *The Russian Journals of Martha and Catherine Wilmot*, 1803–1808) of still another Scottish medico—Dr. John Rogerson, Physician to the Russian Court, of whom Catherine II said that "to put oneself in Rogerson's hands is to be a dead man", and of whom the story is told that he played whist so badly that a Russian noble once ordered the cannons to fire whenever he revoked in the course of the game!

Scotsmen have been responsible for important inventions in every direction—Henry Bell with the first sea-going steam-boat; James Watt "fathering" the steam-engine; Andrew Meikle, inventor of the threshing mill; William Murdoch, inventor of coal-gas lighting; Kirkpatrick McMullen, converting the hobby-horse into the pedal cycle; Sir Charles Stuart-Menteith making railway travel easier in its early days with his simple device of the flange on engine and coach wheels; Neilson and his "hot blast"; Nasmyth and his steam hammer; Dr. Patrick Bell and the first practical reaping machine complete with binder; James Small and the swing plough; Andrew Graham Bell and the telephone . . . and scores of others right down to to-day and J. L. Baird with his television.

Particularly interesting is John Clerk of Eldin. In a fragment of an intended life of Clerk, published in the *Transactions of the Royal Society of Edinburgh*, Professor Playfair remarks that Clerk was one of those men (whom the present author has already remarked have been notably numerous in Scotland) who have carried great improvements into professions not properly their own. Playfair shows how in many professions the individual regularly bred to it is apt to become blindly habituated to particular modes of procedure, and thus is unfitted for suggesting any improvement in it, while a man of talent, not belonging to it, may see possibilities of improvement and instruct those who are apt to think themselves beyond instruction. "Mr Clerk", he says, "was precisely the kind of man by whom a successful inroad into a foreign territory was likely to be made. He possessed a strong and inventive mind, to which the love of knowledge and the pleasure derived from the acquisition of it were always sufficient motives for application. *He had naturally no great respect for authority, or for opinions, either speculative or practical, which rested only on fashion or custom.* He had never circumscribed his studies by the circle of things immediately useful to himself; and was more guided in his pursuits by the inclinations and capacities of his own mind and less by circumstances than any man I have ever known. Thus it was that he studied the surface of the land as if he had been a general, and the surface of the sea as an admiral, though he had no direct connection with the profession either of the one or of the other."

A fortunate instinct directed his mind to naval affairs before he had seen a ship or even the sea at a less distance than four or five miles. This interest developed steadily through model ships constructed by himself and the study of Robinson Crusoe and books of sea-voyages generally. The upshot was Mr Clerk made himself very extensively and accurately acquainted with both the theory and practice of naval tactics and in the solitude of his country house where after dinner he would get up a mimic fight with bits of cork upon the table he discovered the grand principle of attack, which Bonaparte afterwards brought into such successful practice by land—that is to say, he saw the absurdity of an attacking force extending itself over the whole line of the enemy, by which the amount of resistance became everywhere as great as the force of attack, when it was possible, by bringing the force to bear upon a particular point, and carrying that by an irresistible weight, to introduce confusion and defeat over the whole. Mr Clerk, whose essay on Naval Tactics was not published for sale (though a few copies had previously been struck off and distributed privately) till 1790, thus conceived, on land and without the least experience of sea life (he never enjoyed any longer sail than to the Isle of Arran in the Firth of Clyde), the manœuvre of breaking the line at a period antecedent to the time that idea was put into practice, and his system became a guide to all the operations of the British Navy subsequent to the particular victory in 1782 in which, under Lord Rodney, it first seemed to be acted upon.

So much for a glimpse of the great and varied parade of Scottish scientists throughout the generations. Nothing has been said of Scotland's soldiers of fortune, prominent in all the great European armies, or of its wandering scholars found in every European university; nor does space permit any account of these. Scottish destinies were entangled in an extraordinary way with every aspect of European affairs for centuries, and one of the results of that—if it was not rather one of the causes of this international adventuring—was the Scot's splendid linguistic facility. Countless Scots throughout several centuries were multi-lingual, and in the rapid acquiring, and proficiency in, foreign tongues Scots have always been greatly superior to the English. I do not know that Scots to-day have much multi-linguistic faculty. They are not nearly so actively and intimately bound up with Europe as they were before our modern days of so-called internationalism which has substituted newspaper tittle-tattle of foreign countries for the old close vital connection and actual experience in them in a better capacity than mere tourists. It is needless to rehearse a list of Scots adept in five, ten, fifteen languages. The Admirable Crichton, who died at twenty-two years of age, knew twelve different languages. But James Bonaventura Hepburn, of the Order of the Minims, knew no fewer than seventy-two. We have among these the Cussian, the Virgilian, the Hetruscan, the Saracen, the Assyrian, the Armenian, the Syro-Armenian, the Gothic, and also the Getic, the Scythian, and the Moeso-Gothic, according to Dr. George Mackenzie's account in his *Lives of Scottish Writers*. Then he leaves such modern labourers as Champolion and Dr. Young deeply in the shade for his knowledge of the Coptic, the Hieroglyphic, the Egyptian, the Mercurial Egyptiac, the Isiac-Egyptiac, and the Babylonish. He then turns towards the Chaldaic, the Palestinian, the Turkish, the Rabbinical, the German Rabbinical, the Galilean, the Spanish-Rabbinical, the Afro-Rabbinical, and what seems the most appropriate tongue of all, the "Mystical".[1] Gradually the biographer rises with the dignity of his subject and begins to leave the firm earth. He proceeds to tell us how Hepburn wrote in the "Noahic", the "Adamean", the "Solomonic", the "Mosaic", the "Hulo-Rabbinic", the "Seraphic", the "Angelical", and the "Supercelestial". "Now", continues Mackenzie, with much complacency at the successful exhibition he has made of our countrymen's powers, but certainly with much modesty considering their extent, "these are all the languages (and they are the most of the whole *habitable world*) in which our author has given us a specimen of his knowledge, and which evidently demonstrates that he was not only the greatest linguist of his own age, but of any age that has been since the creation of the world, and may be reckoned amongst those prodigies of mankind that seem to go beyond the ordinary limits of nature."

There is an exception, however, to the Scot's facility in the acquisition of foreign tongues. Sir John Malcolm tells how when John Leyden, another Scot of singularly varied genius and accomplishment, arrived in Calcutta in 1805, "I entreat you, my good friend," I said to him, "to be

[1] Perhaps Mackenzie may in naming this alphabet have had some confused idea in his mind of an arrangement of the celestial bodies, by alternate contortion, into something resembling the letters of the Hebrew alphabet, followed by some of the worshippers of the secret sciences. The arrangement was called the celestial alphabet.

careful of the impression you make on your entering this community; for God's sake learn a little English, and be silent upon literary subjects except among literary men". "Learn English!" he exclaimed, "No, never; it was trying to learn that language that spoilt my Scotch; and as to being silent I will promise to hold my tongue, if you will make fools hold theirs."

The intromissions of the Scots with all nations, with every department of arts and affairs, and with all the languages of men and of angels being of the kind that has been indicated in the foregoing paragraphs, it is not surprising to find that they have some exceedingly curious ideas about themselves and their own country. It is impossible to give any comprehensive account of these views and the peculiar and little-known literature in which they are embodied here, but as a sample of the rest reference may be made to the beliefs of John Pinkerton, a voluminous historian and critic (1758–1825).

In 1787 he produced *A Dissertation on the Origin of the Scythians or Goths*. In the compilation of this small treatise, he boasts of having employed himself eight hours per day for one year in the examination of classical authors: the period occupied in consulting those of the Gothic period, whom he found to be "a mass of superfluity and error", he does not venture to limit. This production was suggested by his reading for his celebrated account of the early history of Scotland, and was devised for the laudable purpose of proving that the Celtic race was more degraded than the Gothic, as a prefatory position to the arguments maintained in that work. He accordingly shows the Greeks to have been a Gothic race, in as far as they were descended from the Palasgi, who were Scythians or Goths, and, by a similar progress, he showed the Gothic origin of the Romans. Distinct from the general account of the progress of the Goths, which is certainly full of information and acuteness, he had a particular object to gain, in fixing on an island formed by the influx of the Danube, in the Euxine Sea, termed by the ancient geographers "Peuke" and inhabited by Peukini. From this little island, of the importance of which he produced many highly respectable certificates, he brings the Peukini along the Danube, whence, passing to the Baltic, they afterwards appear in Scotland as the Picts or Pechts. In 1790 appeared his *Inquiry into the History of Scotland, preceding the Reign of Malcolm III, or* 1056. This work contained a sort of concentration of all his peculiarities. It may be said to have been the first work which thoroughly sifted the great "Pictish question", the question whether the Picts were Goths or Celts. In pursuance of his line of argument in the progress of the Goths, he takes up the latter position; and in the minds of those who have no opinions of their own, and have consulted no other authorities, by means of his confidence and his hard terms he may be said to have taken the point by storm. But he went further in his proofs. It was an undoubted fact that the Scots were Celts, and all old authorities bore that the Scots had subdued the Picts. This was something which Pinkerton could not patiently contemplate; but he found no readier means of overcoming it than by proving that the Picts conquered the Scots; a doctrine founded chiefly on the natural falsehood of the Celtic race, which prompted a man of sense, whenever he heard anything asserted by a Celt, to believe that the converse was the truth.

His numberless observations on the Celts are thus pithily brought to a focus: "Being mere savages, but one degree above brutes, they remain still in much the same state of society as in the days of Julius Caesar; and he who travels among the Scottish Highlanders, the old Welsh, or wild Irish, may see at once the ancient and modern state of women among the Celts when he beholds these savages stretched in their huts, while their poor women toil like beasts of burden for their unmanly husbands". And he thus draws up a comparison betwixt these unfortunates and his favourite Goths. "The Lowlanders are acute, industrious, sensible, erect, free; the

Highlanders, indolent, slavish, strangers to industry. The former have, in short, every attribute of a civilised people; the latter are absolute savages; and like Indians and negroes, will ever continue to be. All we can do is to plant colonies among them, and by this, and encouraging their emigration, try to get rid of the breed."

Pinkerton scoffed at any claim put in for Celtic merit. He would call on the company to name a Celt of eminence. "If one mentioned Burke——" observes a late writer ". . . What?" said he, "a descendant of de Bourg? Class that high Norman chivalry with the riffraff of O's and Mac's? Show me a great O', and I am done."

He delighted to prove that the Scottish Highlanders had never had but a few great captains, such as Montrose, Dundee, and the first Duke of Argyle—and these were all Goths—the first two Lowlanders; the last a Norman, a "*De Campo Bello*."

William Cleland (1661–89), the troubadour of the Covenanters, had no better opinion of the Highland host, judging by this Hudibrastic satire on their expedition of 1678:

> Some might have judged they were the creatures
> Call'd selfies, whose customs and features
> Paracelsus doth descry
> In his occult philosophy,
> Or faunes, or brownies, if ye will,
> Or satyrs, come from Atlas hill;
> Or that the three-tongued tyke was sleeping
> Who had the Stygian door a-keeping:
> Their head, their neck, their legs and thighs
> Are influenced by the skies;
> Without a clout to interrupt them.
> They need not strip them when they whip them
> Nor loose their doublet when they're hanged
>
> . . . . .
>
> But those who were their chief commanders,
> As such who love the pirnie standards,
> Who led the van and drove the rear,
> Were right well mounted of their gear;
> With brogues, and trews, and pirnie plaids
> And good blue bonnets on their heads
> Which on the one side had a flipe

Adorned with a tobacco-pipe,
With dirk, and snap-work, and snuff-mill;
A bag which they with onions fill,
And, as their strict observers say,
A tasse horn filled with usquebay.
A slashed-out coat beneath the plaids,
A targe of timber, nails, and hides;
With a long two-handed sword,
As good's the country can afford—
Had they not need of bulk and bones
Who fight with all these arms at once?
It's marvellous how in such weather
O'er hill and moss they came together;
How in such storms they came so far.
The reason is, they're smeared with tar;
Which doth defend them, heel and heck,
Just as it doth their sheep protect.

. . . . .

Nought like religion they retain,
Of moral honesty they're clean,
In nothing they're accounted sharp
Except in bagpipe and in harp.
For a misobliging word
She'll durk her neighbour o'er the boord,
And then she'll flee like fire from flint.
She'll scarcely ward the second dint.
If any ask her of her thrift
Forsooth, her *nainsell* lives by theft!

If, finally, I were asked to fix upon what to my mind is the best description of a typical Scot I would hesitate between two. The first of these is the impecunious, alcoholic James Tytler—author of some beautiful Scots songs, dabbling in the manufacture of magnesia, experimenting with balloon-flying, compiling a Grammar, a System of Surgery, and other entirely unrelated works, retreating hastily to Ireland and thence to America when cited to answer a charge of sedition. When living in a slum garret in Edinburgh he was visited by a gentleman who, having heard of the extraordinary stock of general knowledge Mr Tytler possessed and with what ease he could write on any subject almost extempore, was anxious to procure as much matter as would form a junction between a certain history and its continuance to a later period. An old crone told him he could not see Tytler as he had gone to bed the worse of liquor. "Determined, however, not to depart without accomplishing his errand, he was shown into Mr Tytler's apartment by the light of a lamp, where he found him in the situation described by the landlady. Being acquainted with the nature of the visit, Mr Tytler called for pen and ink, and in a short time produced about a page and a half of letter-press which answered the end as completely as if it had been the result of the most mature deliberation, previous notice, and a mind undisturbed by any liquid capable of deranging its ideas." In a small mean room, amidst the squalling and squalor of a number of children, on other occasions this singular genius stood at a printer's case (his press was of his own manufacture, too, being "wrought in the direction of a smith's bellows") composing pages of types, either altogether from his own ideas, or perhaps with a volume before him, the language of which he was condensing by a mental process little less difficult. In this way he accomplished the first volume of an abridgement of that colossal work, the Universal History!

The second is Fletcher of Saltoun, of whom the Earl of Buchan says that "Fletcher was uniform and indefatigable in his parliamentary conduct, continually attentive to the rights of the people, and jealous, as every friend of his country must be, of their invasion by the King and his Ministers, for it is as much the nature of kings and ministers to invade and destroy the rights of the people, as it is of foxes and weasels to rifle a poultry yard and destroy the poultry. All of them, therefore, ought to be muzzled." Lockhart says: "The idea of England's domineering over Scotland was what his generous soul could not endure. The indignities and oppression Scotland lay under galled him to the heart, so that, in his learned and elaborate discourses, he exposed them with undaunted courage and pathetic eloquence. He was blessed with a soul that hated and despised whatever was mean and unbecoming a gentleman, and was so steadfast to what he thought right that no hazard or advantage—

not the universal empire, nor the gold of America—could tempt him to yield or desert it. And I may affirm that in all his life, he never once pursued a measure with the least prospect of anything by end to himself, nor further than he judged it for the common benefit and advantage of his country. He was master of the English, Latin, Greek, French, and Italian languages, and well versed in history, the civil law, and all kinds of learning. He had a pentrating, clear, and lively apprehension but so exceedingly wedded to his own opinions, that there were few he could endure to reason against him, and did for the most part closely and unalterably adhere to what he advanced, which was frequently very singular, that he'd break with his party before he'd alter the least jot of his scheme and maxims. He was no doubt an enemy to all monarchical governments; but I do very well believe his aversion to the English and the Union was so great that in revenge to them he'd have sided with the royal family. But, as that was a subject not fit to be entered upon with him, this is only a conjecture from some innuendoes I have heard him make. So far is certain, he liked, commended, and conversed with high flying tories more than any other set of men, acknowledging them to be the best countrymen, and of most honour and integrity."

In conclusion, John Barclay in 1614 published his *Icon Animarum*. "It is", we read, "a delineation of the genius and manners of the European nations, with remarks, moral and philosophical, on the various tempers of men. It is pleasant to observe that in this work he does justice to the Scottish people." I do not know any subsequent writer who has attempted to do so, and assuredly no one has succeeded.

It is a strange, extremely diversified, highly dramatic procession this, through the centuries, of the Scottish people who, amongst all their other achievements, invented the symbolical figure of John Bull, wrote the British National Anthem, founded the Bank of England, and, at the period in which I write, have provided both the Archbishop of Canterbury and the Archbishop of York and given the United Kingdom still another Scottish Prime Minister; for, as George Blake says, however dull the great mass of Anglo-Scots may be, ever and again there comes breaking through "the demoniac strain that is in all Scots, that makes them demons in their cups and terrors before the Lord on the Rugby field; it comes streaking in scarlet threads across the hodden grey of the national life continually; we keep throwing up characters to make even the adventurous English feel hearth-bound and hen-pecked". Here's to us! Wha's like us?

Here's a health to them that's awa',
Here's a health to them that's awa';
And wha winna wish gude luck to our cause
May never gude luck be their fa'.
It's gude to be merry and wise,
It's gude to be honest and true;
It's gude to support Caledonia's cause,
And bide by the buff and the blue.

Here's freedom to them that wad read,
Here's freedom to them that wad write.
There's nane ever fear'd that the truth should be heard
But them whom the truth 'ud indite.

Here's timmer that's red at the heart,
Here's fruit that's sound at the core;
And may he that wad turn the buff and blue coat
Be turned to the back o' the door.

Here's friends on baith sides o' the firth,
And friends on baith sides o' the Tweed;
And wha wad betray old Albion's right
May they never eat of her bread!

It was a true Scot—since all true Scots must be achieving or claiming to be achieving the impossible—to whom an American was showing the Niagara Falls. The Scot was quite unimpressed by the spectacle and the American could awaken no spark of interest in him till he declared that he had seen a man swim up the Falls. "Ay", said the Scot, "That man was me!"

THE CALEDONIAN ANTISYZYGY

"Gott bewahre die aufrechte Schotten."

WHEN a friend of mine heard that I was writing a book on Scottish eccentrics, he said: "Ha, A sort of Dictionary of Scottish National Biography, I presume".

"I admit that we are a most peculiar people," I replied, "But what I am concerned with is simply the fact that such a Dictionary would reveal extraordinary contradictions of character, most dangerous antinomies and antithetical impulses, in the make-up of almost every distinguished Scot, though nowadays these seem to have been relegated to very trivial parts of contemporary Scots personalities, and no longer affect their public work, either in arts or affairs, to anything like the same extent as they did throughout centuries of our history—phases and centuries of our history practically wholly excluded from the present official narrative. Despite the general mask of respectability, however, and all that is said of modern standardisation and the comparative absence of great men nowadays, I think this complicated kink, this lightning-like zig-zag of temper, exists among us as frequently as ever and is perhaps more insidious and widespread in its influence behind the almost impenetrable concealment that has been imposed upon it, or assumed. The general concept of the typical Scot has undergone a very remarkable change (though, to the extent to which we Scots ourselves are responsible for or party to it, that change may itself be only another exemplification of this peculiar working of our national genius). The word "canny" (the main and almost all the subordinate senses of which are best covered by "far ben") has changed its significance—or rather lost all its former very subtle meanings—and become synonymous with gentle or cautious or thrifty. It is in these senses that people now speak of "the canny Scot".

We are regarded for the most part as a very dour, hard-headed, hard-working, tenacious people, devoted to the practical things of life and making little or no contribution to the more dazzling or debatable spheres of human genius. True there are still a few points at which this myth fails to cover very obvious facts. We still drink too much, with drinking habits very different from the sociable beer-swilling of our English friends. M. Benjamin Crémieux has recently put it: "I shall not easily forget the rush of the bourgeois Scottish intellectuals towards the bottles of sherry and whisky. This violent taste for alcohol always remains rather mysterious to a Frenchman from south of the Loire, where people drink brandy and *fine champagne* much as they smell a flower." But M. Crémieux went on to say: "I searched in vain on Saturday afternoon in Glasgow during a greyhound race for something that might distinguish it from a similar gathering in London". Yet we retain, in addition to whisky and our divers "twangs", a certain wild hooching and abandon in our dancing, the time-honoured picturesqueness of our tartans, and the terrible skirling of our pipes; but these do not enliven the general tenor of our lives to any great extent and matter little for practical purposes. They are really curious survivals, strange foibles, and their retention is of little account so long as in all really important respects we are almost wholly assimilated to the English. On the whole, the world thinks it knows where it has us, and, as a recent Whig historian has said, believes (despite the emergence of a handful of extremists among us in recent years and sensational rumours, which seem to have little behind them, of Scottish separatist and Sinn Fein societies) that, though Scotland "has problems to cope with as grave as any which can be found elsewhere, that a unique catastrophe lies around the corner, brought about by the decay of her strength and spirituality, is a nightmare which will not distress men of sanity and vision"—

amongst whom that modest author unhesitatingly includes himself. Still less are "men of sanity and vision" apt to believe, or welcome, the notion that Scotland may yet reassert any unique spirit and proffer any independent contribution towards the solution of those grave problems which, we are told *ad nauseam*, with the most damnable iteration, cannot possibly be solved by any one country but depend on international co-operation. In short, we are all going the same way home, and no longer all in step "save oor Jock". Oor Jock, if he ever belonged to the awkward squad, is now thoroughly disciplined, and, although in the general march-past his accent may still be distinguishable, the sense of anything he has to say does not differ in any material way from that of all other right-thinking people. Well, we will see. All I want to say at the moment is that if it does not differ—and differ in a very sensational fashion—that will be even more astonishing than if it does, for, as Mr Colin Walkinshaw has said, "Our generation must see either the end of Scotland or a new beginning. Can Scotland hope to survive? If she does not, the history of the process whereby the long centuries of her national life have been brought to nothing will be of the strongest intellectual interest. For the final and permanent destruction of a nation once fully established and conscious of itself will be something unique in the records of Western Christendom."

"Yet such an extinction", I continued thoughtfully, "would be a fitting enough end to the curious process of the national spirit with which I am concerned." It is not my business to prophesy but to show that process at work in a few selected cases drawn from divers periods of our history, yet having all something so strangely in common that the eccentric actually becomes the typical and the wildest irregularities combine to manifest the essence of our national spirit and historic function. If, to take up Mr Walkinshaw's speculation, Scotland is to survive, where is the impetus to come from, what invisible reservoir secretes such a startling potentiality? No glimpse of anything of the sort is to be found in the conception of the Scottish character almost universally accepted to-day; certainly nothing seems to be further from the minds of the vast majority of Scots themselves. So far as they are concerned the long centuries of Scotland's national life have long ago been brought to nothing; they are totally unaware of them. Their "race memory" only goes back to the day before yesterday. It is strictly confined to those aspects of the past which have contributed to the present happy state of affairs and are commendable on that account. Every consideration is abjectly adjusted to that. It is agreed that "History had to happen" and there is a general belief in progress—a general belief that everything is working together for good. Any harking back on elements in the past that seem to challenge that popular assumption—any insistence on the significance of elements customarily left out—any attempt to undermine the conventional acceptance of history and get down to fundamentals—is deprecated, resented, misrepresented, or laughed out of court in the extremely limited circle privy to such activities. So far as the great mass of the people is concerned the newspapers and other great agencies carry on the good work begun with *compulsory* education in the schools and they are incapable of being swung out of the racing "main-stream of contemporary life" into any such vexing and unnecessary side-issues. Particularly in Scotland. All that every other European nation strives at whatever cost to retain and further means nothing to Scotland. The Scots attempt to compensate themselves in the fervour of their protestations for what they willingly relinquish in actual fact. They have allowed their languages—Gaelic and Scots—and the literatures in them, to lapse almost completely, though every other European nation or national minority has fought most desperately to keep and use its distinctive language. The Scots alone have never generated any effective or even considerable Nationalist movement. No serious Scottish issue has induced them to put up more than a very temporary sham fight. They have acquiesced in the progressive depopulation and relegation for sporting purposes of what now amounts to over a third of their country. They have—since the Reformation or since the Union with England—failed to erect distinctive national arts on the splendid foundations their ancestors had created for them; and they become irritated and indignant when this is pointed out to them. Scottish literature and history (even in those accepted forms which so carefully leave out of account all that would suggest that the present state of affairs is not highly creditable, and, blessed word, inevitable) are taught only to a negligible extent, if at all, in Scottish schools and Universities.

All this is no new development since the Reformation or the Union. The strains in the national disposition that made this aversion to their own affairs—this tendency to "keep their eyes on the ends of the earth"—have been so strongly marked through the whole course of Scottish history that, in works of national biography, accounts of great Scots almost invariably begin, "one of the great band of whom we read 'nothing is known except their birth *in Scotland* and their transactions in public life *out of it*' " (Note I).

It can be said of no contemporary Scottish politician as was said of Henry Dundas, Lord Melville: "Perhaps the most *remarkable peculiarity* in his character was his intimate acquaintance with the actual state of Scotland, and its inhabitants, and all their affairs". The documentation of Scotland is hopelessly inadequate; in all kinds of important directions the statistical and other material necessary to form a judgement is simply not available without the devotion of years to difficult first-hand research. And even such research would be hampered by the deplorable state into which the Scottish records have been allowed to fall and, in more recent times, the way in which the Scottish returns have been lumped indistinguishably with English. Moreover a great deal of the apparent material can only be used with the utmost reserve owing to the propagandist falsification it reflects. Still a little progress has been made in the last few years (though the Old Gang and the English-controlled newspapers have obstructed it at every point in an absurd and almost incredible fashion). As Mr R. B. Cunninghame Graham says: "For a century Scotsmen have been content to remain pale copies of our 'ancient enemy from beyond the Tweed'. Some degenerate sons of Scotia, even to-day, attribute the economic progress of Scotland to the Act of Union and forget their own share in the job. Mesopotamia is a blessed word. When you have said Act of Union there are still sporadic Scots who put on the same kind of long face as they assume on reading aloud the genealogy of King David. Mercifully they are becoming rare, as rare as those who think John Knox invented Scotland, almost without the assistance of the Deity." Scottish History is indeed being rewritten, but it is necessarily a long and difficult task, so massive is the overgrowth of error that encumbers it. "It was no doubt", as *The Modern Scot* says, "out of a purely religious zeal that the reformers sought the help of England, but no one can deny the wholesale Anglicisation that ensued. The early orientation of the Scottish Protestants was all towards England. Knox was the first Scottish writer to discard his native language for English. 'The major theological documents of the day . . . were all compiled in English and by Englishmen.' And in a negative way, too, the Presbyterians cut the Scot off from his past, for it is in its arts that the nationality of a people is most clearly enshrined and these the Presbyterians destroyed, at first half-heartedly (for even Knox went to see a play about the capture of Edinburgh Castle), but eventually with a ruthless zeal. They killed the architectural movement of the Renaissance that had so many gracious achievements to its credit, and strangled the drama that was so promising. In routing Catholicism, they destroyed more of the indigenous culture of the country than, say, the Bolshevists have in Russia. They erected barriers against the dispassionate study of Scottish history that made it comparatively easy for latter-day historians to distort it in the cause of the English ascendency, and it is only with the pulling down of those barriers by such workers as Major M. V. Hay that long perspectives into Scottish history are becoming possible." But the University professors and lecturers and the school-teachers are not going to explore these perspectives, these tortuous labyrinths, if they can possibly help it; they prefer to pass on the ready-made article.

Robert Chambers in his *Biographical Dictionary of Eminent Scotsmen* has very hard things to say about the old fabulous histories. He rails in particular at Dempster for amassing, for the honour of his country as he foolishly imagined, an "immense mass of incredible fictions"—"losing in the brilliancy of his imagination any little spark of integrity that illumined his understanding, when the reputation of his native country was concerned he seems to have been incapable of distinguishing between truth and falsehood". And he rejoices when Father Innes initiates a more modern mode of history and lops away some forty mythical kings from the overloaded monarchical line of οἱ κατ' ἐξοχήν, "the ancient kingdom". But at least the inventions of Dempster, Boece, and others were fine wild tales and they lied nobly to the glory of Scotland. In our humdrum rationalising days the tide of mendacity is running far higher than ever. Newspapers trouble little about consistency. "The public memory is short", and they say one thing one day and the opposite the next with complete indifference. There is everywhere more humbug and imposture—and of a far more sordid kind. A case in point is the latest History of Scotland. It proudly claims to be the first attempt to describe in detail the forces which have gone to the shaping of the Scotland of to-day—the first to discuss the evolution of modern Scotland at length. There is length enough but little else (Note II); the style, in its unrelieved clumsy dullness, is itself one of the forces that have gone to the shaping of modern Scotland—it has obvious affinities with Malinowski's "phatic communion", and is a natural enough product of a country with no conventions, only *clichés*. The significance of the damning fact that it is the first History of modern Scotland is, of course, entirely missed. As to its author—amusingly named Pryde—that a country like Scotland could secrete in its tiny population such a redoubtable polymath, utterly unknown to the vast majority of its people and vouchsafing nothing to prepare one for his sudden emergence—attached to the department of Scottish History and Literature in Glasgow University of all places—is a phenomenon significantly at variance with the appeal to "common sense" on which so much of his book avowedly relies. Even he, however, is constrained to admit that the young protagonists of the present Scottish Movement at least deserve credit for "deepening the nation's interest in its destinies, material and spiritual". The point is well made, but Dr. Pryde does not revive the ancient supernumerary kings. He gravely discusses, *inter alia*, the poetry of a man who has never written any, and eulogistically reviews a novel not only unpublished at the time he wrote but no more than half written—to which MSS. he had, to my knowledge, no access. It is only natural that a writer capable of such ludicrous and inexcusable errors should abound in unsubstantiated charges of untruth, exaggeration, partisanship (synonymous with any difference of view from his own), opinionatedness, extremism, ignorance, and so forth against carefully unspecified opponents, while taking his own perfect balance and impartiality for granted—particularly in his baseless sectarian charges against the Irish in Scotland, in which he repeats libels that have been repeatedly and incontrovertibly exposed. Newspapers of any standing are not edited with such careless inconsistency as Dr. Pryde displays when he defends the press in one place (by a mere assertion) against the charges of not being nationally representative, and in another naïvely confesses that "the general difficulty of assessing current trends of public opinion is accentuated, as regards

Scotland and the first two years' record of the National Government by *the almost unanimously favourable attitude of the Press*". In trying to justify the leading Scottish newspapers he does not account for the way in which the writers who are "deepening the nation's interest in its destinies" are almost wholly excluded from their columns in favour of those who are not in the inconvenient condition of having "opinions of their own". Nor does he reconcile his claim that these papers (though the *Scotsman* and the *Glasgow Herald* go into precious few working-class houses and the vast majority of the Scottish votes belong to the working-class) have still "an enormous power of moulding public opinion, especially at general elections", with the fact, which he elsewhere establishes, that the bulk of the Scottish electorate vote in precisely the opposite direction to that which these journals advocate, unaffected by the frantic campaigns of misrepresentation which they conduct, and despite the lack of any effective opposition press. The whole volume is full of similar illogicalities. But Dr. Pryde's climax in this sort is his suggestion that "English public opinion is probably now over-influenced by the Renaissance group". If English thought is amenable to a handful of extremists in this way, what becomes of Dr. Pryde's praise of it in other connections as a necessity to balance the Scots—his basic argument in fact for the continuance of the Union? The real fun of the book is richest where Dr. Pryde touches upon cultural matters, invariably with a *gaucherie* that beggars description. No one but an Anglo-Scot of his type could display such an excruciating incapacity for the matters in question. In music he says "the evidence shows Scotland, while not leading any new movement like France or England, is in a state not dissimilar to that of other countries". What other countries? Italy? Germany? Russia? What new movement is England leading in music? He holds that Burns (who incidentally was not a composer) "marks the peak of Scottish achievement in the only branch of music in which the national genius may be said to have succeeded" (which is like attributing the musical value of Schubert's settings not to Schubert but to the writers of the poems he set to music),—and he ignores alike the superlative significance of the *Ceol Mor* of the great period and the magnificent art-song achievement of our living composer, Mr F. G. Scott, of whom a great critic recently said that his work was the most outstanding artistic achievement of these islands in our time. Dr. Pryde regards the criticism of the late Mrs Kennedy Fraser's *Hebridean Songs* (Note III)—*i.e.* the foisting of a foreign and inappropriate musical technique on the folk-song originals—as "inept and ungracious". But Dr. Pryde is no greater authority on aptness, generosity, and graciousness than on other matters. His comments on literary matters have to be seen in cold print to be believed. It is particularly significant of the continuing time-lag in all cultural connections in Scotland that at this juncture Dr. Pryde should be solemnly announcing that "Scottish literature like any other must stand or fall by its output of fiction". (Stand or fall is good.) He goes on to make the diverting confession that "it would be going too far to say that Sir Walter Scott fixed the type of the entire novel form". This "going too far" is certainly the type of most of Dr. Pryde's elephantine subtleties of perception. I shall say nothing about his animadversions on political, social, economic, and religious matters except that they are all of like sort to his flat-footed forays into the realms of music and literature. He is the Glasgow business man's retort to "all this nonsense about a Scottish cultural revival". He'll "larn" these young fellows. His treatment of his subject in every phase has a slipshodness, a lack of dignity, incompatible with a worthy or useful attitude to any country. His trick of taking for granted that "all right-thinking people" are opposed to Communism, Catholicism, etc., and that there is accordingly no need to argue such matters out, and his habit of "no case—abuse plaintiff's attorney", are much in evidence, together with an attitude of "any stick will do to beat an adversary". The last-mentioned leads Dr. Pryde to say that "distance meant isolation or at least very imperfect contact (of Scotland) with the main stream of European thought and progress"—though the distance of Scotland is obviously not much greater than the distance of England. Scotland's countless close independent European associations in the old days are conveniently forgotten, of course.

I have not made all these comments on Dr. Pryde's egregious tome without maintaining a shrewd bearing on my theme of Scottish Eccentricity. Dr. Pryde's perversity is in fact the present Anglo-Scottish inversion of the old Scottish spirit. His book, as associated with the Glasgow chair of Scottish History and Literature, is a typical product of that state of affairs which disguises behind nominally Scottish functions and prepossessions a determination to see that they never become more than nominal and actually subserve the opposite policy to that which would seem their natural concern. The fact that such a book "devoted to" Scotland by a writer never previously heard of in relation to Scottish arts and affairs should appear in a magnificent series which includes G. P. Gooch's *Germany*, Sir Valentine Chirol's *India*, Stephen Gwynn's *Ireland*, S. de Madariaga's *Spain*, speaks for itself. It is a characteristic manœuvre, carried through in this case, however, with a brutality that indicates the alarm in certain quarters at the new tendencies in Scottish arts and affairs which they affect to belittle. Happily it has completely overreached itself. Dr. Pryde's style is far from learned, complex, and allusive; I have quoted his weighty pronouncement with regard to Sir Walter Scott. It would have been more in keeping with the authentic Scottish spirit if he could have written more after the manner of Mr Arthur Machen who can recall how "I had just read *Waverley* with huge relish, and was full of the silver Bear that held a quart of claret, of the Tappit Hen that devoured the few crumbs of reason that the Bear had left, of the distinction between *ebrius* (drunk) and *ebriolus* (slightly fuddled), of the Baron who held his lands by the tenure *detrahendi seu removendi caligas Regis post battaliam*''. Now, alas, we are living in days when Sir J. M. Barrie of all people can give a Scottish University Lord Rector's address on Courage. And General Smuts another in the same University on Freedom, though "General Smuts' country stands in the forefront of practitioners of those sterilising tyrannies which he here so loudly bemoans. No doubt the beam in his own eye makes him peculiarly sensitive to the mote in other people's. But one can marvel at the hardihood with which an envoy from such a quarter composes dithyrambs upon the favourite themes of Rousseau—a hardihood that, like Hassan's in Flecker's play, has a monstrous beauty, as of the hindquarters of an elephant. Would it not be fitting if we, following an ancient custom, were to anoint this poet with myrrh, bind a chaplet of wool about his temples, and, having praised his eloquence, request him to pass homeward to his native land that he may there apply and carry into effect the first principles of which he sings? For his need is greater than ours." Dr. Pryde, like Barrie and Smuts, is not eccentric with the old Scottish eccentricity which is my theme. Like them he is merely an abominable intrusion into a sphere that is not his. My Scots of an elder day had "language at large''. Dr. Pryde's language—and the language of Anglo-Scotland to-day as a whole—is of a different sort—it is not meant for examination. It has only a humbug imitation of a meaning wrought out of the stuff of sheer verbalism. It is meant to reassure those whose shibboleths are just such mumblings; all they need to do is to hear the familiar sound—the policeman on his beat.

What accounts for the touchiness, the refusal, the inability of the Scot when any attempt is made to make him concentrate his attention on Scottish affairs—to make him give these the consideration he is only too willing to devote to the affairs of the Empire or of any other country under the sun? Is it a case of bad conscience? Is it a psychological compensation? Does this account for that incessant protestation of excessive love of country which has no practical coefficient? Is this the reason for that exaggerated insistence on the mere frills, the externals, of nationality to the exclusion of any regard for or recognition of the realities? Is an unexampled attachment to the affairs of the Parish Pump an escape, an excuse for failing to promote Scottish issues on any higher plane? These studies of a few Scottish Eccentrics may, at least, throw a little light on these questions. Whatever the explanation may be it is certainly true—and has always been true—of an amazing number of Scots that, like Donald Farfrae in *The Mayor of Casterbridge*, they have "loved their country so much as never to have revisited it". In every other sense, except physically, all but an infinitesimal minority of modern Scots have never seen it and have taken every possible precaution to ensure that they never should. And in this all the powers that be have ably abetted them.

Buckle, in his *History of Civilisation*, propounds a thesis that the Scots are more under the thumb of their clergy than any other European nation. He wonders why "men capable of a bold and inquisitive literature . . . should constantly withstand their kings and as constantly succumb to their clergy . . . why men who display a shrewdness and boldness rarely equalled in practical life should, nevertheless, in speculative life tremble like sheep before their pastors". Well, you will see from my account of these Eccentrics where the full play of their eccentricity led them in matters of religion, morals, and practical life. Even now Scotsmen must work it off somehow—into a MacConochie like Barrie, or through some such safety-valve as the Burns cult which caused an English writer to protest that an end should be put to this annual laudation by gatherings in all parts of the world in whose midst appear some of the most eminent in the Church, the Law, literature, and politics, of "one of the lewdest, most drunken and most dissolute libertines who ever stained human records. . . . To drink a toast to a man like Burns ought properly to be considered as an affront to every decent thing in life. . . . In all the long erratic history of hero-worship there is probably not such another example where a reprobate, a deliberate, boasting defaulter from ordinary human decency, has carried his excesses to such repulsive extremes. No excuse whatever can be made for Burns' calculated violation all through his life of human decency. He was a deliberate moral anarchist."

Evidently the Scot is not so well understood in some quarters as those who subscribe to the general myth regarding our national character confidently assume. Moral anarchy, in fact, says a great deal about it. May it not be that we have here the key to the whole problem—the anti-national attitude of the Scottish Church, the explanation alike of the Anglicising policy and of the acquiescence in it of a people only too devastatingly aware of their real propensities and terrified to give rein to them? Has the whole trend of modern Scots history depended on the same realisation as, according to George Bernard Shaw, prompted the massacre after Culloden? "After Culloden", he says, in his preface to *On the Rocks*, "the defeated Highland chiefs and their clansmen were butchered like sheep in the field. Had they been merely prisoners this would have been murder. But as they were also *Incompatibles with British Civilisation* . . . it was only liquidation." Incompatibles with British Civilisation. Is this the secret of the Unspeakable Scot, the clue to that element in the Scottish character towards the elimination of which, at all costs, every effort in modern Scottish history has been devoted? Is this the reason for the Scotsman's vigorous concentration in modern times on "the main chance"; and for the extent to which Scotsmen have gone into the Army and the Police Force, well content like young King James the Second to go to the war in Flanders, and to exchange the complications of human intercourse and of religious and political intrigue for the steady discipline and unquestioning comradeship of army life? Why, even David Hume "for a short time hesitated whether he should continue his studies, or at once relinquish the pursuit of philosophical fame by joining the army".

What has happened to Scotland, the horrible psychological revolution effected, reminds me rather of the article in *Blackwood's Magazine* for September 1822, which had for its text Mrs Barbauld's tender line: 'Pity the sorrows of the Poor Old Stot'. The Scot has almost without exception it seems to me been turned during the past century and more into the Stot. The article I refer to said: "The term Stot, as applied to the Scotsman, was, we believe, first used in this magazine. It immediately acquired great popularity. . . . It appears to us a figurative or metaphorical expression, and to involve nothing personal. . . . In the first place a Stot is, most frequently, a sour, surly, dogged animal. He retains a most absurd resemblance to a Bull, and the absurdity is augmented by the idea that he once absolutely was a Bull. . . . His forehead lowers, and his eye is swarthy; but look him in the face, and you discern the malice of emasculation and the cowardice of his curtailed estate. . . ."

I noticed that my friend was following my argument very intently, and not wishing for the time being to go further afield, but to keep my remarks for the most part well within the circle of my subject-matter in *Scottish Eccentrics*, I said: "But we'll not go into that just now, though that is really what the Scottish Renaissance Movement is driving at—a liberation of qualities resembling the strange volcanic eruptions of Christopher North's convivial genius. The confinement of the Scottish spirit within these narrow limits, these rather sordid ruts, for the last century or two; this strange distemper, this bleak and horrible disease of the human spirit that has affected us so devastatingly, is, as Mr Walkinshaw indicates, as curious a phenomenon as the putting of a gallon of liquid into a pint bottle. But, on the other hand, if it is once again threatening to measure up to the issue I have just suggested, we shall witness the emergence of a djinn from a bottle with a vengeance. Either is a miracle. The point is that the Scottish spirit is capable of both performances —alternately, and often almost simultaneously. We are the people who always best realised the truth of what Schopenhauer says: 'Whatever course of action we take in life there is always some element in our nature which could only find satisfaction in an exactly contrary course'. Or as Havelock Ellis says: 'It seems to be too often forgotten that repression and license are two sides of the same fact'." It has been said of Wagner that he had in him the instinct of an ascetic and of a satyr, and the first is just as necessary as the second to the making of a great artist. As matters stand in Scotland, however, in all connections and not merely the religious, "I think", as William Ridge of Adderny said, "that the Church of Scotland is just like Adam in Paradise, that cannot continue in integrity a moment". It is a fool's paradise. The old energy has gone almost entirely; few people in Scotland to-day, in Euphan M'Cullen's phrase, "have the tar pig by their belt and are ready to give a smott to every one of Christ's sheep as they come in their way". Nor are they like Alexander Gordon of Earlston, a man of great spirit, much subdued by inward exercise, who attained the most rare experiences of downcasting and uplifting; nor like Lady Robertland, "one deeply exercised in her mind and who often got as rare outgates". Least of all can they cry with Andrew Melville, who, when some blamed him as fiery, said: "If you see my fire go downward, set your feet on it and put it out; but if it go upward, let it return to its own place".

I am making all these allusions and assembling all these instances as a means of creating a historical picture of the Scottish spirit as a background to my specific studies. D. H. Lawrence was undoubtedly on the right track when he remarked, apropos Donald Carswell's book, *Brother Scots*: "You admire a little overmuch English detachment. It is often a mere indifference and lack of life. And you are a bit contemptuous of your Scotch; one feels they are miserable specimens all told by the time one winds up with Robertson Nicoll. It's because you underestimate the vital quality, and overestimate the English detached efficiency, which is not very vital."

There you have it. Modern Scotland has been devitalised as much as possible. Progress. The advantages Scotland has derived from the Union with England.

Professor R. D. Jameson in his *A Comparison of Literatures* attempts to discover how the English, French, German, and American literatures have described the universe and satisfied temperamental needs, and how each of these national imaginations has absorbed the phantasies of the others and been influenced by them. His view of the four national literatures, whose development he considers from the early Middle Ages to the nineteenth century, suggests that the French are particularly concerned with problems of behaviour interpreted psychologically: that the Germans have been especially concerned with dreams about God and the mystery of the Universe: that the English, descending from both the Germans and the French, have a dual nature. English phantasy is particularly concerned with the things of the physical universe (love of nature), the ethics of action, and laughter, which may to some extent be the result of a clash between the two contrasting types of phantasy. And what of the modern Scottish phantasy? Probably the best hint of it, in these days when the Anglicised Scot is so much more English than any Englishman—"unScotched and become a damned bad Englishman"—is to recall what Professor Pellizzi says in his *Il Teatro Inglese*: "He who does not understand that Peter Pan is a serious work, and in a certain sense one that is *fundamental to the English mind*, must give up trying to understand England or anything to do with her". If Professor Pellizzi's theory is correct about the English—that they become "intensely dramatic" whenever compromise fails in their souls—it is to be hoped that they may be forced very soon to suffer from this fecund "social remorse" with regard to Scotland. The "*grande terribile populo*" will have to find some better refuge from mental discomfort in their imagination than Peter Pan. When England reaches the point where the daemon of its race becomes naturally dramatic in this connection something prodigious will surely emerge; and its nature may perhaps be glimpsed in these studies of mine of Scottish eccentricity.

Professor Gregory Smith has said: "It is never easy to describe national idiosyncrasy, but Englishmen think they know their Scot. He has long been a very near neighbour, and every habit of his has become familiar. In his literature he stands so self-confessed that any man of intelligence can—as they phrase it in the high place of Jargon—'discern the true Scottish note'. Yet sometimes one wonders what these words are intended to mean, and whether they are not used in an off-hand impressionist way to turn the reader from sterile enquiry. For criticism has learnt as much from that sacred bird the lapwing as from the sacred ostrich." Whatever the attempted explanation may be, Scotland to-day offers no material for any repetition of the remark made by an eighteenth-century London visitor to the printer William Smellie: "Here stand I at what is called the Cross of Edinburgh, and can in a few minutes take fifty men of genius by the hand"; or of that other comment made by Matthew Bramble in *Humphry Clinker*: "Edinburgh is a hotbed of genius". Just as Scottish historians have been at vast pains to exclude from their vision any glimpse of whole tracts of Scottish history and to refrain from acquiring the languages (Scots, and in particular Gaelic) used in the periods in question—without which their conceptions of these periods are pretty much like those of an English-speaking Frenchman trying to relate the substance of the remarks made to him by a Dorset yokel—so Scottish *littérateurs* rejoice in the limitations of Scottish literature as manifested in what remains when similar prejudices have whittled it down to a comfortable little corpus, agreeable to their idea of what is typically Scottish. Thus we have Mr R. L. Mackie complacently observing, in the preface to his *Book of Scottish Verse* in the World's Classics Series, that "of the poems assembled here—the salvage of six centuries—none is conceived on a grand scale. The Scottish poet is seldom subtle or profound; he lives a life of sensations, not of thoughts. Thus in spite of the supposed preoccupation of the Scot with philosophy and religion, Scotland has not produced any great religious poetry. This is not said to deter the reader. He would court only disappointment if he looked for Alpine splendours in the 'honest grey hills' to which Scott gave his heart."

What is the desperate fear that dictates this anxiety to appear humble and inoffensive? Why this insistence on "simple common sense", applying psychology and reason in their abecedarian implications, yet ridiculing any application of them in their higher developments? There is no mere supposedness about the abnormal preoccupation of the Scot with psychology and religion. Mr Mackie should not generalise about his countrymen on the basis of his own personal experience. A very little thought would have shown him that England lacks the variety, wild grandeurs, and startling juxtapositions of scenery to be found in Scotland. Is English poetry then tamer still—still more destitute of Alpine splendours? He has cited Scott and Stevenson. Scott was not wholly confined to the "honest grey hills". His masterpiece was that "wildest and most rueful of dreams", Wandering Willie's tale, in *Redgauntlet*, yet, as Professor Gregory Smith says, "its wildness and ruefulness hardly compensate us for Scott's disappointing surrender to the bourgeois sentiment which tolerates 'mystery' only as material to be explained by the literary detective". It is this disappointing surrender that is complete in Mr Mackie and all his kind—in contemporary Scotland as a whole. "Even Kilmeny's magic journey must be explained in the *Noctes* by twaddle about 'inspired dwawms' and by a theory of the 'social affections'. Fortunately, there is no confession of this in Hogg's poem, and the Ambrosian commentary is now quite forgotten." A very different and much better anthology of Scottish poetry than Mr Mackie's could easily be made, and afford grounds for the very opposite conclusions to those he has drawn. The real Scotland, having been "presumed dead", cannot be admitted to be alive no matter how obviously it may demonstrate that it is. It is the victim of a legal fiction, and, for the most part, a very willing victim. The whole inwardness of Mr Mackie's remarks is at one with the professed sentiments of the vast majority of Scots to-day. To them, the nature of their literature, the history of their country, is as unintelligible as the theories of Einstein or the paintings of Paul Klee; and for the same reason. Their constant appeal is to common sense in the lowest sense of the term. The uncanny Scot, examples of whom are the subjects of my essays, has been everywhere transformed into, or all but indetectibly disguised as, the Canny Scot of modern acceptance.

But, in view of all that went before, his transformation or disguising is itself a still more uncanny and questionable performance. Startling psychological propensities may have been neatly tucked away or confined to trivial spheres; but the centrifugal traits of the Scottish people —what Mr Power calls our persistent "externalism"— remain as obvious as ever, and that, in itself, is eccentric enough in all conscience. Hence the schismatic passions, the almost insane individualism, the insistence on such artificial distinctions as the gulf between Highlanders and Lowlanders. To-day it is the plane upon which that dispersion operates—the quality of the elements that fly to extremes—that has so sadly changed. The motivation remains the same. The manifestation has become trivial except when one realises that the sum of its trivialities is the betrayal of Scotland and the submergence of the

Scottish spirit in the English, although, as one of our ancient historians pointed out, neighbours as they are, there are no two peoples in the world so utterly different as the Scots and the English. It was the same spirit as Mr Mackie's and Dr. Pryde's—this need to "domesticate the issue", this insistence on the established fiction which indicates the insecurity with which it is now maintained—that led the music critic of the *Glasgow Herald* to the inanity of saying of the song-settings of Francis George Scott: "The sudden outbursts that he indulges in are not characteristic of our nation: but reflect rather the mercurial and almost volcanic natures that are to be found in Eastern Europe. The true Scot makes his meaning clear in more subtle ways, and can be, for that reason, more impressive because more controlled." Another writer promptly retorted: "Before anyone thus dismisses the idea that the Scot is capable of extremes of feeling, he surely ought to have paused to consider some of the landmarks in the history of the Scottish arts—the 'flytings' of Dunbar, Burns's whirling clouds of words, the music of the pibrochs, Urquhart's Rabelais. The *Glasgow Herald* writer's remarks are born of ignorance or a wilful misreading of the Scottish tradition; of such a fear of anything with life in it as prompted Roy Campbell to write to a third-rate novelist:

> They praise the firm restraint with which you write.
> I'm with them there, of course.
> You use the snaffle and the curb all right—
> But where's the bloody horse?"

There is no need to seek the refutation of such a statement in any wide consideration of the Scottish spirit. Music, the subject in question, provides instances enough. The landmarks in Scottish music are sufficiently few and far between, and such a critic ought to have known them all, though they are generally quite unknown, and it is highly questionable whether he knew any of them. I will only quote what is said by his biographer of Thomas Erskine, the sixth Earl of Kellie (born 1732), one of the few musical geniuses Scotland has so far produced, and you have only to compare my quotation with the *Glasgow Herald* critic's remarks to understand the obligation imposed by the established fiction to insist that everything really Scottish is un-Scottish. "In his works", we read, "the *fervidum ingenium* of his country bursts forth, and elegance is mingled with fire. From the singular ardour and impetuosity of his temperament, joined to his German education, under the celebrated Stamitz, and at a time when the German overture, or symphony, consisting of a grand chorus of violins and wind instruments, was in its highest vogue, this great composer has employed himself chiefly in symphonies, but in a style peculiar to himself. While others please and amuse, it is his province to rouse and almost overset his hearer. Loudness, rapidity, enthusiasm, announced the Earl of Kellie. What appears singularly peculiar in this musician is what may be called the velocity of his talents."

This also explains why Scots in the arts have lacked architectonic faculty and purpose. As Professor Gregory Smith says: "Stevenson found it hard to sustain a plot, and good judges have been willing to agree. Sir James Barrie has confessed his inability to plan a long tale. Lang who, with all his vagrancy, had the classicist's sense of proportion, failed notoriously." The Scottish genius plays a similar rôle to that of the refrain singer in a Cossack quartet whose function it is to vary "the refrain in a whimsical manner, mostly in descant interpolated with laughing, howling, whistling, and yodelling. The Cossacks speak, not of singing, but of 'playing', a song, and this refrain-singer plays on his voice as on a quivering stringed instrument, or, rather, several different instruments, while his long and intricate refrains wind round the singing of the others like freely waving tendrils, and with their wildness incite and lash the passions." That is just the function and the practice of the true Scottish spirit in relation to human consciousness as a whole. Above all, it must be remembered that the Scottish spirit is in general brilliantly improvisatory. This is true of a great deal of what it has produced, as it was of the sermons of David Dickson, of whom Principal Baillie said that "he refuted all these errors (of Arminianism) in a new way of his own —Mr Dickson's discourse was much, as all his things, extempore; so he could give no double of it, and his labour went away with his speech".

Take the common idea of the essential Scotsman today. Compare it with the following descriptions of two typical Scots drawn from widely separated periods of our history. The first is from the sixteenth century and goes as follows:

"He had hardly passed his twelfth year when he took his degree of bachelor of arts; two years afterwards, that of master of arts; being then esteemed the third scholar in the university for talents and proficiency. His excellence did not stop there. Before attaining the age of twenty, besides becoming master of the sciences, he had attained to the knowledge of ten different languages, which he could write and speak to perfection. He had every accomplishment which it is befitting or ornamental in a gentleman to have. He practised the arts of drawing and painting, and improved himself to the highest degree in riding, fencing, dancing, singing, and in playing upon all sort of musical instruments. It remains only to add that this extraordinary person possessed a form and face of great beauty and symmetry; and was unequalled in every exertion requiring activity and strength. He would spring at one bound the space of twenty or twenty-four feet in closing with his antagonist; and he added to a perfect science in the sword, such strength and dexterity that none could rival him. He was likewise an excellent horseman."

The second is from the nineteenth century and runs thus:

"What can be said of him worthy of his various merits? Nothing. . . . A poet, who having had the calamity of obtaining Oxford prizes, and incurred the misfortune of having been praised by the *Edinburgh Review* for some juvenile indiscretions in the way of rhyme, wrote *The City of the Plague*, which even the envious Lord Byron placed among the great works of the age, and which all real critics put higher than his poetical lordship's best productions in the way of tragedy; a moral professor who dings down the fame of Dugald Stewart . . . an orator who, sober or convivial, morning and evening, can pour forth gushes of eloquence the most stirring, and fun the most rejoicing; a novelist who has chosen a somewhat peculiar department, but who, in his *Lights and Shadows*, etc., gives forth continually fine touches of original thought, and bursts of real pathos; a sixteen stoner who has tried it without the gloves with the game chicken and got none the worse, a cocker, a racer, a sixbottler, a twenty-four tumblerer, an out and outer, a true, upright, knocking-down, poetical, prosaic, moral, professional, hard-drinking, fierce-eating, good-looking, honourable, straightforward Tory. . . . A Gipsy, a magazine, a wit, a six-foot club man, an unflinching ultra in the worst of times. In what is he not great?"

You may be reluctant to accept my assurance that these two *are* typical and that I can adduce description of scores of other Scots all of whom would be as like each other as these two are, so, leaving out of account the subjects of my essays, let me just run very rapidly over a host of witnesses, and mark the concurrence of the epithets applied to them. Of Duns Scotus we read: "Among all the scholastic doctors I must regard John Duns Scotus as a splendid sun, obscuring all the stars of heaven, by the piercing acuteness of his genius; by the subtlety and the depth of the most wide, the most hidden, the most wonderful learning, this most subtle doctor surpasses all others, his productions, the admiration and despair of even the most learned among the learned, being of such extreme acuteness that they exercise, excite, and sharpen even the brightest talents to a more sublime knowledge of divine objects. . . . Scotus was so consummate a philosopher that he could have been the inventor of philosophy if it had not before existed. He described the divine nature as if he had seen God; the attributes of the celestial spirits as if he had been an angel; the felicities of the future state as if he had enjoyed them; and the ways of providence as if he had penetrated into all its secrets. He wrote so many books that one man is hardly able to read them and no one man is able to understand them. Such was our immortal Scotus, the most ingenious, acute, and subtle of the sons of men."

So much for the Subtle Doctor; another Scot, John Bassol, was not called *Doctor Ordinatissimus* with less good reason. His endless nicety in starting questions and objections, his powers of hair-splitting, are well known as a general characteristic of the fissiparous, argumentative Scot. Bassol was the Most Methodical Doctor of scholastic circles which included that *illustrissimus* one of whose arguments was declared to be enough to puzzle all posterity and who himself wept in his old age because he had become unable to understand his own works. Thomas Dempster, a man of fabulous propensity, was one whose powers of memory were so great that he himself was in the habit of saying that he did not know what it was to forget. James Elphinstone was "a Quixote in whatever he judged right—the force of custom or a host of foes made no impression upon him", an early advocate of phonetic spelling and a follower of literature "who did little to secure the approbation of mankind". Robert Bruce, the seventeenth-century divine, whose manner of delivery was an earthquake to his hearers, had "that fantastic obstinacy which caused him to lose the means of extensive usefulness for a trifling point of punctilio; with a mind only a little more accommodating to the circumstances of the time he must have become the first man of his age and country instead of spending the latter half of his life in exile, but if it had been so it is to be feared he would not have been the really great man he was". Abyssinian Bruce, his descendant in the sixth degree, was a man "whose person was majestic and whose mind, while diminished a little in utility by hasty passion and a want of accommodation to circumstances, was also of the most powerful cast and calculated to produce a great impression upon those around it". John Brown, the artist, brought down at the first shot even the celebrated Piranese who, being unable to sit two moments in one posture, reduced his portrait-painter to the necessity of shooting him flying like a bat or a snipe.

Dr. John Brown, the founder of the Brunonian system in medicine, was an eccentric genius "whose system simply consists in the administration of a course of stimulants, instead of the usual anti-phlogistic remedies, as a means of producing that change in the system necessary to a cure, the idea being perhaps suggested by his own habits in life which were unfortunately so very dissolute as to deprive him of all personal respect; he was, perhaps, the only great drinker who ever exulted in that degrading vice, as justified by philosophical principles; in truth he lived at a time when men of genius did not conceive it to be appropriate to their character to conduct themselves with decency; he was the founder of a peculiar lodge in Edinburgh, called the Roman Eagle, where no language but Latin was allowed to be spoken; one of his friends remarked with astonishment the readiness with which he could translate the technicalities and slang of masonry into this language, which however he at all times spoke with the same fluency as his vernacular Scotch; it affords a lamentable view of the state of literary society in Edinburgh between 1780 and 1790 that this learned lodge was perhaps characterised by a deeper system of debauch than any other."

Another John Brown, author of *The Self-Interpreting Bible*, indulged in such excesses of exertion in pursuit of knowledge and extraordinary acquisition of it that he was under the suspicion, more generally entertained than would appear credible, that he received a secret aid from the enemy of man upon the pledge of his own soul.

Thomas Brown, a philosophical writer, at six years of age was found with the Family Bible, and explained that he "only wished to see what the evangelists differ in, for truly they do not all give the same account of Christ". His pamphlet, *Observations upon Dr. Darwin's Zoonomia*, in 1798, was justly characterised as "one of the most remarkable exemplifications of premature intellect ever exhibited". Of Dr. Arbuthnott, Swift said that "he has more wit than we all have and more humanity than wit", and of Lord Orrery that "his very sarcasms are the satirical strokes of good nature; they are like slaps on the face, given in jest, the effects of which may raise blushes, but no blackness will appear after the blow; he laughs as jovially as an attendant upon Bacchus, but continues as sober and considerate as a disciple of Socrates", one who had "too much sympathy *and worth* to profit by the expedients of life", or, in Swift's words, "He knew his art, but not his trade".

Professor John Millar, author of a *Historical View of the English Government*, gaily set out "to trace back the history of society to its most simple and universal elements; to resolve almost all that has been ascribed to positive institution to the spontaneous and irresistible development of certain obvious principles; and to show with how little contrivance or political wisdom the most complicated and apparently artificial schemes of policy might have been erected". Of Patrick Murray, the fifth Lord Elibank, Dr. Johnson declared he never met him without going away "a wiser man". John Ogilvie was described as one "with powers far above the common order, who did not know how to use them with effect; he was an able man lost; his intellectual wealth and industry were wasted in huge unhappy speculations; had the same talent which Ogilvie threw away upon a number of objects been concentrated on one, and that one chosen with judgment and taste, he might have rivalled in popularity the most renowned of his contemporaries". Then there was the restless and acrid Pinkerton, one in whom the proud spirit of the great historian, Gibbon, seemed to find something congenial. Himself a literary impostor, he regarded literary imposture as a crime of the most degraded order and used the whole force of his nature and power over the language to describe his loathing and contempt of it, above all, in the case of "Ossian" Macpherson. He it was who pithily remarked of the Celts, that "being mere savages but one degree above brutes, they remain still in much the same state of society as in the days of Julius Caesar, and, like the Indians, and negroes, ever will continue".

John Rollock (born 1555) was an early and zealous promoter of Scottish literature, one of whom we are told that he was "a diligent and acceptable minister of the gospel, but, with literary ardour almost boundless and the warmest piety, Mr Rollock's simplicity of character degenerated into, or originally possessed, a natural imbecility, not at all uncommon in minds of this description, which disqualified him from acting a consistent or a profitable part in the conduct of the public affairs of the Church, which at this period were of a paramount importance, involving at once the civil and the religious rights of the community".

Bishop Sage was a man of great ability, even genius, whose "life and intellect were altogether expended in a wrong position and on a thankless subject; as all the sophisticated ingenuity that ever was exerted would have been unable to convince the great majority of the Scottish people that the order of Bishops was of scriptural institution or that the government of the last two male Stuarts was a humane or just government. Bishop Sage was a man labouring against the great tide of circumstances and public feeling, and, accordingly, those talents which otherwise must have been exerted for the improvement of his fellow-creatures and the fulfilment of the grand designs of providence, were thrown away, without producing either immediate or remote good."

George Sinclair, the scientist, and author of *Satan's Invisible Works Discovered*, was an "extraordinary person in whom science and superstition are so curiously mingled that it is hardly possible to censure delusions which seem to have been entertained with such sincerity and in company with such a zeal for the propagation of real knowledge".

William Wilkie, the "Scottish Homer", and author of the *Epigoniad*, is described as "superior in genius to any man of his time, but rough and unpolished in his manners, and still less accommodating to the decorum of society in the ordinary habits of his life". Charles Townsend well said of him that "he had never met with a man who approached so near to the two extremes of a god and a brute". There is also Alexander Geddes, a very typical Scot indeed, of whom it was justly said that "perhaps there is not in the history of literary men a character that calls more loudly for animadversion, or that requires a more skilful hand to lay it open; he professed a savage sort of straightforward honesty that was at war on multiplied occasions with the common charities of life, yet amid his numerous writings, will any man take it on him to collect what were really his opinions upon the most important subjects of human contemplation? He professed himself a zealous Catholic; yet of all or nearly all that constitutes a Catholic, he has spoken with as much bitterness as it was possible for any Protestant to have done. If it be objected that he added to the adjective catholic the noun Christian, when he says that he admits nothing but what has been taught by Christ, his apostles, and successors *in every age and in every place*, we would ask how much we are the wiser. He professed to believe in Jesus Christ, and in the perfection of his code, but he held Moses to have been a man to be compared only with Numa and Lycurgus; a man who like them pretended to personal intercourse with the Deity, from whom he never received any immediate communication; a man who had the art to take advantage of rarely occurring natural circumstances, and to persuade the Israelites that they were accomplished under his direction by the immediate power of God; a man, in short, conspicuous above all men as a juggling impostor. Now to the divine mission of Moses, we have the direct testimony of Jesus Christ himself, with the express assurance that without believing in Moses it was impossible to believe in him."

Again I might tell you of the Rev. Robert Kirk, M.A., who was kidnapped by elves for betraying the secrets of the polity of their commonwealth. Of Lord Braxfield, the judge, who, when a political prisoner tried to justify his reformist activities by saying that Christianity itself was once an innovation and that all great men had been reformers, even our Saviour himself, chuckled, "Muckle He made o' that—He was hangit". Of William Lauder's amazing and desperately unscrupulous and ingenious hatred of Milton. Of John Donaldson, the painter, who "conceived that in morals, religion, policy, and taste mankind were radically wrong", and, neglecting his profession, employed himself in devising schemes for remedying this universal error; "he was remarkable for a sarcastic and epigrammatic turn, the indiscreet indulgence of which lost him many friends: even while persons of consideration were sitting to him he would get up and leave them that he might finish an epigram or jot down a happy thought". Of James Tytler, an early and unsuccessful aeronaut, author of seven volumes of the second edition of the *Encyclopaedia Britannica*, and of books ranging from an *Edinburgh Geographical Grammar* to a *System of Surgery*, and of at least one excellent song, "I canna come ilka day to woo", who was so regardless of the uttermost extremes of poverty as to feel no desire to conceal his deplorable condition from the world.

I must mention Dr. Alexander Webster, an eminent divine endowed with an extraordinary power of arithmetical calculation, "unrivalled for extent of comprehension, depth of thinking, and accuracy in the profoundest researches". His "convivial powers were enchanting; he had a constitutional strength against intoxication, which made it dangerous in most men to attempt bringing him to such a state; often, when they were unfit for sitting at table, he remained clear, regular, and unaffected". Also Alexander Wedderburn, first Earl of Rosslyn, who "could argue with great ingenuity on either side, so that it was difficult to anticipate his future by his past opinions". I need only remind you of James Watt, the engineer, who was a very versatile person, versed in several of the modern languages, antiquities, law, and the fine arts, and largely read in light literature. His friend Francis Jeffrey tells us that he "was not only one of the most generally well-informed, but one of the best and kindest of human beings. . . . In his eighty-fifth year the alert, kind, benevolent old man had his attention at every one's question, his information at every one's command. His talents and fancy overflowed on every subject. One gentleman was a deep philologist; he talked with him on the origin of the alphabet as if he had been coeval with Cadmus; another was a celebrated critic—you would have said the old man had studied political economy and belles lettres all his life. And yet, Captain Clutterbuck, when he spoke with your countryman, Jedediah Cleishbotham, you would have sworn he had been coeval with Claverse and Burley, with the persecutors and persecuted, and could number every shot the dragoons had fired at the fugitive covenanters. In fact, we discovered that no novel of the least celebrity escaped his perusal, and that the gifted man of science was as much addicted to the productions of your native country (the land of Utopia aforesaid); in other words, as shameless and obstinate a peruser of novels as if he had been a very milliner's apprentice of eighteen."

I have gone on quite long enough, but I could go on almost indefinitely, citing case after case; all brilliantly and diversely gifted, often more or less wasted, all with views of utter recklessness, or strains of high impracticability, or the most violent contradictions of character. Constantly they call for a verdict similar to that passed by a recent reviewer on Sir Walter Scott—"when Sir

Walter Scott is charged with jobbery and shady business transactions it may indeed be best to remember what Stevenson said about D'Artagnan: 'There is nothing of the copybook about his virtues . . . but the whole man rings true like a good sovereign' ".

Frequently these talented Scots boast their knowledge of every country in Europe save only England, to which they had never been attracted and did not account it any loss. And, above all, it could be said of an extraordinarily high percentage of them, wherever we turn in Scottish biography, as was said of "Christopher North": "He was equally persuasive and conclusive upon entirely opposite propositions, and could uphold and decry them with the same cleverness and conviction. He had a versatility of opinion that ultimately amounted to *no* opinion." They also display an essential incongruity like his. We are told: "Christopher North sought to balance the brawniness of his physique by the delicacy of his muse—a muse not so much feminine as ladylike. The pendulum of these diverse elements had too wide an oscillation and swung wildly from a riotous animal activity to the milksop expression of hyper-refined sensibilities. There was between what he did, and what he said and wrote, the incongruity of violent contrast; the physical splendour of the 'beautiful Leopard' that was Christopher North, swinging lithely through the forest, became on the poetical plane merely the pathetic futility of a blind kitten that was John Wilson, author of the *Isle of Palms*." "Another writer", as Professor Gregory Smith points out, "can 'keep his eye' on the Paisley of his youth and wander through an eerie Dominion of Dreams, with less risk of artistic strabism than the Good Man in the *Night Thoughts* encounters in his spiritual activities:

> One eye on Death and one full fixed on Heaven
> Become a mortal and immortal man."

The music critic of the *Glasgow Herald* and all his kind who would fain persuade us that the adjective Scottish is strictly synonymous with circumspect, not to say genteel, had his typical predecessor in another Scot, the poet Campbell, who thought that Burns was "the most un-Scotch like of Scotchmen" because he was so free in confession to the world.

Dreaming of a "total alteration in philosophy" and holding that "all distinctions between virtue and vice were merely imaginary", Hume brilliantly exemplifies the dialectical dexterity I have been stressing. "His great views of being singular, and a vanity to show himself superior to most people, led him to advance many axioms that were dissonant to the opinions of others and led him into sceptical doctrines, only to show how minute and puzzling they were to other folk; in so far, that I have often seen him (in various companies, according as he saw some enthusiastic person there) combat either their religious or political principles; nay, after he had struck them dumb, take up the argument on their side, with equal good humour, wit, and jocoseness, all to show his pre-eminency." The same writer mentions that while he never gambled he had a natural liking to whist playing, and was so accomplished a player "as to be the subject of a shameless proposal on the part of a needy man of rank, for bettering their mutual fortunes, which it need not be said was repelled". "He had," according to Henry Mackenzie, the Man of Feeling, "it might be said in the language which the Grecian historian applies to an illustrious Roman, two minds." And like not a few great Scotsmen his incongruities also manifested themselves in his personal appearance. "Nature I believe never formed any man more unlike his real character than David Hume", wrote Lord Charlemont. "The powers of physiognomy were baffled by his countenance; neither could the most skilful in that science pretend to discover the smallest trace of the faculties of his mind, in the unmeaning features of his visage. His face was broad and fat, his mouth wide, and without any other expression than that of imbecility. His eyes vacant and spiritless; and the corpulence of his whole person was far better fitted to communicate the idea of a turtle-eating alderman than of a refined philosopher. His speech in English was rendered ridiculous by the broadest Scottish accent, and his French was, if possible, still more laughable; so that wisdom, most certainly, never disguised herself before in so uncouth a garb."

It may be objected that my examples are almost all literary and that the same liability to inconsistency, to sudden apostasy, has not characterised the Scot in other affairs. The answer is simply that it has, but here I cite only the case of James, fourth Duke of Hamilton: "Hamilton was the first to fail in the performance of the anti-Unionist scheme which he had taken so much pains to persuade his coadjutors to consent to. On the morning appointed for the execution of their plan when the members of opposition had mustered all their forces and were about to go to Parliament, attended by great numbers of gentlemen and citizens, prepared to assist them if there should be an attempt to arrest any of their number, they learned that the Duke of Hamilton was so much affected with the toothache that he could not attend the House that morning. His friends hastened to his chambers and remonstrated with him so bitterly on this conduct that he at length came down to the house, but it was only to astonish them by asking whom they had pitched upon to present their protestation. They answered, with extreme surprise, that they had reckoned on his grace. The Duke persisted, however, in refusing to expose himself to the displeasure of the court, by being foremost in breaking their favourite measure, but offered to second anyone whom the party might appoint to offer the protest. During this altercation, the business of the day was so far advanced that the vote was put and carried on the disputed article respecting the representation, and the opportunity of carrying the scheme into effect was totally lost. The members who had hitherto opposed the Union, being thus three times disappointed in their measures by the unexpected conduct of the Duke of Hamilton, now felt themselves deserted and betrayed. Shortly afterwards most of them retired altogether from their attendance in Parliament, and those who favoured the treaty were suffered to proceed in their own way, little encumbered either by remonstrance or opposition. . . . Such is the story of the Duke of Hamilton's share in these two great measures. It presents a curious view of perseverance and firmness of purpose at one time, and of the utmost instability at another, in the same person, both concurring to produce a great and important change in the feelings and interests of two nations. The conspicuous and decided manner in which the Duke of Hamilton stood forward, as the advocate of the act of security, carried it through a stormy opposition and placed the kingdom in a state of declared but legalised defiance of England; while the unsteadiness of his opposition to the union paved the way for the reconciliation of the two nations." And what of the brilliant rise and subsequent collapse of politicians like Lord George Gordon (Note VI) and Lord Rosebery?

In summary of all these contentions with regard to the nature of the Scottish genius I cannot do better than quote Professor Gregory Smith, who puts the whole matter in a nutshell when he says: "Scottish literature is remarkably varied and becomes, under the stress of foreign influence and native division and reaction, almost a zigzag of contradictions. The antithesis need not, however, disconcert us. Perhaps in the very combination of opposites—what either of the two Sir Thomases, of Norwich and Cromarty, might have been willing to call 'the Caledonian antisyzygy'—we have a reflection of the contrasts which the Scot shows at every turn, in his political and ecclesiastical history, in his polemical restlessness, in his adaptability. There is more in the Scottish antithesis of the real and fantastic than is to be explained by the familiar rules of rhetoric. The sudden jostling of contraries seems to preclude any relationship by literary suggestion. The one invades the other without warning.

They are the 'polar twins' of the Scottish Muse. . . . This mingling, even of the most eccentric kind, is an indication to us that the Scot, in that mediaeval fashion which takes all things as granted, is at his ease in both 'rooms of life', and turns to fun, and even profanity, with no misgivings. For Scottish literature is more mediaeval in habit than criticism has suspected, and owes some part of its picturesque strength to this freedom in passing from one mood to another. It takes some people more time than they can spare to see the absolute propriety of a gargoyle's grinning at the elbow of a kneeling saint."

NOTES

I.—For example, of William Bellenden, the historian, we read: "one of those learned and ingenious Scotsmen of a former age, who are esteemed in the general literary world as an honour to their country but with whom that country itself is scarcely at all acquainted. As there were many great but unrecorded before Agamemnon, so may it be said that there have flourished, *out of Scotland*, many illustrious Scotsmen, whose names have not been celebrated in that country." Indeed the works, and even the very names, of the great majority of the eminent Scotsmen to whom I refer in this essay are unknown in Scotland to-day to all but a very small number of specialists.

II.—I am not referring to the "Inglis lyis" which Buchanan complained had cost him so much trouble to purge out of "the story of Scotland", but which—if of a different, and deadlier, sort—are far more numerous in it to-day than they were before he began his patriotic cleansing.

III.—The most diverting comment I have encountered in this connection is Ezra Pound's declaration that "the Kennedy-Frasers have dug up music that fits the *Beowulf*. It was being used for heroic song in the Hebrides."

IV.—I have drawn attention in my volume of essays, *At the Sign of the Thistle*, to egregious errors in glossing of Scots poems by reputed authorities on the Scots vernacular, but since I wrote that —and we are told that Scots scholarship is improving nowadays—I have encountered the most appalling example in the "explanation" of the meaning of certain Scots phrases in Dunbar's *Kynd Kittok* in Dr. W. Mackay Mackenzie's new edition of *Dunbar's Poems*. Nothing could be further from the mark, or more destructive of the sense of the passage in question, than his interpretations in this instance; and the fact throws a lurid light on the prevalence in Scottish scholarship to-day of what Ezra Pound calls the gentle art of "how to seem to know it when you don't".

V.—My countrymen have happily never been afraid to encounter such indignant comments as Dr. Johnson's on Hume: "And as to Hume—a man who has so much conceit as to tell all mankind that they have been bubbled for ages, and he is the wise man who sees better than they—a man who has so little scrupulosity as to venture to oppose those principles which have been thought necessary to human happiness—is he to be surprised if another man comes and laughs at him? If he is the great man he thinks himself, all this cannot hurt him; it is like throwing peas against a rock."

VI.—Readers interested in extraordinary concurrences of effect in entirely unrelated cases may be interested to compare the particularly remarkable effect at the close of Gerard Manley Hopkins's sonnet, *Carrion Comfort*:

That night, that year,
Of now done darkness I wretch lay wrestling with
(my God!) my God,

and the amazing effect produced by Mr Erskine, afterwards Lord Erskine, during his great speech for the man of the people, Lord George Gordon, at the Old Bailey. "After reciting a variety of circumstances in Lord George's conduct which tended to prove that the idea of resorting to absolute force and compulsion by armed violence never was contemplated by the prisoner, he breaks out with this extraordinary exclamation: 'I say, by God, that man is a ruffian who shall after this presume to build upon such honest, artless conduct as an evidence of guilt'. But for the sympathy which the orator must have felt to exist at the moment, between himself and his audience, this singular effort must have been fatal to the cause it was designed to support; as it was, however, the sensation produced by these words, and the look, voice, gesture, and whole manner of the speaker, were tremendous."